Earth 2012

Time of the Awakening Soul

Praise for the Earth 2012 Series

This series will speak to hearts around the world. It will quicken the Awakening in many people who have tried to make sense of similar experiences. It will bring relief to those who have pictured a negative future. It will help others realize the potential that is being birthed within us all in this extraordinary time. After working closely with Dr. Aurora Juliana Ariel on this project, I am excited to see the powerful ramifications this book will have on people around the world. —*Jack Canfield, Author of Success Principles and Co-Author of the Chicken Soup For The Soul Series*

This inspiring, prophetic book speaks to a Soul Awakening that if embraced, can take humanity through a quantum leap into a future Eden that has forever lived as a vision in the hearts of humanity. —*John Gray, Author of Men Are From Mars, Women Are From Venus*

A clarion call to consciousness awakening to itself, Earth 2012 quickens spiritual unfolding by lovingly guiding you through one of the most difficult and transformative periods in human history. --*Leonard Laskow, M.D., Author of Healing With Love*

This book rises to the heights of poetry, unveiling a majesty of human potential like a torch in the morning light. It adds its brilliance to what is silently arising all around us. —*Jonathan Kolber*

This book will guide you inward to remember your truth and why you were born at this glorious moment in time! —*Jared Rosen, Author of The Flip: Turn Your World Around, and Inner Security And Infinite Wealth*

This powerful, practical book will guide you through one of the most challenging periods in our collective history. Read it please! —*Harold H. Bloomfield, M.D., N.Y. Times bestselling author of 19 books.*

In this exciting book you are immediately transformed by Aurora's passionate wisdom and captivated in a fascinating wake-up call to humankind. This masterpiece is a must to read! —*Karina Schelde, Author of Soul Voice*

This book is filled with love, clarity, and reverence... a breath of Light and air. It is a wonderful offering! Truly Inspiring! What a gift! It is food for the soul. —*Allan Cohen, Author of 20 books including* The Dragon Doesn't Live Here Anymore

In the book, *Earth 2012*, Aurora Juliana Ariel graces us with the wisdom and inspiration of her clear channel to Spirit. The truths that we hear in her writing are echoes of the free, expansive and Radiant Being that is the Eternal Self. We are fortunate to have pure souls like Aurora on this planet to remind us of who we really are. Her book is a great gift for those who would travel the path of spiritual transcendence, awakening and its abiding peace. —*Kamala Allen, PhD, Author of* A Woman's Guide to Opening A Man's Heart.

This book is so full of light! Our collective objective as spiritual beings is to increase the vibratory rate of all whom we come in contact with and to those whom we reach out to. The energy field this comprehensive body of work emits is very empowering and humanity will benefit greatly from it. In a world shrouded in darkness, it will help to light the way to peace, love and understanding. —*Bruce Robert Travis, Author of* My Past Life As Jesus: An Autobiography Of Two Lifetimes

Aurora's work goes directly to the core issues that humanity needs to address in order to shift into the new paradigm. Her experience and insights into the evolution of the soul shines a healing light and balm into areas of the human psyche that need healing, transmutation, and release. Her techniques for clearing and raising our frequencies to accelerate our process of Self-Mastery and Ascension are most effective and transforming. —*Aeoliah, Composer, Author, Reiki Master*

An inspirational book that will help give you guidance and inner peace in a world filled with so many adversities, Dr. Ariel will bring balance to your world through her writings. —*Mariah Napenthe Brown, Co-owner of Da Kitchen Restaurants*

Words cannot adequately express the wisdom, majesty and beauty of the inspired information in this book. As I read the uplifting and empowering words, I "feel" how important it is that this wondrous message be distributed far and wide to awaken and empower the millions of people that have been waiting for these words all their lives. It is sacred work! Humanity is at a time of ripeness for this awakening. This book of spiritual teaching and encouragement can help facilitate this awakening. This exquisitely beautiful work will truly enlighten the world. —*Sharon Huffman, Contributing Author of Ten Traits of Highly Effective Teachers; and Chicken Soup For the Soul*

This exquisitely crafted body of knowledge is a profound embrace of the spiritual history of humanity, offering insights into the power of TheQuest™ to conquer all obstacles... returning us quickly to the joyful expression of our Divine Nature. The triumphant arrival of the long-awaited Violet Race is celebrated as we traverse the Divine Romance of the journey of our hearts through time. The story of The Great Adventure is our true story, for we are the Heroes of the new Heaven on Earth. For all who wish to undertake the challenge of this time of transformation, this book is a guide and a blessing! —*Mirra Rose, Internationally renowned Spiritual Teacher and Healer*

An uplifting beautifully written book, with much more than prophecies and predictions, *Earth 2012, The Ultimate Quest*, reminds us of our mission, our destiny, and most importantly, that the world needs us. —*Marci Winters, editor for the Maui Vision magazine,writer, screen-writer, director, and producer.*

2012 is prophesied by many to be the end of the World, but what does it mean on a spiritual level? "*Earth 2012: The Ultimate Quest - How to Find Peace in a World of Chaos*" encourages readers to embark on a personal quest to push themselves to find inner peace. With many ideas fresh and new to readers throughout, "Earth 2012," would be excellent reading for anyone who feels like their lives are at the end times, and thinks it could be better. —*Midwest Book Review (Oregon, WI USA) (also posted on Amazon.com). Gave a 5 Star rating.*

Congratulations and thank you for sharing these wonderful dis-coveries with us – it reads like a very precious spiritual guide and such insightful journey into the realm of the soul and psyche. I wish you great success with it – it vibrates like a bestseller! —*Marius Michael George, Artist*

Praise for TheQuest™

Jack Canfield, author of 'Success Principles' and co-author of the 'Chicken Soup for the Soul' Series: TheQuest™ session with Aurora was a magical and helpful experience. It unblocked a subtle but powerful limitation in my life. I am grateful to her for her work and for her safe and gentle way of being.

Jared Rosen, Co-Author of 'The Flip' and, 'Inner Security And Infinite Wealth': TheQuest™ is a rarified healing system that works at such a core level, that ancient subconscious patterns clear at lightning speed. Aurora is truly a master!

Randolph Craft, founder, Pacific Planning Institute, and Pacific International Aging Center: The space Aurora holds for healing is so powerful that one has no choice but to move forward in her Presence.

Aeoliah, Author, Artist, Composer, Recording Artist: I was pleasantly surprised to find Aurora's Quest work to be so simple and straightforward, yet at the same time so dynamic and powerful in helping to shift deep-seated limiting energy patterns hidden within my subconscious. I found it to be a most healing experience to give a voice to my deeper feelings and express how I really felt about certain things in my life in a supportive, caring and non-judgmental setting that helped me to transform those patterns into the fulfillment that I desire. During the session I also enjoyed and appreciated the balance between voicing and openly expressing my feelings, and then later tuning into my Higher Self to allow and receive the messages from my own God Presence which made the experience my own personal empowerment that I cherish in my heart forever.

A Physical Therapist and former Christian Evangelist in California: The diminishment of the human condition is based on lack of self worth and esteem, and no amount of verbal affirmation will transform us. It has to come from an Alchemy within. In TheQuest™ sessions, the very molecules are rearranged, as cells not nourished are now nourished from within. We are truly cleansed from this inner work. This is like a soul clean up, or 50,000 mile check up for the inner being. The best part is that the changes are permanent. I can't believe how changed I am. People notice a calm and clarity. I have not reverted to the pattern since our last session. I cannot think of a better birthday gift than a chance to heal the inner soul of the grief and debris from our years before. —*D.J. Martinovich, Physical Therapist, Palm Springs, California*

Christopher Connolly, Composer, Recording Artist: Dr. Aurora Juliana Ariel's abilities as a Healer are so remarkable it is hard to put into words. My work with her was so profoundly deeply moving and transformational that I felt as if I had literally been bathed in the serene waters of the Holy Spirit. Her voice and presence guided me to a Divine place of Inner Peace.

A former nurse manager in Wisconsin: TheQuest™ process is awesome. I have been through a lot of counseling since the age of 18. I knew as an adult child of alcoholics, without a good role model, I was going to need guidance to overcome my past even at that young age. As a nurse, I have also been exposed to mental heath treatment methods in my career. I have never experienced anything as impressive and empowering. Aurora is a wonderful, loving person who creates a safe space for the deepest healing. —*Virginia Furumo, who is now living her dream life in Hawaii*

Michele Gold, Author of 'Angels of the Sea', Artist and Musician: I had been feeling very sad, almost hopeless, which is very unlike my Nature, for quite awhile, and within 24 hours of my Quest Counseling session with Aurora, it just lifted. Nothing outwardly changed and yet, I felt happy inside, a peace with where I was at. It was huge. Aurora's healing gifts are very powerful! The energy that had been suppressed inside me came forward and new projects began moving and many new creative ideas were bursting forth. I felt freer than I had felt in many years, happier, and filled with a quiet confidence that was battered for so long, and now was emerging from an ancient cocoon, with new shimmering wings with which to soar. Aurora Juliana Ariel is a rare radiant treasure. Her magnificent alchemical gifts will embrace you and guide you in a manner filled with so much love and compassion, you will feel free, your most profound self validated to emerge and shine. To experience Aurora's powerful healing work is to sit in the center of an exquisite circle of angels, supporting your soul's deepest wish to transform and live the most exceptional, magical life you were born to live.

Kamala Allen, PhD, Author of 'A Woman's Guide to Opening a Man's Heart': Aurora Juliana Ariel channels Mother Mary energy in an atmosphere of unconditional love and profound peace. Her gentle, effective approach to healing is a deep experience of nurturance and transformation.

A Police Office and High School Teacher in Aspen: Dr. Ariel's method of going inside one's self and healing past issues or gaining self-realizations is really quite amazingly simple, yet very valuable. Almost like finding a key to a hidden treasure. *—Brad Onsgard, Aspen, Colorado*

A teen in Hawaii: TheQuest™ is a great way to get things off your chest and deal with feelings that have been deep inside and yet are effecting us in a negative way. It really works! *—Aradeus Zachariah Daffin, 16 years old, Maui, Hawaii (Dr. Ariel's youngest son, now 21, received TheQuest™ Master Counselor Training with Dr. Ariel for 18 months and co-facilitated the first Quest Teen Forum with her in Aspen)*

A mother of an angry, violent eight-year-old: My daughter is doing really well! Thank you so much for working with her, I can really tell a difference in her self-esteem and overall well-being. I can see she really feels great about her appointments with you! After two sessions, three teachers called and asked what happened to her, she had changed so much! Namaste. *—Kelly Sundstrum, Carbondale, Colorado*

A mother whose son was traumatized by a fatal accident where he was the driver: Aurora, you are our angel. You accomplished in five days what doctors and other professionals around us believed would take 8 months for my son to fully recover and get to. Being with you this short time, my son is a changed person. I am very grateful! *—Patti S., Colorado Springs, Colorado*

And others....

Aurora's mastery shines as she navigates us through the terrain of our soul, allowing all of our self to be seen and expressed, thus granting greater freedom, wisdom, and insight. With her keenly trained mind, she lovingly and compassionately guides us in and through the closed doors and murky waters of our unexpressed parts, revealing hidden resources that bring solutions to our every day life, catalyzing deep awakening and a greater understanding of our self. —*Rev. Adrianna Levinson, Vibrant Life Center, Maui, Hawaii*

After years of being in and out of therapy I had changed my life very little but after four Counseling sessions with Aurora I was a new person. I had come to the first session a skeptic, but by the time we were done I was totally amazed by the amount of healing that took place. I had been hitting my head against the wall not getting any movement in my years of therapy. Traditional therapy had only scratched the surface, whereas TheQuest™ dove right into the root of the issue, uncovered the truth, and healed that aspect of my inner self. The sessions have been the most powerful events in my life. I'm finally free of the unhealthy part of myself that was holding me back for years. I never thought transformation like this was truly possible. I'm no longer a victim of the past and my emotional traumas have been set free. I have my life back! I've made more progress in a few sessions with Dr. Ariel than I have in years of therapy. —*Lance Koberlein, Programmer Real Estate Broker Entrepreneur, Denver, Colorado*

I had pronated knees since I was a little girl. Continually aggravating the condition through a very active and full life, it became a life long affliction. By 25 years old I had to stop running, a great passion in my life! I also loved to ski, hike, and bike, but my knees would get so sore that my lifestyle was greatly hindered. At TheQuest™ Life Mastery Training Course in Aspen, I had the opportunity to work with Dr. Ariel. In my session we traced a pattern back to early childhood where I had suffered severe abuse. As we unlocked and healed the pattern, I felt a tremendous release. The very next day I was working out at the Aspen Club gym when, looking in the mirror, I noticed my legs were straight. My trainer came over and could hardly believe his eyes. The condition was healed! —*Diane Argenzio, Estate Manager, Aspen, Colorado*

Gone are the days of long drawn out traditional therapies! With Aurora's 'TheQuest™' work, I have found a way to heal and transform any pattern or history from ancient to present times. The space she creates in her sessions is nurturing, loving, empowering and safe. I have found a new sense of purpose in life with each healing of the darker aspects of myself, a greater love for all that I am. TheQuest™ allows me to address issues as they come up and access the core of the issue to transform it all in one session! I am so grateful for Aurora's dedication to the healing arts and her loving presence, which has empowered me as a wife, mother, businesswoman, healer, and human being. —*Colleen Lisowski, Business Owner/Healer, Kula, Hawaii*

Since the session I have a very clear mind, not used to it. All energy is there and the creativity is fully able to explode into any direction it needs to without any interruption. Wow! Still settling in the experience and taking apart the system for a deeper grasp and understanding. —*Arben Kryeziu, Business, Marketing, and Internet Consultant*

I thank the Angels for the day Aurora walked into my life! —*Jason Kitchens, Entrepreneur, Grants Pass, Oregon*

My heart is so open and full from this work. Being gently led through the deepest, darkest places leaves only gratitude, love and freedom. In every session we come quickly to the taproot of the issue, create safety for its exposure and transformation, and watch the magic with awe as the entire tree is healed. This work helps me feel so purposeful; proud to be a human, finally. The tools that Aurora uses for healing are pure magic, like laser surgery for the soul. The operation is fast, relatively painless and totally effective. People would not choose to live with pain if they knew this was available. Miracles with Aurora are commonplace. In every session I have the experience that something very profound has taken place, something life changing of a permanent nature. The power of love to heal used to be an expression. After working with Aurora it is a fact. This gentle, precise soul surgeon is a master at healing. —*Miriam Mara, Business Consultant, Boca Raton, Florida*

I feel differently. My attitude has changed. I definitely have transcended my pattern. I am a whole new being! TheQuest™ session was like an exorcism, casting a demon out of my being that was like a leach, sucking the lifeforce out of me, and preventing me from being who I am as a person. After one session, I am a completely different person. —*Bruce Travis, Author, Real Estate Broker, Wailea, Hawaii*

After 20 years of being intimately involved in the human potential movement, reading endless material, attending every conference I could, listening to speakers, reading their books, and applying their principles, I was never taken to the places I was told they would take me. They just didn't hold up and I would soon be back into my old patterns without knowing why things were not working for me. Then I met Aurora and started receiving TheQuest™ sessions. Right away, after the 1st session, I realized there was a deeper place I needed to go to resolve the issues in my life. I learned of the imporatance of finding the root of the problem instead of adopting a philosophy which doesn't eliminate the effect things have had on my life. My life has changed considerably with the elimination of stress, eliminating guilt and frustration, and knowing I can be completely honest with myself and those around me. My self-esteem has been restored to a new high. Each day I look forward to meeting new people, making friends, creating relationships, and enjoying new, and exciting experiences. There is a new outlook on life that has never been there before, and I am free to achieve my goals and aspirations. I am so grateful for this life changing experience of TheQuest™. —*Bill Mollring, Business Owner*

Aurora brings a special presence to her work as higher energies work through her causing transformation for the individual. I have personally experienced this and have benefited by releasing, clearing, and transforming at a very deep level. Experiencing her work has helped me to take my own healing work to a deeper and more powerful level. —*Lisbeth Johnson, Certified Rolfer, Columbus, Ohio*

I went from panic to peace in my session. It was incredible. Through this work, I'm feeling a new sense of well being. Everything is shifting. Sometimes I don't even recognize this new person. I am healing after 57 years in life, finally getting 'it' with the help of my guide, Dr. Ariel. —*Kamalia Vonlixfeld, Owner, Lotus Galleries, Kauai*

The session was incredible! I am so much less fearful. Even though it seems that nothing has changed in the physical, I see things differently. —*Mary Miller, Editor*

My life is very changed. I am showing up differently in my relationship with my husband, my son and others. TheQuest™ has brought me a renewed sense of faith in the Divine. —DB. *Healer/Mother, Maui, Hawaii*

Aurora embodies the violet flame. Transformation and healing occur in her presence. She is a miracle as is every experience I have with her. Colors are brighter, scents are sweeter, sounds are crisper, air is clearer. Working with Aurora is like buying a shuttle pass to Heaven. The entire experience of being human is a greater joy as a result of these clearings. —*Julie Mara, Business Consultant, Kihei, Hawaii*

I thank Aurora you for her deep and compassionate listening. She has a very special gift and I feel grateful to get to connect and experience it. I was able to be more honest with myself about my feelings and needs in my relationship with a very close friend with a life threatening illness. My opening up with her brought us closer together. TheQuest™ also enhanced my meditation experience, which was really great. They go together very well. —*Paula Mantel, Owner/Educator/ Producer, Discovery Learning Systems, Honolulu, Hawaii*

My work and life has really changed and continuing to change because of working with Dr. Ariel. On top of that I have felt really seen by her which has encouraged me to come out more with who I am in the world, something most others cannot do for me since they are not where I am, and don't understand. Her style of counseling resonates with me because it feels very organic to me, creative and natural in working with the psyche and what wants to be seen, acknowledged, transformed, and that our beings want this and know how to do it with help and encouragement and love. This has been an incredible door for me, and my clients are really benefiting. It is helping me to become who I am and what I am here to do. I'm feeling rather teary now with gratitude for divine guidance in meeting Dr. Ariel and the serendipity of life when we open to spirit. —*Lisbeth Walters, Rolpher and Cranial Sacral Practitioner, Columbus, Ohio*

I feel lighter... I loved the process! I have been thinking so much about everything I experienced! Many thoughtful doors have opened and I love the unfolding. It has been helping to shape the way I think and feel about my loves in my life and the lesson they bring. —*Elli Clauson, Special Ed Teacher, Aspen, Colorado*

TheQuest™ is a gift to our planet from the Angelic Realms, which transforms and blesses all who choose to surrender to the Love and Grace of the Soul. Aurora holds the keys to this sacred process, which liberates energies trapped for lifetimes, allowing true Freedom and Peace to become the basis for a happy, fulfilling life. —*Mirra Rose, Spiritual Teacher, International Speaker, Healer, Wailea, Hawaii*

In my class I got to see a side of Aurora that impresses me to no end. Both the spiritual side, but also the vulnerable sharing and compassionate side that has such great love, desire, energy, and compassion to help the world and a great mind to go with all that. She really connected to the kids and I guarantee that is not an easy thing to do these days. She will make a difference and I feel very fortunate I somehow was blessed I got to meet her. My hat's off to her in a big way. —*Brad Onsgard, Aspen High School Teacher and Law Enforcement Officer*

The tools Aurora shared about in her TV interview are so simple, flow easily and have helped me already. I sent an email about her work to others, and several of us have instantly benefited. The arrangement of her process was much easier than others I've tried. Maybe it is just time for things to be easy. I especially was touched that Aurora allowed the interviewer to be a facilitator, as this shows others that even amateurs can assist healing. I was also impressed that she allowed herself to be the subject. This sends a great message that healers need healing too. I commend her for that openness. —*Libby Coulter, Maui*

When meeting with a court-ordered youth, I noticed an enormous shift in his attitude and responsibility in a very short period of time... So I asked him, "What has happened to cause you to mature so quickly?" and that's when he told me that he was in a program for teens (TheQuest™ Teen Forum) that was making a huge difference for him. While he still has a way to go in his life, I have not seen such a huge internal shift in a youth like this in a very long time. My interest in the TheQuest™ came from seeing results, not from hearing about the program. Fantastic work! —*Shawn Stevenson, MSW, Youth At Risk Counselor, Case Manager for Youth Zone*

AURORA JULIANA ARIEL PhD

Time of the Awakening Soul

How millions of people are changing our future

A Worldwide Awakening,
Global Renaissance & Glorious Destiny Unveiled

A New Frontier In Multimedia Arts
Inspired Music, Books, & Films

Publisher: AEOS, Inc.
PO Box 532539, Wailea, Hi 96753
Ph: 310-591-8799 Fax: 413-521-8799
Email: Info@AEOS.ws
Website: http://www.AEOS.ws

Bio Photo by Christian Cooper
Art Direction by Aurora Juliana Ariel
Cover Design by Aurora Juliana Ariel
Interior Design by Kareen Ross http://www.KareenRoss.com
Editing by Edward Ellsworth http://mystereproductions.com

Printed in the USA by Lightening Source

FIRST EDITION
Library of Congress
ISBN 978-0-9816501-3-5

Dedication

I dedicate this book to

all the valiant souls who have risen up to

assist the planet at this important and historic time

Acknowledgments

With the deepest gratitude
I acknowledge and thank...

The many incredible teachers who have shed light on my pathway, too numerous to name.

Everyone who shared their inspiring stories in this book: Dr. Vernon Woolf, Dr. John Upledger, Dr. Ann West, Dr. Doreen Virtue, Dr. Joe Vitale, Kamala Allen, Gary Voss, Kiara Windrider, Michelle Gold, Peter Sterling, Mirra Rose, Caitlin and Sika, Trish Regan, Marius Michael-George, Robin Miller, Lee Shapiro, Mellen-Thomas Benedict, Richard N. Schooping, Kaitlyn Keyt, Christopher Connolly, Araphiel Brown, Peter Sterling, Boriska, and Gennady Belimo. Your stories have been an important addition to this treatise on the Awakening.

Jack Canfield, for your support, trust in my life's work and vision for humanity. Thank you for assisting me with the Earth 2012 series.

Marc Ivey, for your timely support of AEOS, which allowed this series to be released in its most exquisite form, and for your support and continual belief in me.

Tara Grace, for your friendship and support of AEOS, undying belief in me, and for holding the vision with me that the Earth 2012 series, TheQuest™, my music, and other products will reach everyone they are meant for.

Joe Sugarman, for your timely support of this book and AEOS. Thank you for your friendship and belief in me all these years.

Chris Collins, for your excellent branding advice.

Ed Ellsworth, for your assistance with the editing.

Christian Cooper, for the great photography shoot.

Margaret Phanes, for your timely assistance with the last edit and preparing the documents for print.

My daughter, Mariah, for all your love and support while I wrote this book and birthed my life's work.

My children, Araphiel, Gabriel, and Aradeus, and daughter in law, Becky, for your unwavering belief in me.

Becky Brown, for all your generosity of time and energy helping me with AEOS, and your assistance with marketing, PR, bookkeeping, and fulfillment.

Bruce BecVar, for your friendship and creative collaboration on our music CDs, and your continual love and support.

Vaz Andreas, for all the romantic adventures you created while I was writing this book.

Shakti Navran, Linda Deslauriers, Shalandra Abbey, and Toby Neal of my writer's group on Maui, for all your insights, enthusiasm, and support while wriiing this book.

And my dearest friends, Bernadette and Chester, Melea, and Vajra, for all your love and support over the years as I birthed the Earth 2012 series and gifted TheQuest™ to the world.

Contents

.

The world must
be ready to receive this vision,
for at long last life is compelling me to share it.
I can do nothing less.
It has burned within me like a silent fire for too long.
I know that what I am about to reveal is important.
It must be written,
even though it is very different from the
prophecies and predictions
filling the airwaves of earth today.

It is a unique perspective of a
future potential I have witnessed becoming
a reality for some time.
It is a vision that lives in my heart and inspires my soul.
It is a glimmer of hope for humanity,
a sacred offering to a world in transition.
It is a Sacred Vision whose time has come
to be released to the world.

As you follow the thread
of Violet Stories in this book,
may it reveal a Tapestry of Truth that illumines your soul
and awakens you to the glorious Destiny
that is being birthed at this historic time on earth.

Introduction

The stories in this book are true. As miraculous as they many seem, they are written by credible people. Even if similar experiences have not yet happened to you, reading this book with an open mind can expand your awareness to the infinite wonders that many are now experiencing worldwide. This is the mystical side of our present planetary equation... a doorway that is open to each one of us.

In the first book of the Earth 2012 series, *Earth 2012: The Ultimate Quest, How To Find Peace in a World of Chaos*, I spoke of the glorious time we are in as we reach what is perhaps Earth's most epic moment in history on our journey through the gateway of 2012. I revealed the signs of the times, the portent in the skies, and the prophetic wisdom of the Elders, as earth inhabitants are being prepared at inner levels to make the Shift of the Ages.

We journeyed deep into the dire prophecies and potentials before us to the subconscious patterning that is at the heart of suffering in our world and found a remedy in TheQuest™, the breakthrough healing system I developed.

In this second book of the series, I share many of the incredible phenomena that are helping facilitate The Awakening, catalyzing an advancement in the soul evolution of the planet unparalleled in Earth history. These mystical stories, shared by people from every walk of life and from all over the planet, reveal the unseen hand in the exciting destiny that is unfolding for humanity and the Earth. As more stories pour in, the evidence is clear. We are in an unprecedented and significant time, the outcome of which, will be up to us.

Part One

The Awakening

CHAPTER ONE

The Unseen Hand in Earth's Destiny

Today we stand on the edge of an exciting destiny that is being fulfilled by an unseen force so brilliant in its design that it defies imagination. An Awakening is occurring in millions of people so vast and incomprehensible, it is changing the world around us. You may not even realize it is taking place and yet, this silent force of dynamic intention is forging a New Reality and you are a part of it, whether you are consciously aware of it or not.

In the following chapters, I bring evidence that these largely unnoticed millions are a mystic culture, who by the very nature of their unique destiny, are compelled to change the outcome of our planet's future. Shining a Rainbow of Divine Promise on our horizon, the Awakening of millions of people simultaneously across the planet is the unseen hand in a planetary destiny that could move us out of the grip of dire planetary potentials into a more enlightened world.

As the planet hurls towards destruction and people throughout the world are in the throes of darkness and despair, Awakening Souls are breaking the secret code of their unique destiny and transforming the human programming that has brought us to the brink of disaster.

Inspired by a 'Vision of a Transformed World,' they are changing life on earth, as we know it, dedicating their lives to a planetary restoration project vast in its implementation and yet, largely unnoticed by a majority of Earth's inhabitants who are sadly caught up in Earth's present challenging dramas. From the evidence I've gathered, I believe Awakening Souls are here to turn the tide at the 11th hour. The question is, will they succeed?

Two Futures

I received visions of the future and its many dire potentials beginning in my teens. Later I would read Edgar Cayce's visions and other prophecies similar to what I had been shown. Prophecies that spoke of cataclysmic events and a great undoing that would dramatically change our world.

As a young child, I had a reoccurring experience. I saw myself in the future, telling my grandchildren about the way the world used to be. "We had stores and could buy and sell things," I was saying as I reminisced a lost past. Wide eyed, they barely comprehended what I spoke of because the world was so changed. Could that future be before us? A world where everything we have built through millennia of time has come undone?

Having led an idyllic childhood, the planetary potentials in my visions were foreign to me. I grew up in Malibu, California with parents who were like Barbie and Ken, wonderful and fun and yet, who didn't have the depth they gained in later years. Consequently, I never heard about challenging planetary conditions, wars, disease, or suffering, nor did I watch much television. Secluded in my Malibu Colony world, in creative play or galloping my horse beside the ocean, I was an innocent.

As I journeyed forth at sixteen with my mother's blessing, I had extraordinary experiences that awakened me to the seriousness of the time. I saw how stressed people were and learned about hardship and pain. This was all new to me.

Then my mother became severely ill when I was seventeen and I had my first experience of real suffering. In that one day my life changed. I lost my mother in the role I had known her and became her parent, counselor and guide. This reversal of roles along with my father also abandoning me left me to forge my way alone. In one way this was hard because I had no one to turn to for guidance or help. In another, it left me completely free to follow my own Inner Guidance, which led me on an incredible journey into a new frontier, the Inner World of the Soul.

The Earth became my mother then. I remember feeling safe in her arms as I traveled to many regions, slept beside hot springs, or traversed ancient ruins. I was led to the Indian Nations, to their reservations, culture, and symbolism. I journeyed to other nations and received more visions about the coming earth changes. Against the backdrop of dark potentials, I also received visions of another future. It was as if two distinct pathways lay before us, two ways our world could go at this crucial time, one very disastrous and bleak, the other a shining future.

One set of visions revealed cataclysm and demise, another was of masses of people becoming enlightened. In one vision, I saw the earth in darkness. Suddenly, lights began to appear all over the planet. These points of light began to form circles of light and then became patches of light. The patches filled in until our once dark world was illumined in light.

As I grew to understand the meaning behind these visions, I was also becoming aware of the shift in my own consciousness and that of many others and the impact it was having on the planet.

Later, I delved deeply into the psyche and uncovered the cause of suffering and a way to heal it from within. This birthed TheQuest™. I also saw the answer to the dire potentials before us in The Awakening that was occurring worldwide. As more people awakened to their higher purpose, healed their lives and became a part of this Light Potential, we would witness the healing of our world, and the cataclysmic prophecies for our time would be averted.

CHAPTER THREE

Remembrance

There was a formative experience in my teens that changed the landscape of my life and set me on a powerful destiny course. Transported back to right before this life, I found myself in a Soul School along with many others. We were excited about coming to Earth. Seated in a large Grecian Hall with high ceilings, we were watching a movie on a big screen that was evoking human emotions like love, caring, and compassion in preparation for our life on Earth.

There was great excitement as we prepared to embark upon this exciting adventure, though we had a sense it would not be easy. We knew we would be born into a serious time. Our saving grace would be knowing that this timea around, we would all come in together, though we would be born throughout the Earth. This was very different from the past when there had only been a handful of advanced souls or one illumined individual born to help the planet move forward at a given time.

Our preparation was momentous and joyous, as many of us knew we would ascend in this life. This word was new to me. I had never heard the word 'Ascension' before, but it seems to be part of the unique and clearly distinctive vocabulary of Awakening Souls. We would all be 'ascending' together, our collective consciousness rising each year. Knowing this was happening to all of us together would be our comfort in a troubled world, a source of great inspiration, connectedness, and purpose.

As the years have passed, I have witnessed my vision coming true. There is an acceleration in my consciousness that I similarly witness in others. An internal refining process is taking place that is powerful and profound, the reality of which cannot be denied. Each year we emerge more awake and illumined, rising to each new level, all of us together across the Earth. This is a significantly violet energetic of great import, because it is behind the personal and planetary transformation that is changing the landscape of our world. We have entered a 'Violet' Age where nothing will remain the same, as we advance light years in consciousness into a future that is very different than the dire one presently looming before us.

Through the years, I've met people all over the world who share a similar vision of a transformed world. It is as if we immediately know each other, though we might not be able to understand each other's native language. As we break through Earth Language barriers, we find we share a similar consciousness language that becomes our special bond. This has given me a sense of peace, knowing so many of us are here on earth together at this time, undergoing the immense challenges of this grand adventure as we turn our world on a more positive course.

CHAPTER FOUR

The Inner World

My early visions had a profound impact at such a young age, their immensity propelling me into a life of study and research. A host of excruciating challenges arrived in quick succession, further catalyzing my Quest for Truth. This led me into my Inner World.

My journey into the shadowlands of the psyche opened up a world of untapped knowledge. As I traversed ancient histories in countless clients and myself, a reoccurring theme emerged. Earth was a sorrowful planet where souls came to suffer. Despite humanity's highest dreams and aspirations, there was continual hardship and strife here. Delving deeply to find the answer why, I discovered that suffering is a direct result of a rift in the human psyche that began millennia ago.

Humanity became disconnected from their True Identity and link with Source when they began forming beliefs about their existence and the nature of life. These caused distortions in the quantum physics of the planet as consciousness affected physical reality, reshaping the very molecules of our world. The Legend of Eden could be more than a myth. We very well could be descendents of an enlightened world who have lost our way.

In thousands of sessions I found the same equation. Contrary to many religious beliefs, I discovered no outer force or deity regulating us to suffering. Suffering is the direct result of subconscious programming that can be healed and I found a way.

Over many years, I traced every dire condition (pain, illness, job stress, relationship problems, financial strain) to inner belief systems born of misinterpretations. Sub-personalities formed as they broke away from the Core Self under stress or pain, took on beliefs that formed patterns and these created distortions in physical reality.

These distorted patterns have passed down through our family lineages, until today only legends remain of the glorious ages of Earth's Edenic past. Even the most positive person cannot elude the miscreation of the subconscious. That is why good people can have bad things happen to them and why you can follow all the spiritual formulas of the world and still experience painful circumstances.

Humanity's disconnection from Authentic Selfhood continues to cast its shadow upon our world. The question is, "Will we wake up in time?" Will we pull out of the dire potentials looming before us and avert the Great Travail long prophesied and fast appearing in our world?

I found, to do that, we must return to our Edenic Nature. How is that possible? The answer is to heal the shadowed awareness that has covered over our True Self.

Addressing this dilemma, I spent years developing a Counseling Theory and Healing Practice that could go right to core beliefs and the patterns they set in motion, and heal them. I call this breakthrough Healing System, TheQuest™. You can read more about TheQuest™ in the Addendum, and learn how to apply it in your life in book one, *Earth 2012: The Ultimate Quest.*)

CHAPTER FIVE

Time of the Awakening

Long prophesied, the Time of the Awakening was well underway when the new millennium dawned. Heralding in the coming new cycle known as the Aquarian Age, millions of souls began undergoing a major shift in consciousness. Piscean ideals that fostered dependence on outer forces and dictates gave way to universal ideals that empowered Self-Actualization. A planetary shift occurred in the consciousness of a people as Awakening Souls began understanding that 'peace begins with me,' and that 'together we are responsible for our planet.' This vast and comprehensive change in the psyche of humanity began a rippling effect on Earth that many are now calling the Shift of the Ages.

Millions of people worldwide began waking up from the slumbers of a mass programming behind the human dilemma. They began breaking out of the grip of societal patterns that limited their self-expression and created misery in their lives. There was a mass exodus from religious doctrines promoting Suffering as a Way of Life, as millions turned their attention to personal empowerment and claiming the Abundant Life as their Divine Birthright. Marches for World Peace became the signature of a generation of souls who were no longer willing to perpetuate suffering, war, and strife on the planet. A Human Potential Movement was born.

Today, the Awakening has changed the lives of millions of people throughout the earth who are waking up to their planetary responsibility in time to address the dire potentials before us. The unconsciousness of past eras that drove humanity to create wars, plunder nations, and to hold material acquisition as the highest attainment in life is giving way to a more conscious reality, where we become wise stewards of the Earth and extend love and respect to all inhabitants.

The Awakening is a shift in consciousness where we move out of the grip of our unconscious wounding and awaken to the true self beyond our human programming. This Authentic Reality is a bastion of knowledge, wisdom, and peace within us that compels us to refine our natures, emulate noble qualities, create harmony in all our relationships, and to express ourselves in ways that are a blessing to others and the planet.

The Awakening has ignited millions of people throughout the world with a new vision and planetary awareness. This has launched a Global Renaissance that is birthing new inventions and cures, a host of inspired media in music, books and films, and sustainable models that are being implemented in communities around the globe.

An Enlightened Age is being birthed out of an old order, in the midst of chaos and travail, and even though the dire circumstances that beset our world have many quaking in fear, anything can happen. The prophecies of doom are not set in stone. Infinite possibilities await us as we change the future from within.

CHAPTER SIX

A Mystic Equation

There are many phenomena facilitating The Awakening at this time. This is the mystical side of our planetary equation, and it is huge in its ramification for positive planetary change. Through extraordinary encounters and life changing experiences, consciousness is shifting to where we are seeing a leap in human evolution way beyond the norm.

This book is filled with these stories. Though many of them are so mystical they defy reality, exemplary individuals from all walks of life lend credibility to the extraordinary experiences that inspired them to live more conscious lives and make a difference on the planet.

Over the years, profound experiences have inspired my own journey through a troubled world. I've included many of them in this book as well. They have brought hope at the darkest hours and lifted me into heights I never knew were available or attainable.

When we awaken to the fact that we are in the midst of a Great Happening, our perspective on the planetary equation shifts. We realize all is not lost. We are not doomed to extinction as was the fate of lost civilizations of Earth's past. We are not in the grip of dire circumstances without remedy. There is a way out and that is what The Awakening is about. It is a change in thinking and values from within the psyche of humanity, a shift so powerful and profound it changes the world around us.

Many patriots have believed it is better to 'Live Free or Die.' Dedicating their lives to an exemplary service, they paved the way for our freedoms today. We must hold to this sacred trust, for freedom to be all of who we are is how we will realize our full potential. To soar like eagles on Earth, we must align with our Soul Purpose and strengthen our will so that we stay focused on being a vehicle of positive change in the world.

Each one of us is making a difference to our planetary outcome and we must not underestimate our potential, for it is a powerful force of good that can drive our lives and those around us into a better future. We may never know the full extent of the lives we are touching and the great good we are doing, but we will feel an inner sense of fulfillment when we know we are making a difference.

CHAPTER SEVEN

An Illumined Pathway

Out of the Dark Night, a light has appeared on the horizon. It is calling us onto an Illumined Pathway into a New World. It is summoning us to participate in an exciting destiny for our planet. It is calling each of us to do our part.

This New Light is bathing the earth with a bright promise. Significantly violet, it is compelling a planetary transformation unparalleled in earth history, awakening and illumining millions of souls across the Earth. This is the mysterious equation in a planetary hand that is amazing, for here at our darkest hour in the midst of planetary travail, people from every walk of life are coming into higher awareness.

For years I've delved deeply into this passage through 2012 and uncovered at the heart of it, an emergence of souls who are having a great impact on our planet. I call them the Violet People because of their focus on personal and planetary transformation, a distinctly violet quality.

Nahari wrote, "Violet symbolizes the creative force, beauty, inspiration and artistry. Energetically, violet inspires the receptive soul to express itself in art, music, spiritual ideals and selfless acts of love. It is the universal call to excellence that inspires great things and works of art."

I first introduced the Violet People in my book, *Earth 2012: The Ultimate Quest, How to Find Peace in a World of Chaos* and shared how the internal shift in Awakening Souls is having a rippling effect on the collective consciousness of the planet.

Alchemists of old knew the power of the Violet Light. The highest frequency of the seven rays, it holds the energetic of transformation. There was a revival of this Sacred Knowledge beginning in the late nineteenth century. In recent times, advanced healing instruments have been invented that emit ultra violet light.

Today millions of Violet People are breaking down the human

encoded barriers to realizing and empowering their Authentic Self. As they transcend the archaic patterns that have perpetuated suffering in our world, a vast and almost incomprehensible leap in human evolution is taking place.

Uncovering the mystery of our present age, I unlocked the secret code to this vast planetary transformation and am providing a powerful technology to accelerate healing with TheQuest™. This alchemical process is easy to apply and can completely transform your life. (TheQuest™ 7 Step Self Counseling Technique is available in book one, *Earth 2012: The Ultimate Quest*).

It is the Violet People today, who are the Avant Guarde. They are opening new doorways of thought and are leading the masses into a new awareness. They are activating an ancient encoding within the human psyche that can birth a glorious Eden in the midst of a troubled world.

The world is rapidly changing, because a host of Violet People have embodied on Earth at this critical moment. Because they are here, much suffering that has been predicted for our time can be averted.

Violet People show us that sanity can return to the inhabitants of Earth and a new consciousness can rule the world. Their presence is a light at the end of the tunnel, a glimmer of hope in our present Dark Night.

A Divine Hand is playing out and its greatest card is the millions of Awakening Souls who are turning our world around and setting us on a safer course. By healing their lives, they are transforming the future.

So, who are these Ilustrious Souls who are having such a dramatic impact on our planet? Read on, and see if you are one of them.

Part Two

The Violet People

CHAPTER ONE

The Violet People

*Usually each universal age is accompanied by a life color,
and during each such age there is a prevalence of people
born during that time with that corresponding life color.*

*-Genevieve Richards
Author and Freelance writer*

The world was a very different place before Violet People arrived.
It is almost as if everything was black and white and then, in a twinkling
of an eye, became living color. Citizens of the earth, for the most part,
held to their national identities, eating the foods and wearing the clothing of their native lands. Each followed the dictates of the predominant
religions in their respective areas. The Quest for Enlightenment, Human
Empowerment, and Spiritual Awakening was relatively unheard of.

People lived more limited lives in line with the status quo.
Societal programming was strong and for the most part, adhered to.
Thinking "outside the box" was left to the rare scientist or philosopher
who, often ridiculed for bringing forward new information, was rarely
applauded or acknowledged.

Through the ages, a saint or sage might seek to enlighten their
community. In some cases, religious factions would jealously guard
the history as their "own" lineage and the "only way" to salvation.
Separation between these religious factions created wars and this continues today.

The ideals of unity, harmony, and peace have been sentiments
left to religious manuscripts, while humanity has continued to fight for
their separatist beliefs. And sadly, universal laws have seldom been the
true ideal behind planetary movements.

Respect for other religious traditions has been a concept embraced
by only a few scholars and people of a philosophical nature, and though

advancements in technologies gave the feeling that humanity was progressing into a more enlightened era, it was still very much the dark ages when Violet Souls arrived.

It has been in relatively recent history that Violet People appeared on Earth. The threads of their unique vision can be seen in past centuries, but the real impact of their presence was not felt until the 1960's when a host of movements were launched reflecting Violet Ideals. Since that time, the world has been undergoing a major shift as consciousness breaks through the darkness, and fiery intention replaces apathy in those once relegated to an unhappy fate.

There have been many prophecies of a Coming Race destined to take the planet through a profound change. Some of the most powerful prophecies come from the Indian Nations, who saw a new culture rise at a time of darkness on the planet that would be born from every race and nation. They called this multi-cultured group the Warriors of the Rainbow.

Standing Bear of the Manataka Indian Council said, "Our Prophecies foretell of a people who will rise from earth's ashes like the thunderbird symbolizing rebirth. They will bring balance and harmony back to Mother Earth. The first of these beings will come as teachers and storytellers to remind us of the ancient truths of the star people and beyond. They will be pathfinders leading the way to a new universe, a new reality. Great Leaders, Warriors and Shamans of many nations will be born and they will cleanse the Earth for rebirth. Next will come the Planters sowing seeds of truth, justice and freedom. The Storytellers, Warriors and Planters will live in the way of the Great Spirit and teach ways to keep Mother of the Ground sacred forevermore. They will be called Rainbow Warriors for they will gather the four sacred directions, all distinctly separate but forever connected in the Circle of Life. They will bring together the four races of man to live in peace. The four sacred directions and the four races of man are symbolized by the magnificence and glory of the rainbow. The neo-indigenous people of the Rainbow will give praise for the blessings of the Creator's loving grace."

The spectacular nature of these 'Rainbow' Violets is that they catalyze change, inspire new systems, create new approaches, and address dilemmas in new ways. They share a similar vision of Earth's future potential and unique insight into present world conditions. Though they have been born in different locations throughout the world, have been raised with different values, and have completely different back-grounds, they share a common vision and mission. They even speak their own consciousness language.

Violet People have an uncanny ability to find each other through-out the planet, joining into groups with shared missions, visions, and creative endeavors. They create global conferences and trek to sacred sites where they share in sacred moments. They love to get into groups of a spiritual or healing nature and join together in global meditations or marches for world peace. They move on an inner quest for truth, inspiring the lives of everyone around them.

Powerful in its ramifications for planetary change, Violet Inspiration is igniting a revolution in consciousness that is reverberat-ing throughout the planet. Light, color, and sound have become the elements used by the 21st Century Alchemist to uplift, heal, and inspire as Creative Artists transform the landscape of the human mind, moving humanity from unconsciousness to self-actualization.

A host of transformational media in music, books, art, and film is weaving its magic upon the human psyche launching a global renais-sance unparalleled in Earth time. This, along with inventions, green technologies, and sustainable projects, are laying the foundation for an Enlightened World.

Born to fulfill an extraordinary destiny, the Violet Race is a col-lective consciousness that moves from an inner calling to heal and transform the planet. This mission has inspired a massive Restoration Earth Project that has compelled Violets to heal and transform the pat-terns of the past so that they can bring their authentic power into the equation. In this way, Violet People come of age and realize their full potential. And yet, one of the most intriguing facets of the Violet Soul Mystery is that the Violet Person many times doesn't know who they are or the power that they wield to transform a world. They, like the rest of humanity, have undergone the amnesia inherent in this earth experi-ence. Until they go through an awakening process, their true identity and purpose for being on the planet remains hidden.

The Violet Soul phenomenon is a silent force of positive intention, a shared destiny unparalleled in earth's history that could completely change our world. It is as if the Violet Race has come from a future, more advanced time. They cannot abide the soul amnesia other gen-erations of Earth have complacently accepted. They are not content to remain in the dark. They enter a quest for self-identity early on, exploring the mystery of the soul. They seek freedom from the personality dysfunctions of their family lineage. They are compelled to realize their Full Potential.

While Violet People have a quiet power, their presence is emanating throughout the Earth. The world has undergone vast changes since their arrival, and this is only the beginning. Their focus on Personal and Planetary Transformation is a signpost of the Violet Age, a time foretold when humanity would go through the Great Purification and the planet would be restored. The change in values on Earth since their coming has been nothing less than miraculous. Since Violet Souls arrived, the world has never been the same.

Wayshowers Of A New Millennium

Violet Souls are the inspirational visionaries,
leaders and teachers who are here to help save the planet.

-Pamela Oslie
Author of Life Colors

Nicholas Tesla, Albert Einstein, Gandhi, Jules Verne and other brilliant minds of a previous generation opened us to New Frontiers followed by an influx of millions of new Wayshowers who have joined the fray. Today Violet People are on the leading edge, inspiring New Archetypes for the New Society. They are carrying the torches with advances in medicine, pioneering work in psychology, green technologies, inventions and cures, which are restoring the planet and releasing humanity from its bondage.

Some of the most prominent people of our time could be Violets. These are the individuals who are paving a new way for humanity, who are bringing forth new thought and advanced technologies, who are the leaders in the Human Potential Movement working for global change. Scientists, Innovators, and Inventors, Pioneers of the Psyche, Leaders in the Green Movement, Yogis and Medicine People, are all 21st Century Visionaries and Architects of Planetary Change. I've listed some of them here.

Queen Noor of Jordan and her beloved, the King of Jordan, embodied the New Relationship Archetype, where out of a great love a gift flows forth to humanity. Their vision of Peace in the Middle East gave them a shared mission. They educated the people of Jordan bringing new thought and timely advances to their country. Today, Queen Noor continues to work tirelessly for world peace and the betterment of our world.

Mother Teresa, viewed by many as a contemporary saint, brought global awareness to some of the greatest issues of our time. Tending to the sick, poor, and needy, she reminded the world of the importance of caring compassionately for those in distress, and that each life on earth is precious.

Robert F. Kennedy, Jr's reputation as a resolute defender of the environment stems from a litany of successful legal actions. He was named one of Time magazine's "Heroes for the Planet" for his success helping Riverkeeper lead the fight to restore the Hudson River. The group's achievement helped spawn more than 130 Waterkeeper organizations across the globe. He has worked on environmental issues across the Americas and has assisted several indigenous tribes in Latin America and Canada in successfully negotiating treaties protecting traditional homelands. The New York City watershed agreement is regarded as an international model in sustainable development. Among Mr. Kennedy's published books are the New York Times bestseller, *Crimes Against Nature*, and *St. Francis of Assisi: A Life of Joy,* showing both his activist and mystical side.

Al Gore, former Vice President, won the Nobel Peace Award for helping awaken humanity to the dire potentials of global warming. In the wake of defeat in the 2000 presidential election, he re-set the course of his life to focus on a last-ditch, all-out effort to help save the planet from irrevocable change. The film, *An Inconvenient Truth*, takes a passionate and inspirational look at this man's fervent crusade to halt global warming's deadly progress by exposing the myths and misconceptions that surround it. Through his 'traveling global warming show' he is bringing what he calls a "planetary emergency" into global awareness.

Princess Diana brought the world's attention to timely issues and concerns such as landmines and AIDs. She demonstrated love and compassion as she traveled to hospitals and hugged AIDs patients. She was interested in astrology, delving deeply into the mysteries of life, and serving a higher purpose. Her life inspired millions around the world.

Oprah Winfrey rose from humble beginnings knowing she had a special purpose to fulfill. She is one of the most avant garde women on the planet, helping awaken millions of people who tune into her television show daily from across the world. Many of her shows are on Violet Topics including The Power of Now with Eckhart Tolle, Spiritual Partnership with Gary Zukav, and 'The Secret.' Her programs not only bring awareness of timely issues, they help people live their 'best lives.'

Angelina Jolie and Brad Pitt's relationship represents sacred partnership in planetary service. As Ambassadors of Peace, they have awakened us to the plights of orphans, to the suffering and starvation of many peoples, and to the dire circumstances of many nations.

Paul and Linda McCartney's spiritual partnership was displayed in their great love, devotion to family, and concert performances together, while Linda's animal rights activism focused on a solution through the promotion of vegetarianism via her multimillion-dollar vegeburger business.

Leonardo Di'Caprio, the latest emissary for planetary awareness to rise from the stars, produced and narrated the film, *The 11th Hour*, which brings a dire warning that we've almost reached the point of no return. The film explores humanity's impact on the Earth's ecosystems and what we can do to change our course before it is too late.

John and Yoko, perhaps one of the most controversial couples in recent history, promoted their revolutionary ideas helping launch the Peace Movement. In his song, *Imagine*, John shares the Vision of a Transformed World encoded in the Violet Race.

Martin Luther King's vision of unity and equality resounded around the world and came alive in the hearts of many who followed him to change laws and way of life in America. To this day, his 'new thought' and timely philosophies have inspired positive change in countless lives.

Prominent Leaders in the Human Potential Movement: Tony Robbins, Jack Canfield, Mark Victor Hansen, Marianne Williamsen, Shakti Gawain, Wayne Dyer, Alan Cohen, Reverend Michael Beckwith, and others.

Some of the Pioneers in Psychology and Mind Body Medicine: Carl Rogers (developed Client Centered Therapy), Rollo May (Art of Counseling), Carl Jung (founder of Analytical Psychology), Deepak Chopra (best selling author and leader in Mind, Body Medicine), Fritz and Laura Perls (developed Gestalt Therapy), Roberto Assagioli (developed Psychosynthesis), Dr. Bernie Segal (pioneering doctor and author of Love, Medicine, and Miracles), Ron and Mary Hulnick (Founders of USM (University of Santa Monica) and its Spiritual Psychology, Consicousness, Health and Healing, M.A. and PsyD Courses.)

Archetypes of the New Relationship: Authors John Gray (Men Are From Mars, Women Are From Venus), Gay and Kathlyn Hendricks (Conscious Loving), Harville Hendricks (Getting the Love Your Want), John Welwood (Journey of the Heart: The Path of Conscious Love), and many others.

CHAPTER THREE

Signature of the Violet Soul

Though Violet People have been born into every culture throughout the planet, it has been interesting to find that they share similar attributes. The following are the 22 Master Qualities that give Violet People a unique signature. See how many describe you. If you feel a resonance with these qualities you are definitely a Violet Person.

1. Unique. Growing up, many Violet People feel they are different than others. Alone, and often misunderstood, many feel that they don't fit in. They can be born into families, go to schools, or be surrounded by people they cannot relate to, or live in areas where they feel no one is like them. Many of these souls are highly creative, have special talents, or gifts. This can cause challenges in their ability to follow the 'status quo' or live up to societal or family standards. Many have a heart for humanity, are very compassionate and caring. Many Violet People go in a different direction than their parents would like them to, turning away from the family business, the economic standard, or lifestyle of their upbringing to seek a new way that is a reflection of their true nature, talents and gifts.

2. Sensitive. Many Violets are highly sensitive. They need to live serene lives and renew themselves in solitude, especially the highly creative ones. They find relief and healing in nature. Some are recluses, withdrawing from the craziness of the world and from people they have felt were unkind. This can cause them to feel alone at times, or to embrace an aloneness that allows them their individuality and a fuller creative expression.

3. Seek Altered States. Meditation has been widely embraced by the Violet Person, bringing them into altered states that have had profound ramifications and which have led them to follow extraordinary visions or insights. Prayer, reflection, and inner communion with the Divine are common among these souls. Some Violet People use drugs or alcohol to escape the wounds from a painful childhood, challenging relationship, or a troubled world. Others use drugs to experience altered states of awareness, to find themselves, the deeper meaning of their life, or to get a different perspective than what they've been taught or told. Many times the drug use leads to addictions or personality disorders that they must then overcome. In healing these conditions, many come through the ordeal having a unique offering for others.

4. Creative. Many Violet Souls are extremely talented and are brimming with unbridled creativity. They lend their unique vision to the Global Renaissance presently underway. A host of inspired books, music, films, and art, healing modalities, self help techniques, unique architecture, planet friendly products, conscious businesses and more are changing the world we are living in through these 'Cultural Creatives.'

5. Free Spirits. Violet People walk away from conventions and confines of society that do not appeal to their free spirited natures. Instead they go on spiritual journeys and quests, living completely different lives than their families and communities. They are seekers on the path, looking for new, more enlightened ways to live. Many remove themselves from the solemn dictates of society and from religions that seem unloving or out of date. Freedom is a strong theme in the Violet Race and is the prevailing energy behind the Violet Age. In this Age of Freedom, humanity releases itself from enslavement to outdated belief systems and patterns, entering a time of greater enlightenment and noble achievement.

6. Individuality. Seeking to go where no one else has gone before and to live free of codes and beliefs that are confining, Violet People adopt an eclectic view of life, embracing many different paths, ways of being, spiritual traditions, diets, clothing, and lifestyles that are reflective of their true natures. They will eat food from a different country every night, wear clothing from different cultures around the world, will delve deeply into different religious traditions incorporating what they resonate with into their own practices, will travel widely, explore new horizons, and will adopt new ways of thinking inspired from different traditions throughout the planet.

7. **Conscious.** Violet People are striving to be conscious in every area of their lives including their diets, health, the environment, their business, workplace, and relationship. They feel troubled when they fall short of their higher ideals or behave unconsciously and hurt others. They strive for higher standards, excellence, and awareness in all their relationships and like to be present, centered, and clear. This intention has launched a host of movements and media speaking to a conscious way of life that is a strong theme in the Violet Soul.

8. **Self-Discovering.** Self-inquiry is important to these souls. The Violet Person wants to know where they came from and why they are here. They enter paths of discovery to uncover who they are beyond their human existence. They are not content to adhere to the beliefs of others. They want a personal experience, a personal knowledge that they can only gain from a quest within. This puts them on a unique journey of self-discovery that can take them into many interesting experiences and through many life changes that may seem abnormal to others who are not having a similar experience. The more self evolved, the more these souls bring their newfound awareness and insights to help others. The quest for their lost identity has sparked a universal interest in the Legend of the Holy Grail, sacred scriptures, ancient texts, and apocryphal works. It has immersed them in the mystical traditions of the world religions and the healing practices of shamans and medicine people. It has inspired a yearning for sacred knowledge, a personal experience of God, and a reconnection with their Authentic Self.

9. **Quest For Truth.** The Violet Person is interested in uncovering the truth. They study ancient history, go to ruins and sacred sites, they are interested in phenomena and the mystical aspects of life, they study different traditions and love to delve deeply into mysteries and the miraculous. They want to know what is happening behind the scenes, what is the deeper message and meaning to their life experience. Many

are up on the latest exposes, advances, inventions, technologies, and healing modalities.

10. **Learn From Challenges.** The life of the Violet Person can be very challenging, giving them much growth and learning. Consequently, many Violets are very strong because they've been through so much. Many realize that the challenges they've faced have given them a unique perspective about the world around them and have helped them to develop a compassion for humanity they might not have had if their lives had been easier. In many cases, overcoming these life challenges compels them to assist others similarly afflicted. A reoccurring theme is the choice to be born into family dynamics with challenges that are scarring, giving the Violet Person a 'Mount Everest' of adversity to overcome. By healing their childhood wounds, they come out of the experience with an extraordinary wisdom to share and a special gift for humanity. Many Violets like self-imposed challenges. It helps strengthen their character as they forge their unique identity. We saw this with the advent of fire walking and a host of X-Games and extreme sports. There is a thrill for jumping off mountains, racing down rapids, going through ropes courses, delving deeply into their shadow self, and living on the edge.

11. **Self-Improving.** The Violet Person continually strives to better their self. They delve deeply to find the answers to their life dilemmas and strive to make positive changes in their lives. They are not content to carry on the family patterns as generations before them have done. Instead, they receive psychotherapy, go to healers or shamans to clear the past and to free themselves of ways of being they may have taken on that are not akin to their True Nature. Self help books and empowerment seminars become a way of life, assisting them to make sense of each new level of their awakening. Those who have gained great mastery in their respective areas love to share their knowledge with others. They become teachers of the highest order.

12. **Purposeful.** The Violet Soul seeks to find their unique purpose in life and fulfill it. They follow their inner voice and calling, inwardly guided as their Soul Purpose unfolds. They may feel they have special gifts or talents that they must bring forth to help others. Developing

these gifts gives them a unique journey that is exciting and fulfilling. They feel they are here to fulfill a mission and can be very focused and purposeful. Oftentimes they will feel frustrated when their life conditions block them from fulfilling something meaningful. The Violet Person becomes discontent when working in a job that is contrary to their interests and talents. They can feel stifled in relationships that are not deep and constantly evolving, and can get bored easily with the mundane aspects of life. These souls are not content to just drift along or to get lost in meaningless pursuits. If they have done this, they may feel depressed, lose incentive, or feel like their life has no meaning. This lack of fulfillment will cause them to seek answers to their dilemma, which can then lead them to make changes to create a more purposeful and empowering life. Many who have done this become teachers sharing their experience, knowledge, and wisdom with others.

13. Service Oriented. Many Violets have felt lost in a world that is driven by money and accumulating possessions because they like to be of service to others. They may love the finer things in life, but many of them would rather be of service and be on a path of self discovery and awakening than to seek money, status, and possessions as their main drive in life. The Violet Person likes to be a master of manifestation, drawing in the resources they need rather than working hard for a living just to barely get by. Many renounce the world for a time, retreating in ashrams, communes, religious orders, or spiritual communities where they can be free to find themselves, make sense of the earthly dilemma, and realize their purpose in life.

14. Loving Parents. Violet People are constantly striving to be conscious, loving parents, and many times feel ashamed when they make the same mistakes as their parents. They are ever focused on their child's greatest welfare, advancement and creative expression. They feed their children healthy foods, raise them in safe environments, inspire higher intelligence by teaching them when they are very young. Some even read to their unborn child or play inspiring music for them while they are in the womb. They love to enhance their child's creative expression, interact with them in empowering ways, and are dedicated to helping their children reach their highest potential.

15. Authentic. It is the authenticity of the Violet Person that is their charm. Open and caring, these people love to share their truth, discuss their issues, and work things out. They continually strive to better themselves and shy away from any form of dishonesty, falsehood, and fakeness, usually feeling a great sense of remorse or failure when they lie or behave unconsciously.

16. Experiential. The Violet Person loves to have a direct experience of life and acquire much of their knowledge by personal experience. These people venture out on journeys, partake of ceremonies, experience the magic of other cultures, and experiment with various healing modalities, spiritual techniques, and traditions from different planetary cultures.

17. Spiritual. Violet People are ever on a quest. Some enter a spiritual path at a young age that takes them into the deeper mysteries of life. They delve deeply into the mystical aspects of their religion or move away from traditional religious thought on a journey of self-awakening and discovery. Self-realization is sought through meditation, psychotherapy, shamanic journeys, transformational healing, and treks to sacred sites. Violets love to experience different spiritual practices and traditions incorporating them into their own spiritual practice. Rituals are adopted from many different religions, as are spiritual icons, creating a unique blend that appeals to their own individuality and unique essence. Their homes are many times filled with spiritual pictures and sacred art. One of the signatures of Violets is an altar in their home that reflects their own spiritual path, with statues or pictures of saints, sages and spiritual traditions they resonate with.

18. Mystics. Violet People around the world are having mystical experiences that are profound and life changing. In past centuries, a saint, sage, medicine man or woman was a rare gift to a community. In the new millennium, the practices, soul searching, and inner experiences of the saints are now being experienced by a multitude of Violets, birthing us into a very unique time where communion with angels and divine realms, once a signpost of the mystic, is fast becoming a commonplace practice experienced by Violet People throughout the globe.

19. Visionaries. Encoded in the heart of the Violet Race is the Utopian Ideal. Violets not only have a clear vision of this potential, but will work very hard towards it. They inspire others to high ideals and noble endeavors, paving the way for millions of souls who, on fire with a Sacred Vision, can rise to play their own unique roles in birthing a New World. The Violet Person has hope for humanity and cares what happens to the Earth. They are troubled with the world condition and sometimes fall under the weight of planetary burdens. They hold great visions of the future and speak of a higher purpose and potential for humanity that they themselves are striving for. This many times can make them a bit serious, because they are very dedicated and committed to helping others and to furthering the positive direction of our planet. They strive for perfection, love to inspire others to realize their full potential, and feel chagrined when they and others around them fall short of their ideals.

20. Humanitarian. The Violet Person wants to make a difference. They are advocates for positive change. They will work tirelessly to accomplish goals that will directly affect the areas they are concerned about. Their passion about causes has launched a host of organizations dedicated to benefiting humanity, saving starving children and people, finding new cures and innovations, implementing green technologies, stopping pollution, and educating the masses. These people tend to be workaholics striving for a cause that never gives them rest, until they learn that they must live a more balanced life if they want the planet to reflect this harmony and balance as well.

21. Environmentalists. The Violet Person has a deep concern for the direction our planet is taking and the effects modern society has upon the environment. This has spawned groups in every nation who have a concentrated focus on protecting our natural resources, national parks, the rainforest, wildlife, and endangered species. Violet People are committed to bringing awareness, inspiring others in timely actions that can bring ecological balance back into our world. Imagine if they succeed! We could have crystal clear streams, oceans, and skies and be living in an unpolluted world filled with pristine natural environments!

22. Universal Thinkers. The Violet Person loves universal principles and ideals. Unity and oneness is a celebrated theme. They are universal in their thinking and in their spiritual beliefs, incorporating what feels right to them from the different world religions. Violets tend to create personally tailored daily practices, set up altars in their homes that represent many different traditions, and fill their homes with décor that is sacred and spiritual. Many are into meditation and practices that inspire self-realization, self-transformation, and self-actualization.

How many Violet Qualities described you?

1 – 5 **A Hint of Violet**: You have some Violet Qualities and may be exploring or open to Violet Ideologies.

6 – 10 **Budding Violet**: You are awakening to your Violet Nature.

11 – 17 **Blossoming Violet**: You know you have a special purpose to fulfill. You have tapped into your True Identity. You live with purpose and are committed to Violet Ideologies.

18 – 22 **Full Blown Violet**: You are awake. You live consciously. You are aware of your unique destiny and are fulfilling your Soul Purpose.

CHAPTER FOUR

21st Century Sages

Today, millions of 21st Century Sages make up a Violet Culture that was prophesied long before its arrival by the Indian Nations and others seers for our time. How did the ancient ones know we were coming to such an apocryphal moment, and that millions of souls would arrive to help the Earth at the 11th hour? Their visions help us understand that the destiny of our planet is not set in stone. We have a grand opportunity to be part of a collective intention that can change the future.

Unique in every respect, this is not a culture born of one religious ideology or from one region on earth. This is a multi-cultured group of souls who have been born into every country and religious background. They have embodied on earth at an historic moment in time to help humanity awaken to a greater destiny and their presence is a glimmer of light in a dark world.

No one person is heading this group, nor is it a human made monument in any form and yet, millions of people today are on this quest, creating an exponential leap in human consciousness across the planet. These legions are fulfilling a destiny born of the fathomless inner kingdom from which all divine purpose has sprung, and it is manifesting its glorious hand in the future of our planet.

This great influx of mysticism is unparalleled in earth history. It heralds a time of great change as 21st Century Sages impact the inhabitants of Earth and change the direction of our planet. This Mystic Culture is igniting a fire to make a difference and this is compelling people worldwide to make an extraordinary effort at a time when our planet is in dire need of assistance if we are going to make it through the gateway of 2012.

Extraordinary stories of mystic encounters fill the pages of this book. They may resonate strongly with you, or seem beyond the scope of possibility. I felt the same way when I first learned that people were being healed by the dolphins and that these encounters were taking place in increasing numbers all over the world.

Whether you believe you are a Violet or not, you have gifts and talents to lend to the present planetary equation and you can make a difference, but you must begin now. If you remain immobilized under the weight of too many personal and planetary problems, not knowing where to begin, you will never play your unique role and fulfill your destiny for this time.

When you move beyond overwhelm and begin positive action in the area you are most qualified and that is aligned with your soul purpose, you will find your greatest joy in a cause you are the most passionate about. Then you can lend an extraordinary effort that will inspire others to do the same.

When you realize that the efforts of the few can translate into a far-reaching positive planetary change, you are no longer daunted by a lack in numbers. The unconscious apathy of the masses will no longer set you back, making you feel that your effort does not count.

We are in an exciting time, where light and dark are increasing exponentially, and where we are seeing this same drama playing out within us. It is time for each of us to take command and lend our creative energies to end the Reign of Darkness so that we can birth a New World.

CHAPTER FIVE

Prophetic Visions

The rich ancient heritage the Indian Nations bring to this study is seen in their prophetic visions of a coming race, who in a time of turmoil, would restore balance to the earth. The significance of these prophecies is that each of these nations individually received a similar vision. Each one speaks of a rainbow people (from all races) who would be born throughout the earth at a crucial point in earth's history, assisting the world to avert certain disaster.

It has been very exciting to delve deeply into these rich, ancient prophecies and to find that the arrival of the Violet Race was foretold. The elders knew the Rainbow Warriors were coming. They foresaw a time of advancement when the earth would enter perilous times, but before it was destroyed, a New Race would be born within the nations of the world and bring the people of Earth out of danger, leading them back into a balanced way of life. I thank the Indian Nations for sharing their beautiful prophecies in this book.

The Prophecies

Manataka Prophecy: Manataka is home of the Rainbow Woman who sleeps deep within the sacred mountain in the Place of Peace. During the Awakening, she will emerge once more to give rebirth to this new tribe of people who will sing and dance praises to the Great Spirit - Creator under the rainbow. Warriors of the Rainbow will be pathfinders of the principles the people will follow to achieve unity, understanding and love.

Prophecy of the Hopi People: When the Earth is dying there shall arise a new tribe of all colors and all creeds. This tribe shall be called the Warriors of the Rainbow and it will put its faith in actions not words.

Sioux Prophecy: There will come a time when the Earth is sick and the animals and plants begin to die. Then the Indians will regain their spirit and gather people of all nations, colors and beliefs (The Rainbow Warriors) to join together in the fight to save the Earth.

American Indian Ancient Prophecy: A day will come when the beautiful rainbow will disappear because people will not remember to keep the Mother Earth sacred and will destroy its beauty. Children of the Rainbow Warriors will come before all is destroyed and they will love the trees and the animals. They will love and respect each other and they will help people to live in peace with all creation. The rainbow in the sky will return as a sign of the Creator's grace.

Zuni Legend of the Rainbow Warrior: There is a symbol known to the Zuni Indians as Rainbow Man. Found on a Zuni War Shield, it is a symbol of protection.

Cree Indian Nation Prophecy: 100 years ago, an old Indian Woman named "Eyes of Fire" had a vision of the future. She prophesied that one day, because of the White Mans' greed, there would come a time when the earth was being ravaged and polluted, forests destroyed, birds falling from the air, waters blackened, fish poisoned in the streams, and trees would no longer be. Mankind, as we know it, would all but cease to exist.

Then would come the time when the "Keepers of the Legend, stories, culture rituals, and myths, and all the Ancient Tribal Customs" would be needed to restore us to health, making the Earth green again. They were the "Warriors of the Rainbow" and mankind's key to survival.

A day of Awakening would come, when all the peoples of all the tribes would form a New World of Justice, Peace, Freedom and recognition of the Great Spirit. The "Warriors of the Rainbow" would spread these messages and teach all peoples of the Earth or "Elohi." They would teach them how to live the "Way of the Great Spirit." They would tell them of how the world today has turned away from the Great Spirit and that is why our Earth is "Sick".

The "Warriors of the Rainbow" would show the peoples that this "Ancient Being" (the Great Spirit), is full of love and understanding, and teach them how to make the Earth beautiful again. These Warriors would give the people principles or rules to follow to make their path right with the world. These principles would be those of the Ancient Tribes. The Warriors of the Rainbow would teach the people of the ancient practices of Unity, Love and Understanding and teach of Harmony among people in all four corners of the Earth.

Ancient Hawaiian Petroglyphs: The "Anuenue Wahine" (Rainbow Woman) is found in several locations. The arch over her head represents a rainbow, which means she is an honored and respected wise woman or the Woman Who Sees All. Many women held active positions in the Ali'i and many were highly respected Kahuna.

The "Anuenue Kane" (Rainbow Man) is one of the best known among the Hawaiian petroglyphs. Found at Nuuanu, Oahu, the "Rainbow Man" depicts a man with a rainbow resting on his shoulders representing each person's responsibility to 'shoulder' the task of protecting Mother Earth, the land "Aina." The arc of the rainbow means the person is honorable and respected.

Today, Hawaiian craft people frequently use the symbol of the Rainbow Woman and Rainbow Man in their work found in market places throughout the Hawaiian Islands.

A Mysterious Origin

There are compelling questions about the Violet People and their arrival at this historic time. Having undergone the same amnesia as the rest of humanity, their true origin remains locked within their psyche, a soul memory that must be excavated to fully comprehend the magnitude of their unique destiny.

It has been a puzzling mystery how one generation of people can be so different from all the generations before. How children born into this time have such a unique perspective and set of ideologies that they challenge their parent's core values and society's dictates to pave a new way. Whether they come from the future, the stars, higher realms, or are highly advanced souls who've embodied on Earth over time, Violet People are distinctly different from the normal Earth population.

I have often wondered, "Did Violet Souls meet in councils in higher worlds? Did they look into the dire potentials facing our planet and determine that if something drastic weren't done, the world as we know it, could be completely destroyed? And, if not annihilated, set back another 10,000 years as supposedly happened with the sinking of Atlantis?"

Did Violets join together in a grand alliance to save the planet? Is their plan a Restoration Earth Experiment? And if so, did these valiant souls choose to take on the lineage of darkness inherent in Earth's populations by taking over for other souls who would not have been able to make such a dramatic leap in their own soul evolution in time to save the planet?

Did they take on some kind of encoding as they entered the womb that carried all the patterns of that soul's past records with its embodiments of pain? Like a virtual reality video game, did they begin where the other soul left off knowing they would be able to make the quantum leap in consciousness imperative to the present age?

Did they make such a choice, taking over for less evolved souls, because they knew they would not sit under the same amnesia with the same patterns as past generations had done? That somehow their fiery natures would be a safeguard against living unconscious lives satisfied with the status quo? That instead, they would strive for a higher destiny, overcome the circumstances created by their human patterns, and seek ways to free themselves of the human conditioning? Is this what birthed the Human Potential Movement? If so, the ramifications are great. Whatever their origin or reason for embodying on Earth at this time, one thing is clear. Violet People are on a serious mission.

CHAPTER SEVEN

Conscious Stewardship of the Earth

Extinction or advancement? That is the question of the hour looming before humanity at one of the most serious times in Earth's history.

On the light side, humanity is breaking through bonds that have kept individuals enslaved to a perceptual reality and limited their potential. A change in values is birthing a new Way of Life that is fast replacing the outdated systems of a past era. We are seeing this change in every area of life as Violets rise like phoenixes from the ashes of a millennia of unconsciousness to birth a New World.

During thirteen years of research, Paul H. Ray, PhD and Sherry Ruth Anderson, PhD, authors of *The Cultural Creatives*, concluded that a powerful subculture is emerging. According to their study, over 100 million people in the US and Europe, and countless others around the world have made a "comprehensive shift in their worldview, values, and way of life" since the 1960's.

They write, "These creative, optimistic millions are at the leading edge of several kinds of cultural change, deeply affecting not only their own lives but our larger society as well." Anderson and Ray believe that innovation-by-innovation, they are shaping a new kind of culture for the twenty-first century.

I was excited to find that Violet People bear a remarkable resemblance to the core group identified in their statistics. These are activists who delve deeply into the Inner World to find a deeper purpose for their life. My estimate is that there are 80 to 100 million Violet People on the planet today, with more waves of Violets birthing each year. The amount of Violet Children being born show us that this violet energetic is destined to continue until Violets have laid a new path for humanity.

As Violet People began coming of age in the 60's, we saw a host of movements launched. Conscious stewards of the Earth emerged who care about the condition of our planet and the serious direction we are heading. Through their Vision of a Transformed World, they have opened the door to the change we have seen in environmental awareness and the advent of green technologies now being embraced as a solution for global warming.

As the impact of Violet Soul influence began making sweeping changes to the landscape of Planet Earth in the later part of the 20th century, consciences were quickened worldwide, and positive planetary change became a focal point of many valiant souls who began working together to affect a shift in global affairs.

Women's rights helped shift values in a tremendous sweep of feminine advancement into new fields and endeavors, signifying a unifying action from a powerful inner change, as many people worldwide embraced their feminine side. Heart entered a largely left brained society and with it, a new conscience to care for the planet and restore its ecological balance.

Similarly, indigenous cultures around the world emerged out of their Dark Night to receive acknowledgment of the wisdom of their ancient heritage. Races suppressed and labeled inferior, like the Hawaiians, were able to rise into their rightful place as citizens of the Earth. And, steadily, we moved out of the dark ages of our past into a new planetary conscience that is paving the way to a New World of equality and peace. There is a glimmer of light on the horizon as heart and mind unite, and new advancements coupled with planetary awareness recreate the world at the 11th hour.

Standing Bear of the Manataka American Indian Council said, "If we were to look from above at the Circle of Life it would appear as a gigantic spiral. Each age, or Revolution of the Circle moves the next Circle to a plane in perfect concentric alignment with the last, but on a higher level in the spiral. Those souls who walk the path to higher awareness, consciousness and spirituality move with the spiral to the next plane."

Against the backdrop of planetary challenge and in some perspectives, imminent planetary demise, Violet People have been inspiring positive actions and creating sweeping changes. We saw this with the movements launched that have now translated into over 144,000 companies, organizations, ministries, and projects working towards positive planetary change.

Crises worldwide have called us to take timely actions and millions of Violets have risen to the call. Solar and windmill stations are moving us from dependency on oil. Electric cars are on the horizon. Our innovations are taking us out of the grip of increasing oil prices and pollution. Technological advancements are releasing us from an arduous past and there's been a return to 'health' emotionally as well as physically as we've entered the last frontier and explored the Science of the Soul, Psychology.

Violet Movements

The following are some of the movements, technologies, and advances that have sprung from Violet Idealogy since the 60's. The magnitude of these movements is far reaching in their ability to affect powerful changes for our future in our lifetime.

The Environment Movement

Environmental Groups
Earth Friendly Products
Recycling
Hybrid Cars powered by electricity
Solar Power and other Alternative Energies
Inventions to clean up toxic waste
Soil Replenishment
Water Purification
Protection of our Environment
Protection of National Parks, Rivers, Waterways, and Oceans
Protection of endangered species and plants
Save the dolphins, whales, and marine eco systems programs
Eco Tourism
Eco Adventures

Healing and Health Movement

Organic, Vegetarian, Raw Food, Macrobiotic, and Vegan diets
Alternative Health Care, Cutting Edge Treatments, and Cures
Healthy Lifestyle Magazines and Programs
Work Out Programs, Spas and Gyms
Eco Hotels, Healing Retreats, Wellness Centers, Yoga Retreats
Rehabilitation and Counseling Centers, Youth At Risk Retreats
12 Step Programs, AA, Al Anon, Grieving Groups, etc.
Cutting Edge Counseling Theories and Practices
Alternative Medicine and Ancient Healing Methods
Resurgence of Shamanic, Huna and other Indigenous Healing
Advances in Medicine and Cutting Edge Healing Modalities

Human Potential Movement

New Psychology, Self Help, Spirituality, and New Age Movement
Meditation, Yoga, Tai Chi, Eastern Religion, Martial Arts
Spiritual Techniques and Traditions
Consciousness Conferences, Seminars, Workshops, Trainings
Conscious Media
Spiritual Cinema
Transformational Products
Visionary Art
Healing Music

Social Reform Movements

Freedom and Patriot Movements
Peace Movement
Women's Movement
Protection of the Unborn Child
Civil Rights Movement
Anti-Nuclear Movement
Equality and Equal Rights Movements
Enlightened Politics and Economics
Conscious Participation In Global Affairs

Advances and New Technologies

Solar and Wind Power
Hybrid, Hydrogen, Electric, and Solar Cars
Sonic Bloom
Soil Replenishment Technologies
Water Purification Systems
Desalinization Technology
Healing Frequency Machines
Laser Surgery
Light Healing Technologies
Fish and shrimp farms
And more!

Part Three

A Journey Into The Miraculous

CHAPTER ONE

Ascension Earth

A New World is being birthed out of an old order as humanity comes of age and departs from archaic traditions, patterns, and belief systems, to leave the old ways behind. Timely assistance is coming from the most amazing sources to support this effort. As the stories in the coming chapters reveal, millions of people are experiencing extraordinary encounters, divine interventions, and profound healings. These stories are evidence that a powerful force is guiding the destiny of humanity.

To some, the stories in this book may seem impossible. Do Angels exist and are they really concerned about what is happening on earth? Do dolphins really have the power to heal? Does humanity have an innate divinity that is being unleashed at this time, catalyzed by mystical encounters that once were reserved for the rare mystic or sage?

After years of collecting stories on the mystical side of our present world equation, I can no longer deny that there is an unseen influence drawing millions of souls out of normal lives into the miraculous. These mystical experiences are literally altering the course of our planet, as people throughout the Earth undergo life changes so powerful and profound, it defies imagination.

Ascension is a word used by many Violets to describe the Planetary Awakening we are now undergoing. Forums throughout the world are embracing this Vision for Humanity and many teachers believe the Earth is going through her ascension as well. This is an important key to Earth's destiny. We are transcending the old conditioning that created strife and this is restoring peace on Earth. Soul by soul we are ascending, as each person wakes up and brings their Authentic Self into the equation.

When we embrace the truth behind The Awakening, we find hope for a world in transition and a meaning behind all the travail. With this understanding comes peace. We are at the right place at the right time and each one of us is important to the equation.

In the midst of this glorious passage, the shadow side of human nature continues to reveal itself in planetary affairs and upheavals. A huge panoramic movie of light and dark potentials is being paraded before humanity and we are being called to cast our vote.

The acceleration of the Dark Side allows us to see what has been hidden forever within our psyche so that we can heal it. We must not fall under the weight of planetary despair, nor think it's all over yet. The prophecies and predictions for this time can be changed and our future altered. Nothing is set in stone, and it's not over until it's over. There is still time to turn the tide, even if we are at the 11th hour.

21st Century Visionaries must understand that the dark images rising before us in ever increasing degrees, must be made conscious so that we can deal with them effectively. Otherwise, they remain hidden in the psyche of an unconscious humanity, while spiritual myths arise to make sense of planetary challenges. Archaic beliefs like, "We are being punished for our sins," must be replaced with a new level of responsibility, so we can maturely take command of our lives and move our planet on a more positive course.

The truth is, there is no punishment being inflicted upon humanity. We are punishing ourselves by allowing human destructive programming to continue to ruin the happiness in our lives. The shadow side of life is being played out on such a grand scale that now, everyone on Earth is experiencng it daily via our media. But, the increase of darkness across the Earth is not only increasing suffering, it is also playing a major role in The Awakening. Through mortal, as well as, psychological challenges, we are being compelled into positive movment, within and without. The Shadow is also serving humanity by catalyzing millions of people into action at the same time across the planet. This is resulting in tremendous positive change so quickly that it can completely transform the very nature of our world.

A huge wake up call, the acclerating Dark Night is literally shaking people to their core, waking them up out of their complacency to do their part. As it plays out in our own worlds, it is driving us to heal the schisms in our psyche, and to become more conscious and awake. What we lose, we seek to reclaim. As our peace of mind is taken away, our longing for that lost chord causes us to find our way back to Peace.

Once largely hidden in the human psyche, the Shadow has

become such an overwhelming physical reality that we can now see and feel it more clearly. This gives us the ability to address and change it, rather than being the sad victims of clandestine acts of evil behind closed doors, as in the past. The most important offering we can give to a planet in travail is to heal and transform the inner reflection of these outer happenings, which is our Shadow Nature. This is an essential key to birthing an Enlightened World.

A Golden Age is not going to make its appearance on our planet, while we continue on in the old ways. No one 'out there' is going to gift us Peace on Earth. If we want to live in peace, we must heal our warlike natures, replacing our continual wars with a new peaceful Way of Life.

It is time we stop looking 'out there' for something we must and can give ourselves. An inner shift is needed, for it is the internal structuring of the human psyche that is behind our present Dark Night. These patterns must be healed and their inherent 'evil' transformed to vanquish it from our world.

To witness millions of people undergoing miraculous healings and life transformations is a powerful statement. If this were not happening, we'd be in a lot of trouble. The dire circumstances besetting our world have become so great there would be no hope for a better future.

If only we could be watching the 'Good News' each day instead of ingesting every problem on the planet, how different we would feel. Can you imagine hearing about all the incredible new inventions, cures, projects, and exciting happenings each day? Wouldn't you feel uplifted and inspired?

That is what the Earth 2012 series is about. To bring evidence of the Light Side of our present planetary equation and bring hope to millions of people who are suffering under hardships and constraint. To give real tools to help people live better lives. When we master our psychology, we become masters of our life. When we allow our Authentic Self into the equation, we change our future and begin living our Highest Destiny Potential.

It is time to take the main spotlight off the shadow side of life, so we can focus on the good news. We can still keep track of the challenges that need addressing and also heal our shadow, but without all the stress our indulgence in the bad news is continually creating. This is a level of Self Mastery each of us is being called to. I found a way to live this way and share about it in Part 8: Miracles Of TheQuest™.

CHAPTER TWO

A Journey Into the Miraculous

One of the signatures of the Violet Age is the mystical nature of the Violet Soul experience. It is as if there has been a parting of the veil and through it we find we have entered a once hidden world largely unexcavated by the human mind. People from diverse religious backgrounds are experiencing extraordinary encounters with the Divine, while a host of beings from transcendent realms are making their presence known.

Traversing the initiatic rites of the Violet Age has become a sacred adventure many Violets are sharing, bringing us into an Age of Miracles where a once Divine Initiation reserved for the enlightened few is now taking place in the lives of many worldwide. Manna from Heaven in a focused release of light and healing is flooding the earth, transforming human consciousness and changing our future.

This powerful Divine Orchestration is transforming millions of lives with a radiant energy that is significantly violet. Miracles are abounding, touching people from every walk of life. These violet experiences are leading humanity into uncharted realms, catalyzing them in new directions, and helping them to uncover their Soul Purpose so that they can fulfill a higher destiny.

These personal accounts represent the heart of the Violet Mystery I have been unveiling in the Earth 2012 series. They speak to the vast changes that are presently underway that are first taking place in the psyche of humanity. As miraculous events become ordinary occurrences, divine synchronicities are leading humanity into a connection with a universal energy that is benevolent and which is guiding us into greater mastery and attainment, causing a quantum leap in the soul evolution of the planet. Religious and societal myths are falling away, as a personal connection with the Divine catalyzes a powerful awakening worldwide, reminding souls of their True Origin and that they are spiritual beings having a human experience.

This journey into the "light" side of our present planetary equation is filled with extraordinary encounters, amazing healings, divine synchronicities, and unexpected blessings.

The stories in this book include miraculous cures, divine encounters, and mystical experiences, each life changing and profound, that can give us hope for the extraordinary future before us. They tell us we have entered a remarkable age where magic and mystery abound. They show us we have gone beyond the limits of ordinary life. We have entered the extraordinary and Violet Souls are leading the way. Each one of us is being called to move beyond what we have known to embrace the miraculous.

Walter Cruttenden, author of *The Lost Star and Myth* said, "The higher ages are so much nicer, not because they're dramatically different physically, but because we perceive ourselves so differently and the whole world reflects this higher consciousness and greater attunement with nature."

At this thrilling moment in Earth history, miracles are occurring daily. You hear it on the airwaves. You see it on television and in films. It is in the songs that are being sung. People around you are changing. Many are having miraculous experiences and you are having your own.

At the heart of this Grand Transfiguration, mystical encounters are not only blowing people's minds, they are completely changing lives. These experiences are showing us that there is a universal energy that is benevolent, which is guiding humankind into a greater awareness that can bring us out of our present day dilemma into an era where our highest potential is realized. We can move forward with the confidence that we are in Divine Hands. There is a purpose to all that we are going through. A glorious Divine Plan is taking place and as we align ourselves more fully with it, we are being transported into a world once reserved for the solitary mystic on their Path to Truth.

This far-reaching Divine Influence is releasing us from the prison house of past limitations and opening our minds, not only to the vast outreaches of a Majestic Universe, but also to the Inner Sanctuary of the Soul. Mystical experiences are removing the barriers that once contained us in a limited existence, blocking our creative expression.

Divinely orchestrated events are catapulting us into a life unimaginable, as the miraculous becomes the attainable, and the future potential the present life experience.

These encounters help us believe the visions of our heart are true, our hopes and dreams are possible, and that Eden is our Divine Birthright. They foster trust in the Divine, and help us open our minds to greater truths. They cause us to soar like eagles above our present difficulties, and embrace visions of a glorious future, knowing it is within our reach.

If we allow ourselves to receive the gifts of this time, our life can be miraculously transformed. We can transcend ourselves in ways we never imagined. We can realize our full potential and overcome the limitations of this realm while still living on earth. This is the Magic of the Violet Age, a time when our 'Vision of a Transformed World' becomes a living tangible reality.

David Icke, author of *Infinite Love is the Only Truth,* wrote, "What would have been considered 'miracles' and impossibilities not so long ago are now the commonplace and we have seen nothing yet."

Over the years, many Violet People have shared their miraculous stories with me and I have included many of them in this book. While they may seem unbelievable, they are nevertheless stories from credible people. I have also chosen to share my own.

To reveal this mystical side of my nature is not easy. People tend to ridicule things they cannot believe, but I think it is important to let the world know these things are happening and that I have not merely been an observer, but that they have happened to me as well.

My life's focus has been largely from a scientific inquiry and I have proceeded as any scientist would to gather knowledge that will help humanity. At the same time, the level of mystical experiences I have had feels important to share. For this is a very real part of our Earth Reality, even though these things are of a dimension largely unnoticed by a majority of people. And yet, increasing numbers of people throughout the world are having similar experiences.

I can only hope that you, the reader, will keep an open mind and even if some of these stories are beyond your personal experience, you will feel inspired that they are taking place. I leave it to you to decide.

CHAPTER THREE

Seven Thunders

It was the third day of a powerful spiritual conference focused on healing our world. The Keynote Speaker said there are many illumined beings assisting humanity at this time and that we have all the help we need to enter a more Enlightened World, but the future is in our hands. They said the Angels, Masters, Archangels, and Elohim are simply waiting for our call. They are standing by to help us, and that this sacred service brings them great fulfillment and joy.

As I returned to where I was staying late that night, I felt uplifted and inspired. It had been an incredible day. The hosts of Light had been invoked by thousands of people to help heal many dire conditions on the planet. Everyone present had felt excited to participate in helping the world in that way.

As I was falling asleep, I began to hear a story that became a full blown cinematic experience in living color. Quickly searching for a pen and paper, I wrote it down, realizing afterwards I want to release it as a children's book and animated feature film. Prophetic and significant to this time, I am inspired to share it here.

In the far reaches of the Universe, 'twixt galaxy and shining star, dwelled a little planet called Earth. She did not twinkle and shine like the suns that filled the vast skies, but she did have a little flicker and that was her hope. She wondered how, she too, could become a star, and she wondered long at her destiny.... what would it be?

There were some who called Earth a Dark Star, though there were whispers that once she had shone brilliant as Starfire. There were other whispers, which spoke of a shining radiant people who once filled the Earth with love and light and of days that had sparkled with a transcendent beauty that was rare among even the finest of planets.

The Little Planet sighed. Oh for those glorious days of old when peace and prosperity had reigned, when her gardens had been full and her fruit trees heavy laden, where streams had flowed, their waters clear as crystal, and where all life had lived upon her in perfect harmony.

There had been no dangerous animals then, nor poisonous plants or thorn filled flowers, no sickness, disease, or death. Oh, who were these people who now infested her, throwing fireballs of hatred at one another and always discontent? And what were these masses of shapeless buildings rising up everywhere? How fast was her beauty disappearing!

The sad Little Earth looked out at all the other stars and planets shining in the universes. "Somebody please help me!" she cried. She knew things had gotten way out of control and that she would never be able to change them on her own.

There was a darkness surrounding the Earth and all the Stars and Planets knew that it was the creation of the people who lived there. Through negative thoughts and feelings, words and deeds, Earth was growing darker and darker. Love seldom visited the planet anymore and Peace didn't know when it would come again. Angels stayed away, and the Little Planet wept with a great sadness.

The Great Starry Bodies held their councils and looked to see the problems of the Little Dark Star. Earth awaited their decision anxiously and tried hard to keep faith uppermost in her mind. The Council deliberated long and then finally proclaimed, "THE EARTH SHALL BE SAVED!" A mighty roar of applause, thanksgiving, and praise rang out and filled the universes.

Soon bands of Angels journeyed forth with swords of light in hand, determined to vanquish the darkness from the Earth. Great beams of light in rainbow hue streamed forth from their hearts into the Little Planet. Earth watched them come and rejoiced as she was bathed again and again in the healing light.

Reinforcements came, marching in precision over the earth, sending forth rainbow rays in great streams of light, and bringing vast changes to the planet. Earth began to sparkle as the density cleared away and for a long moment even her inhabitants could breathe free again. Some of her people saw the Angels and took heart. These were the Violet People. They discovered stories of Earth's ancient past when harmony had reigned on the Little Planet. They longed with all their hearts for those days to come again, and they determined to do all that they could to assist their dear planet who they loved greatly. They held the Vision of a Transformed World. Determined to birth a Golden Age on Earth, they kept up their prayers night and day. Very swiftly these ones began to change in their hearts and minds. They tended to their Inner Worlds and began healing age-old patterns. This changed their thinking and how they viewed life. No longer did they think negative thoughts or act unkindly. As they changed inwardly even their countenances began to shine.

This was an inspiration to others who also desired to cleanse themselves so they could live in a pure and lovely planet. They realized how dark and ugly their planet had become and they decided to work a mighty work on behalf of the Little Planet and all the brave souls who had gone before.

As many a life was transformed and many more came to be, Earth began to be covered with patches of light where darkness had once been. Finally there were many safe pockets all over the world where her Children of the Light could safely dwell.

The Little Planet felt a great sense of relief and gratitude welled up from her center. Many of her people were filled with gratitude too. And so, a flood of faith, hope, and thanksgiving streamed forth from the Earth like a great Symphony of Light. The Great Starry Bodies looked on with awe at the changes that had been wrought on the Earth. Soon even they were bathed in the great stream of LOVE that poured forth from the Little Planet and filled the heavens.

As more and more LOVE was sent forth, more and more Angels appeared to assist the Violet People in their work. Legion after legion descended, determined to clear Earth of all unhappiness, hatred, and despair. Great floods of healing flowed forth from their pure and shining hearts and for a time, solace and respite rested upon the Little Planet.

The Little Earth began to twinkle! It was a great moment in the starry heavens and all the Great Bodies of Light bowed their heads at such a miraculous and wondrous sight. The Violet People, who had worked so long and hard, rejoiced too at such a victory.

Now there were some who dwelled on the Earth who lived selfishly. They harmed and took advantage of others because they were disconnected from their hearts and so, lived their lives in darkness. They were not happy about all this Light because it illumined the dark ways they were living. So they wanted to stop it. This caused them to work harder and faster to keep their darkness around them. They lived thoughtless lives, polluting everything they touched. They incited wars that took many lives, created poison foods that were harmful for people, and smelly industries that brought a horrendous stench upon the Earth. All of this, just so they could be wealthy beyond all others. The people, land, airs, and waters cried out in dismay as they felt the weight of this pollution upon them.

The Darkness continued to grow as these people thought only of themselves and no others. For a time, it seemed that the harder the Violet People worked and the more goodness the Angels brought, the swifter these Unconscious Ones worked their havoc, turning every beautiful thing into ugliness. Finally, many of Earth's peoples began crying out in loud voices, so great was the suffering and bondage these Dark Ones had brought them. Though somehow, there were some who through the darkness kept their hearts full of hope and who turned their faith heavenward. Their pleas for salvation rose to the Heavens like the sweetest incense and were gathered up by Holy Angels who lay them before the Altar of the Most High.

And then a day dawned with a roar and great thunders, and the mighty Elohim appeared. So great was their Presence, they filled the skies everywhere. These were Great Beings of Light who had come to assist the planet. The Awakening Souls on the Little Planet waited in expectation while the Great Starry Bodies cried out in unison, "LET THEIR VOICE BE HEARD!"

The Heavens grew quiet and everyone looked on in awe. Out from the Great Silence came a mighty roar of Seven Thunders and a great voice rang out and even thundered, "YOU HAVE CALLED IN YOUR TROUBLES... SO HAVE I COME TO DELIVER YOU!"

As the Elohim descended, rainbow rays flashed across the skies and great outpourings of light streamed forth consuming large pockets of darkness that lay over the Earth. Huge rivers of dark substance gave way to gleaming pools of shining light as Earth began to be cleared.

As the Cleansing continued, the people of the Earth rose up once more with strengthened hearts and renewed determination. "We shall join with the Elohim and Angels of Light to vanquish Darkness from the Earth!" the Violet People cried.

All this excitement made quite a stir in the Heavens and soon many were traveling from far off worlds to see for themselves all that was taking place on the Little Planet and to lend a hand.

Each day that passed the Little Planet grew brighter. Smiling, shining faces filled the Earth, who now gleamed with a crystal radiance all her own. The Work continued, as more and more lent their energies, until the Earth grew so bright that even many of the Dark Ones were transformed. Many were healed as they shed their old ways and began to live conscious lives.

The Earth began to shine in the Heavens with a brilliant radiance, and more of her people began to shine as well. A wonderful creativity sprung forth from the people as magnificent Cities of Light were built, beautiful statues and fountains erected, and fragrant flowers blossomed everywhere. Fruit trees became heavy laden with delicious fruits of every kind and streams flowed forth with crystal clear waters. The most spectacular gardens sprung up everywhere as the people worked on. Joy, Peace, and Love abounded on Earth and songs that were sung with Angel Voices wafted on the air.

As Earth grew more beautiful with each day, so did her people. The cities were magnificent masterpieces, their buildings made of beautiful materials and the streets were paved with gold. Precious jewels lent to the rich decorations everywhere, so great was the abundance every man, woman, and child now shared.

The Earth continually blessed her children with every wonderful gift. Her seasons rolled on in perfect harmony, not too long or too short, each one more magnificent then the one before.

Beauty and Perfection reigned once again as the Earth sparkled amidst her Heavenly Brothers and Sisters. And then one day the bright Little Planet became a Shining Star and she reigned as a Triumphant Sun with her place in the Heavens forevermore.

Could Earth Be a Virtual Experience?

By Gary Voss

Is it possible that the life we are living here on earth is a Virtual Reality and all that we are experiencing is a download? Perhaps it may be that our True Selves never left Heaven and that, who we are here on earth is just a mere "extension" of our other selves that exist on parallel worlds, which are also downloaded experiences as well.

I have had many visions, visitations, and inner journeys where I was taken through the Firmament into what many have referred to as Heaven. In one inner experience, I had the privilege of witnessing what I call "The Hall of Forever." It was like a long hallway that seemed to have no end and went as far as my eyes could see. It was like looking through a mirror, through another mirror, then endless mirrors. On either side of me were these tall arched entrances that would continue throughout the hall, separated from one another, five to seven feet apart.

No matter which entry I stepped into, I found the same events occurring in each one of the rooms at the same time. What was going on inside was people who had passed on from this world were being brought forth from the "Tunnel of Light" by a Delivering Angel, who would drop them off to a Receiving Angel, then jump back through the wall into the tunnel to go get more passing souls. The Receiving Angel would wave their hand above the person arriving through the Tunnel of Light, and they would be instantly healed, glowing and smiling as if "downloaded" all past and present events.

After this remembrance took place, the Receiving Angel would turn about and face the wall behind them, raise his hand above his head and wave towards the wall as another opening appeared. Huge marble steps embedded with a shiny crystalline substance would flow out from the opening, where many other people were waiting to receive or be reunited with their loved ones.

The most peculiar thing that happened was when a woman arrived who had just passed on. Amazingly, she discovered her husband there who she had left back on earth. Her son was also there to greet her, among other long lost relatives, but he had been left back on earth as well, a young boy with only his father to raise him, or so she had thought. He was still on earth, but a part of him, his Higher Self, was in this Heaven world.

I realized that this "Tunnel of Light" was a type of wormhole that could transport us into the future where all of Creation as we know it, has already passed. It confirmed what I had heard many times before, that there is no time in Heaven, only in our world.

Then one more amazing thing took place. The last person she met was herself. It was explained to me that this was her "Higher Self," the part of us that lives in "Christ Consciousness" and is our link to the Heaven Worlds. This Self gives us the ability to communicate with the Divine Realms and connect with God. It is also the part of us that gives us a natural inner self-awareness that knows right from wrong, and a conscious state of awareness.

Remember the old song from Disney's Jimmy the Cricket, "Let your conscious be your guide?" Perhaps this "Higher self" is like our Guardian Angel, and we really have never left Heaven. The life we are experiencing on earth may just be a virtual reality like a giant Holodeck like on Star Trek.

Since this experience I found there is new emerging scientific evidence of many of the things I have experienced, like quantum physics and holographic universes.

Gary Voss is a member/supporter of the Exopolitics team and founder of TAP-TEN Research, an International Think-Tank that explores the latest in advanced aerospace and engineering technologies for the development of alternative energy and propulsion concepts.

As well as hosting his own radio show, Gary was also a featured guest on a variety of other radio programs and social networks discussing his latest venture he calls "Green Aid" which involves recruiting the music industry to bring about educational awareness and provide funding to construct off-grid community projects that utilize the latest cutting edge developments that involve alternative energy and green building technologies.

Gary is also a visionary and a renowned speaker in many circles about his personal experiences including contact with Angelics, ET's, and others from around the world who claim to be Earth embodiments on assignment. You may contact Gary Voss by email: vosstech@yahoo.com or visit his websites: http://peswiki.com/energy/Directory; http://tap-ten.org; and at http://www.myspace.com/tapten

CHAPTER FIVE

Celestial Rays of Colored Light

By Peter Sterling

One of the earliest and most impacting experiences I had as a child, which has seemed to influence my life in its current direction of spiritual and mystical pursuits, occurred when I was six years old. Every Sunday, my mother would go to church, and I would go to Sunday school with the rest of the children.

Most of my memories of Sunday school in the Episcopal Church would center on the telling of Bible stories, the playing of games that illustrated Bible teachings, and the main attraction for me and every other child, the feast of donuts and coffee cake when we rejoined our parents in the church courtyard after the service.

On one particular occasion, I remember it being close to Easter with the warm spring weather and Easter lilies in bloom. This was a special day for me as my mother invited me to stay with her and her best friend and attend the regular church service. I had never attended the regular mass before, so I watched with interest as the priests readied themselves to begin. I remember being struck by the architecture of the chapel with its high vaulted ceiling and ornately carved pillars with religious icons. There was a sense that something special was going to happen, and I was excited to be part of it that day.

As the service began, and the music started with the opening hymns, I was mesmerized by the sacred rites the priests performed dressed in their colorful vestments of gold, purple, and blue. With the blessings of incense and holy water, I watched and listened as the priest recited something from a sacred text, which spoke of the immense power and light of God and the Holy Spirit. As I sat there and took this all in to my childlike mind, I was struck with a feeling of familiarity. It was as if I knew this and had been here before sometime somewhere.

Sitting between my mother and her friend, I remember looking up at the stained glass windows that graced this sanctuary. They were so beautiful with their colorful depictions of different saints and Bible episodes. It seemed as though the sun had moved just enough so that the most glorious beams of colored light began to shine through the window and reach into the church. I had never seen anything so beautiful before in my life.

As the priest spoke of holy things and the music played in glorious accompaniment, I looked up at the beautiful light shining in through the stained glass windows. The colors penetrated me deeply and touched me in a place within that I had never known until this point in time. It was as if I was able to travel up the beams of colored light through the window and into a celestial vision of heavenly grandeur. It was an exhilarating feeling, one of ecstasy and light, of angels and God's glory.

Many years later, I discovered that stained glass windows were put into churches for exactly this reason. They were believed to be windows to the Heavens, and the beams of colored light coming into the church represented the hand of the Holy Spirit.

A heavenly vision was revealed to me in that instant and I knew, without a doubt, that I would be a maker of stained glass windows. I looked up at my mother with my big eyes full of wonder and said, "When I grow up, I want to be a stained glass window maker." I remember my mother smiling at me, putting her arm around me saying, "That's nice, dear."

It was ten years later when I was in high school that the vision in the church came back to me. One afternoon, I wandered into the career counseling office at my high school. I was looking for a part-time job, and they had a bulletin board there that had 3x5 cards tacked up with all sorts of part-time work listings. I remember I looked up at the board with all the cards and almost instantly, one stood out from the rest. It said, "stained glass studio needs help." I stood there for a moment when the vision in the church came back to me. I remembered my declaration that day, ten years in the past, where I announced I would make stained glass windows. I hadn't thought of stained glass in all those years. I suppose I was caught up in all the normal things that teenagers do. But all of a sudden, it all came back to me. I called the number on the card and was invited over for an interview. I was hired on the spot, and that began my apprenticeship with a master stained glass craftsman who showed me the techniques of this ancient art form.

From the beginning, I started making windows with geometrical patterns similar to the rose windows we see in cathedrals around the world. For some reason, I was naturally drawn to this type of design rather than more realistic themes so popular in stained glass. Even at 17, I found the geometrical patterns created a sense of peace and well-being in me. Plus they dazzled the eyes with their color, symmetry, and balance.

A few years later, I was introduced to the concept of the "mandala," which is so prevalent in Asian art forms, especially from Tibet. I began to read and study the techniques of the Tibetan artisans who infuse their designs with prayers of peace and healing. I discovered that in Asia mandalas are used as a tool for meditation. By looking into the center of the mandala with its geometrical patterns and vivid colors, one can attain a sense of balance, peace, and harmony. The geometry also interacts with the brain in such a way as to facilitate spiritual awakening by stimulating the opening of the third eye or psychic center located at center of the brow.

Around the same time, I was introduced to the concept of "sacred geometry." I learned that builders of cathedrals and temples around the world have used the geometrical proportions found in nature for centuries. The patterns found in the unfolding of flower blossoms, the spiraling of sea shells, and the growth patterns of minerals and crystals all reflect the larger design of God's hand found in the greater cosmos.

The Milky Way galaxy in which we live spirals out into space in perfect proportion and symmetry, and is reflected here on earth in so many ways. From the spiraling form of a hurricane to the delicate structure of a rose blossom, to the structure and form of our own DNA, the ancient adage, "As above, so below," reveals the very foundation of existence in this world of form. If one is willing to look at the tiny details of nature with an open mind and receptive heart, the "Codes of Creation" will reveal themselves in magnificent splendor.

As I learned more of the sacred art of the mandala and its sacred geometry, I began to gain a greater insight into and understanding of the power of color to affect varying states of consciousness. From the beginning, I had a strong sense of color harmony. Intuitively I would choose colors that seemed to blend into one another to create an overall hue pleasing to the eye. I learned that different colors would elicit different responses from people who viewed my windows. For instance, the color red will be stimulating for most people as it is aligned with the element of fire. The color green is soothing and healing to the body, as it is associated with the element of earth, like in a green, forested meadow. And, the color blue associated with water and the blue sky overhead can be a bridge linking the elements of heaven and earth.

As my journey into color and form continued, I discovered that different colors have a corresponding musical note. The seven notes of the musical scale have corresponding colors found in the prismatic effect of the rainbow, and also in the energy centers or "chakras" of the body. The mystics and seers of antiquity mapped these relationships and their importance to the process of awakening, healing, and enlightenment. I became fascinated by the interconnectedness of color, light, and sound as a dazzling world of crystalline light sparkled in symphonic grandeur with the sounds of nature and the "music of the spheres."

Around the time of my 28th birthday, I made the decision to devote myself full-time to the pursuit of artistic excellence in stained glass. The visions that had been revealed to me were too compelling, and I knew from a place deep inside that I was to find a way to express the beauty and power I had experienced in a form that others could enjoy as well.

Peter Sterling is a musician and master stained glassmaker, who has created brilliantly beautiful windows and music. There have been timeless musicians throughout history whose hands seem to be guided by unseen forces. Possessing unexplainable musical genius, the exquisite beauty of their songs have delighted and mystified audiences the world over, somehow connecting us closer to heaven. Peter Sterling is one such musical treasure. A harpist of world-class skill, Peter's eclectic music continues to touch the lives of thousands around the world. Devoted listeners over the years have consistently reported greater peace, spiritual visions, and even miraculous healings while listening to Peter's heavenly albums, suggesting the astonishing potential of his uncanny musical gifts. See more at http://www. harpmagic.com

CHAPTER SIX

Mystery of Enlightenment

By Kiara Windrider

There is nothing like being on a journey towards a far land, not knowing the way, not sure the destination exists; yet somehow knowing I am destined to arrive to God. Ever since I can remember I have been fascinated by stories of holy men and women living in the mountain tops and forests of India in enlightened states of divine union. I looked to them with admiration and some envy, recognizing the longing deep in my heart to achieve a similar state of enlightenment, yet unsure whether I had the discipline or the stamina required to seek this most precious of all pearls.

Many years have passed since that boyhood dream. Yet, through all my travels and experiences of life, some part of me has always held onto that dream, which has continually guided my journey. My journey is not so different from that of others, for underneath all of our separate illusions of reality, there is essentially one soul, one mind and one consciousness. As I share this Journey of Awakening, you will perhaps see that it is your journey as well. And more than that, it is also the journey of the vast unified consciousness that is the collective consciousness of this planet.

I begin my story with an incident, which jolted me out of my complacency one beautiful sunny morning when I was 16. I was a student at the Kodai International School in the lushly forested hills of south India. One day a group of us went out on one of our favorite hikes along a beautiful winding mountain stream that led to a steeply cascading waterfall that dropped hundreds of feet into a gorge below. Two of us went ahead of the rest of the group. Somewhat intoxicated by the perfection of the beauty all around us, we decided to climb down the face of the waterfalls. We had climbed several hundred feet when my friend lost his hold and fell. I watched him fall in petrified shock, and in the next moment I lost my grip and fell down.

Fingernails torn and bloody from trying to stop my fall, I bounced rapidly down the steep cliff, realizing that there was nothing I could do. In that moment, I found myself surrendering to the inevitability of death and strangely enough, a great peace washed over me. I entered a time zone where everything seemed to slow down, and in my next moment of conscious awareness I found myself standing in a pool, waist deep in water on a ledge of rock jutting out from the cliff 200 feet below. Amazingly, my friend had also landed in the same pool. Though hurt and dazed, we were inexplicably, gloriously alive!

In the months and years afterwards I embarked on a fervent quest to understand the meaning and purpose of my life. I studied and explored the teachings and practices of just about every world religious tradition that exists. I also delved deeply into the psyche and earned degrees as a Marriage and Family Therapist.

My home at one time was in Mount Shasta in California, considered by many to be one of the most powerful vortexes on the planet. I spent a lot of time up in the alpine meadows, communing with the spirits of the mountain, and with the Ascended Masters whose presence is so tangible there. It was a beautiful time that broadened my vision of what our planetary journey was all about. I also spent time in Hawaii, playing with the dolphins and whales in their ocean world, allowing them to teach me about oneness.

Gradually, I started putting various pieces together that pointed to a world of new possibilities. I studied various calendar systems and prophecies from around the world, I researched little-known scientific findings that indicated huge shifts in consciousness coming our way. I was inspired by future visions that people were having all over the world and I also channeled from other timelines, all of which pointed towards a collective shift that awaited humanity in the near future. I wrote a book based on this information, *"Doorway to Eternity: A Guide to Planetary Ascension"*, which immediately won a number of awards and glowing commendation from people who were beginning to come to the same conclusions.

Later I was guided to a small ashram in south India, the abode of an avatar named Kalki. People call him a "mukti avatar." His life mission is to give 'enlightenment' to the world. He describes enlightenment as a neurobiological process, which can be facilitated by making some adjustments in the brain. This would allow the cosmic energies to flow through so as to dissolve the concept of a Separate Self. Kalki spoke about the nature of the mind, all the judgments, comparisons, and habitual patterns that create so much suffering in our lives, and said that enlightenment was about 'de-clutching' from the mind. It is not that we no longer experience painful or negative thoughts or emotions, but that we are no longer identified with them.

I had always seen enlightenment as the end of my spiritual journey, the ultimate in human attainment. I now see that it is merely another beginning. Consciousness has its own intelligence, its own cycles, and it is an endless Journey of Discovery. There is a sweetness to this state that is extremely joyful. I am told, however, that at some point I should expect to go through a 'Dark Night of the Soul', a period similar to what Jesus experienced in his 40 days in the wilderness, as he 'wrestled with Satan' prior to embarking on his mission. The Dark Night could last for several months, a time during which the unconscious mind could become completely cleared out.

Perhaps it is similar to what the Australian aborigines and shamans in various traditions refer to as 'dismemberment', in which one's entire foundation of being is erased. This is a deeper stage, necessary in order to de-clutch from the collective mind-field of humanity. It is from this state, says Kalki, that Jesus was able to effectively realize his mission.

Kalki says there are as many kinds of enlightenment as there are people on Earth. He emphasizes that it is a biological event, and describes the possibility of anchoring this state into the 'morphogenetic fields', or collective mind-field of human consciousness, which he believes can lead to 'mass enlightenment' by 2012. This date, interestingly, also coincides with the ending of the Mayan calendar.

There is a vast consciousness at play in the world today. The world is a dream in the mind of God, who dreams through us moment by moment in a continuing dance of Creation. It is a beautiful dance, and it is an exciting time to be alive. I no longer feel a need to focus on all the political and ecological traumas in the world around us. I don't think that these problems will be solved until human consciousness undergoes a collective shift, and I sense that this shift is beginning to take place now. With all the drama that is going on today, there is no place I would rather be in all this vast cosmos than right here on Earth during this glorious time of collective awakening. Together, may we dance the dream awake!

Kiara Windrider, MFCC, is a transpersonal psychotherapist and author of the books, Doorway to Eternity: A Guide to Planetary Ascension; Deeksha Fire From Heaven; and Journey into Forever: Surfing 2012 and Beyond.

For more information on his work, travels, and seminars see his website, http://www.deekshafire.com or http://www.ilahinoor.com. He can be reached at: kiara@deekshafire.com

CHAPTER SEVEN

Light At The End of the Tunnel

By Mirra Rose

When I was a little girl, I was abandoned by my parents, not because they were bad people, but because they had a lot of problems and didn't know how to resolve them. And so I was passed on to my grandparents. My father said, "I just can't take care of her," and walked away. My grandmother took me in her arms and rocked me, and I cried and cried and cried and never seemed to stop crying.

All I can remember of my childhood was a great feeling of loss and devastation, loneliness and despair, feeling isolated and alienated from people, misunderstood, different and alone. So that was my beginning. Because I didn't have a lot of human companionship, I began to commune with Nature Spirits, animals and angels. They would come and be with me when I was alone. Through these experiences I established a strong connection to Christ and Mother Mary.

I experienced a sense of true spirituality in nature with my connection with animals and from the kindness I experienced from human beings. My heart would open up when I saw the beauty, love and divinity. For example, if I was reading a book and came to the part where everything is resolved and something beautiful happens, everyone learns their lessons and it is a little bit sad but beautiful, at that moment something would happen inside of me. My heart would just burst and I would feel like I was floating up out of my body.

My favorite times were moments of being lifted up by music, a beautiful sunset or poem. It would feel like a door opened inside my heart and all this joy would come pouring out of me that was so much greater than all of the pain I had experienced in this life. It was as if my conscious self had found a tiny flame deep inside of me. This little flame-like being was like a Tinkerbelle with wings. She would dance spiraling up and up into the ecstasy and beauty of the divine. Each time that happened, I would know I had a purpose for being alive. That is when I experienced real joy. So, in the midst of so much pain and hardship in what was many times a very bleak and lonely life, there were all these amazing spiritual experiences.

When my first love left me after a year, I couldn't handle it because of all the serious abuse and abandonment I had experienced when I was young. I was depressed, devastated and completely lost. The only thing I could do was write poetry. During those times, beings would come and speak with me directly.

Years later, I was going through another Dark Night of the Soul. At one point, I was in the darkest, blackest, deepest dungeon of despair that you can imagine, laying in bed, when I felt a presence and saw Mother Mary with two other beings. One was her mother, Ann, and the other was my own soul, my Higher Self. I was shown we were connected intimately, that somehow I had known them in that other lifetime. They had come to let me know my purpose and deep connection with Christ.

They told me about my mission in this life, that I was meant to carry on the work Christ had begun. In that moment, I knew my life had a purpose and that no matter how difficult it was I had to keep living because I had something important to do.

In this life, even though I've known immense pain and have suffered greatly, there was always a Divine Presence there to comfort me and to lead me out of the darkness back into the Light.

Mirra Rose is an internationally acclaimed spiritual teacher and healer who has been sharing her gifts world-wide for over thirty years, touching thousands of people with her loving Presence. Her primary mission is the empowerment of individuals to attain Divine Consciousness through a direct connection with the Soul. For more information on her work, see http://www.MirraRose.us

Part Four

Angels of the Sea

CHAPTER ONE

Healing Encounters With Dolphins

A lover of nature, I am inspired by the infinite wonders our planet provides. In encountering the extraordinary aspects of dolphin encounters, I was taken beyond a known understanding of animal human interaction, to witness things that seemed beyond imagination. My own experiences were mystical encounters that changed my perception dramatically. I learned a whole new way of relating to and interacting with Life.

Having been driven in my adult years to accomplishments that were challenging and exciting, now I was learning a new way of being, a way of allowing Life to unfold rather than making things happen. I was good at manifesting my visions and dreams. I had had many victories. Now, Life was teaching me another approach. This was exemplified by the dolphin world I had entered and what I witnessed as their Way of Life.

From each encounter, I found myself relaxing into a deep peace in myself and with the world. The challenging aspects of life began to drop away as I came to an empowered, clear place deep inside me. I found that I did not need to persuade Life to do my bidding, or coerce it to become what I thought I wanted and needed.

I let go and began to allow a different experience than I had been taught or had known. It was an experiment that brought me to the realization that Life knows what it is doing. If we can allow Life to do its magic, we will witness a perfect unfolding of events, synchronicities, the miraculous and the sublime. But to encounter this magic, we have to stop driving ourselves to the point where we are no longer 'listening' or following the nudges life is giving us.

I found there was so much more that Life wanted to offer me once

I got off the track of being a 'Super Achiever." I was finally available for the deeper message pervading all my life experiences. I began to see an order to life that was very interesting, a spectacular series of events that had meaning and purpose. I realized that in the years I had been so intensely striving for 'things,' I had missed the Magic of Life's mystery and its ability to blow my mind.

With this new Way of Being came an exquisite joy from deep inside of me. The dolphins, my wayshowers, had inspired an extraordinary and joyful new approach to life. Swimming with them, I would immediately feel euphoric and this would last for days. A truly great "high," but the experiences went even deeper. I felt shifts of consciousness that were profound.

Old patterns and concepts dissolved, giving way to a whole new perspective on life and living. I left my high powered, ever driven 'Type A' workaholic existence, and moved gracefully into an 'AB' type lifestyle that allowed me to still get alot done, but also provided time and space to relax, create, and enjoy life. Many speak of this consciousness shift from their encounters with dolphins, where mystical experiences took them beyond their normal spiritual beliefs into the realm of the miraculous.

The awesome power of the dolphins is incredible to witness and yet, their intelligence, healing and other abilities are manifest in a quiet power that is not forceful or intruding. Rather, many individuals around the world have experienced a subtle, yet powerful healing from swimming and interacting with dolphins that was delivered with a sense of joy and fun, as dolphins splashed, leapt, flipped, and swam over and beneath them.

In my many encounters with the dolphins, I often wondered how I could receive such powerful changes within my mind while the dolphins seemed to just be playing and having fun. Were they aware of the healing they were transmitting, or was their joyful nature and pure, loving consciousness simply a vehicle of a Divine Intention to restore lives? And, if so, what is behind this great mystery?

That dolphins are initiating a connection with humans is amazing, and this is increasing each year. Traveling all over the world, I have encountered many people who have had profound experiences with dolphins. Where dolphin encounters were once rare or even unheard of, now people are being drawn to exotic locations throughout the world to swim with dolphins. The stories I've collected are too numerous to share in this book. If you enjoy the following stories, you will find my complete treatise on this subject in book 3 of the Earth 2012 series.

From Egypt to Peru, Australia, and Costa Rica, Mexico to Hawaii, dolphin encounters have become a worldwide phenomenon. Through these encounters, lives are changing dramatically, consciousness is shifting, and people are becoming more awake, more conscious, loving, and peaceful.

Like my own experiences, people who are interacting with the dolphins speak of a change in their life direction as well as their perception. There seems to be a shift into allowing Life to unfold in its perfect way, rather than an emphasis on trying to make things happen and controlling the events around them. The status quo is fast becoming an old paradigm, while a new consciousness language is forming and is now being shared by many people throughout the world. "Let go, let God, relax, and let life unfold. Be in the present, live in the now. Everything that is meant to happen for you will."

Through my study of the dolphin phenomenon I am seeing that the participants in these extraordinary encounters are entering a whole new way of living that is replacing the driven focus of the world's obsession with accumulating and accomplishing. Somehow a light goes on in the mind of those touched by dolphins, helping to put their once driven life in perspective. Many people have shared how they are experiencing greater happiness and personal fulfillment, enjoying the blessings of friendships and family, as well as allowing more of their unique creative expression to flow forth in a myriad of forms. That has been my experience as well.

There is an ancient legend that says dolphin encounters increased dramatically as Greece entered her Golden Age. Could dolphins be facilitating a similar miracle for our time? From the hundreds of stories I've received from all over the planet, it is clear that dolphins are helping tramsform our world by profoundly affecting the consciousness of humanity.

Significant to this study, Violet People seem to be the ones who have the innate ability to connect with the dolphin world and to enter the transcendent consciousness many say the dolphins inspire. As you read the following stories, you will see this similar thread of shifts in consciousness, unexpected healings, and even enlightenment.

CHAPTER TWO

A Birthday Gift from the Dolphins

I sat overlooking the deserted stretch of white sand beach as the turquoise ocean sparkled invitingly. I had just had one more incredible adventure with the dolphins on the western shores of Oahu, my favorite place. A tall Hawaiian man named John emerged out of the waters with tales of swimming with the sharks. I was impressed. This fifty-year-old man had quite an adventurous life. He had spent a lot of time filming underwater and his favorite topic was the dolphins. He told me they were his friends and he had names for all of them.

Then he began to share a really incredible dolphin story with me. I immediately asked if I could record it for my book. He assented, saying, "Many people have wanted to interview me about my experiences with the dolphins over the years, but you are the first person I am granting an interview to." This is John's remarkable story...

When I was young, I had a really hard time speaking and would stutter most of the time. All the way through high school I hardly ever said a word, because I was so embarrassed by my impediment. I could never do an oral report and felt very nervous whenever I had to give one. So, on those days, I just wouldn't show up at school. I was lucky that I graduated.

I grew up on the Big Island of Hawaii in a Hawaiian family who were all very well spoken. I felt out of place, and so I turned to nature for friendship. Very early on, I made friends with the dolphins. My grandfather had taken me out to meet them when I was very young. The Hawaiian word for dolphin is Naya. I swam with Naya a lot, and came to know the dolphins in the bay near our house by name. They became my closest friends.

I had passed through many years with this condition that had brought me so much pain and discomfort because of the social hindrance. It seemed to be a life-long handicap that I would just have to live with. Unfortunately, it caused me to be a loner and as the years went on, the ocean and the dolphins were my only solace. Looking into their eyes, I felt total and complete acceptance. They knew me for who I really was.

The morning of my nineteenth birthday, I felt drawn to swim with the dolphins. My family wanted to celebrate, and I told them to come down to the beach. The water was crystal clear, a beautiful turquoise you only see in the tropics. As soon as I got out in deeper water, a dolphin began zooming towards me really fast, then another swam over. For a moment I felt scared.

Then the two dolphins swam moved into a strange position in front of me, pointing their rostrums directly at my neck. Immediately, I felt this strong electrical current running up and down my throat. Next, it started to expand outward in some kind of rippling effect. My whole throat had this tingling feeling, almost like a static charge from shuffling your feet over carpet. I had never seen dolphins this intent.

They then broke "formation" as one of them playfully splashed me in the face. For a long time afterwards, we played in the water. I would lift my arm up, and they would lift their pectoral fins in response. I would roll over in the water and they would follow, mimicking my every move. We were having so much fun that I forgot about our earlier encounter.

Finally, I swam back to shore. People on the beach who had been watching us were amazed by my interaction with the dolphins, and someone even asked if I was a dolphin trainer. I could only laugh good-heartedly. Still flushed with excitement, I ran over to greet my family.

"Did you see them playing with me," I yelled to them as I approached. They stopped and stared back at me with their mouths wide open. I continued talking excitedly about my encounter, when I saw that my mother had tears running down her face. Then I realized that I was talking without a stutter. It was a miracle!

Mama said, "What happened out there?" And then I told them how the dolphins had sent electrical energies to my throat. They had healed me! I had received the most incredible birthday gift from the dolphins, and have been able to speak without a stutter ever since.

I remembered that my grandfather had once told me to swim with Naya and that they would help me. When he heard about my miracle, he nodded his head and said, "I knew Naya would help you, when you were ready."

In time I realized that he was right, that I had been swimming with the dolphins for years, but if they had healed me earlier, I might not have formed this incredible bond with them and nature, one that keeps me going today.

After that experience, I went back to the bay looking for those two dolphins, but I have never seen them again. This is unusual. Dolphins swim in the same area, or at least return to the same spots after a while. This is how I became such good friends with the dolphins in the bay by my house. I now wonder if they were "brought" in like outside surgeons to perform an operation, and then went on their way. That's a funny thought.

I will never forget their gift on my birthday. It changed my life and gave me confidence, as did their friendship. I'm grateful to them, and to all of the dolphins and marine life that have played such an important role in my life over the years.

CHAPTER THREE

Wild Dolphin, Wild Woman, Wild Mare

By Caitlin

I came to New Zealand with a dream in my heart to find wild horses and ride across the wilderness of the South Island living wild in nature for a time. After exploring on foot for a week or so, I came across wild horses near Hanmer Springs, and beneath a crescent moon one magnificent summer night, I started to coax them into joining me on my adventure.

To gain their trust, I sang songs to them while combing the burs out of their manes. I had brought some oats and fed them, but these mares could sense my spirit and needed little inducement. Within two days, I had mounted them bareback and rode daily for hours at a time. Finally, we were ready to head out.

We passed through the Faerie Queen Mountains and rode along the wonderful Rainbow Valley, through beech forests, crossing raging rivers, passing beneath waterfalls in the full moonlight, or in the blazing heat of the sun. I had no particular direction in mind, but seemed to be pulled mysteriously northward. Where was the trail leading me?

Over hill and dale, we made our way toward the North West coast, entering new and exciting territory for all three of us. Time and the need for time melted away. I slept beneath the stars, warmed by the glow of my fire and the companionship of my new friends, counting stars and my blessings, our spirits flying high together. My dream had become my reality!

I rode over the mountain into Golden Bay, where its breathtaking beauty lured me on as I peered through the trees of the Rameka

Track and gazed upon the blue ocean beckoning us, welcoming us. We camped by the beach, where the horses stepped out onto the sand and smelled the ocean for the first time in their lives, kicking up their heels. That first morning we galloped along the empty remote beach, sunlight glittering on the dancing waves. We moved on to Onekaka, and that evening as the horses grazed, I thought I saw a dolphin just beyond the breakers watching us.

The next week I watched as the horses filled their bellies with rich clover grass every morning, and then I would ride them through the surf as they got used to water. Afterwards, to cool them off, we would wade just a little farther out into the ocean each day. This was a new experience for them, but their instincts took over, and before long they would go out in water over their heads and swim to stay afloat.

One magical evening, as the rain began to fall, we rode into a great vivid, deeply colored rainbow. Ashka, the Palomino mare, galloped with me clinging to her wet back, and Merlin ran behind us with the storm on his tail. The moon began to shine brightly between the dark billowing clouds. I was mesmerized by such overpowering beauty. The rainbow began to change shape and color until it became a moon bow. Legend has it that the Divine force is with you when you see the Night Rainbow.

The next morning Ashka and I waded out into the ocean. Moments later, a wild, free she-dolphin swam up into the shallows alongside us, clicking in ecstasy at the horse. My mare snorted nervously but soon the huge form beside us seemed to fill her with a deep peace. Ashka waded out further toward the dolphin, with great silent waves swelling against her belly. Then, all three of us swam toward the morning sun while little diamonds flecked and danced on tiny waves. We moved peacefully and swiftly through the water. The dolphin was clicking and sending us images of life in the ocean.

At some point, the dolphin slowed down and then turned and pointed her head at the mare until they were facing each other, nose to rostrum. Immediately, they both became very still and stayed in this silent meditation for a long time. My mind was filled with delightful images from the dolphin and my mare. I felt they were ready to fly. I reached for the thick creamy mane of the mare, and tightened my legs around her slippery silky body. Ashka broke the mind-meld and at my behest started swimming steadily through the waves, only her head above the shimmering surface of the water. The dolphin twitched her tail slightly and spun away swiftly, then returned to our side smiling. She swam along side us, her graceful body almost touching my horse and my legs. We were three females of three different species gliding into oneness through the blue ocean towards the sun in the west. A wild dolphin, wild mare, and wild woman beginning a journey they'll always remember.

For me, I was cognizant of my body, the water splashing in my face, the rocking movement of the mare as we pushed through the water, but some other part of me merged with my wild friends until our minds and hearts became one. The mountains behind us faded away, and all I could feel was an eternal, infinite, blissful love. I was melting into the oneness of a beautiful, enchanting reality of another kind. The faster we splashed through the water, the faster we moved through this other ethereal multi-colored landscape, dancing and merging with an infinite variety of shapes and forms in all the faces of God.

We were together in a realm of perfection. No need for thoughts or words, no feelings of fear or even bliss. Just oneness. The dolphin told us that this formless but all-powerful consciousness was our real essence. The young filly understood and so did I. We are all one. We are all love. This energy touched my heart, and then I started breathing again in union with my companions as the blue liquid light of our reality began to filter through. The one then became three once more, always to carry this essence with us wherever we may wander.

In an instant, I found myself riding this wild mare through the ocean with our dolphin companion in the waters of the Golden Bay. I could now see the green mountains again and the golden sands. The mare had turned toward the shore as the sandy bottom came up. The dolphin chattered and swam touching Ashka's long flowing tail. She knew we could not stay with her in the water much longer, so when it was finally too shallow, she took a swift dive and went on her way, calling her goodbyes to us as she traveled through the blue water out to sea. As we came from the weightlessness of the water, I turned to say goodbye to our dolphin companion with whom we had shared so much, knowing that in our essence, we would never be apart.

Caitlin is a prolific singer, multi-instrumentalist and performer who travels throughout the world with her Beloved, Sika. Together they cre-

ate a blend of their uniquely creative expressions. Between them, they have released ten music CDs to date including *From an Ancient Land* and *Earth Album*. One of Caitlin's latest releases, *Laxmi's Dream* combines sacred mantras with ambient drum sounds and percussion. For more information see http://www.caitlinsika.com

CHAPTER FOUR

Initiation Into Pod Consciousness

by Kiara Windrider

It was in Hawaii that I had a direct experience. I was interested in the concept of the "global brain," the idea that the next stage of our evolution would be to experience ourselves as a single planetary consciousness. The dolphins and whales were the ones who showed me that this was not just an idea in my head. I had moved to Hawaii in early 1999. I lived in a little cabin among the fruit plantations near Kealakekua Bay.

Every morning I would don my flippers and snorkel gear and jump into this beautifully tranquil bay. Kealakekua is a dolphin sanctuary, and wild spinner dolphins would often come into the bay to rest and play among the shallow waters. Over a period of months I got to know them better as they got to know me. I learned to communicate with them through pictures and through the language of the heart. When swimming with them, any sense of personal identity would simply dissolve. I joined with them in a place that was neither human nor dolphin, a place of pure joyful-playful-being.

I learned a lot about myself. Over the years I had built a whole set of identities around myself. I was a spiritual teacher and a healer. I was sensitive and compassionate. I was a good person with much to offer. I was deep. The problem with all this was that I had become so identified with this image of myself that these very identities became a mask. I found myself carefully protecting this image lest someone see through me into a place that was vulnerable or uncertain, angry or unloving or fearful, depressed or shy. I was forever comparing myself to others, and my sense of self came from how I felt others perceived me, and whether I thought I was good enough or lovable enough. And so, of course, I had to put on my best face at all times. I was losing my sense of spontaneity and childlike wonder. I was losing my ability to live from my heart.

The dolphins didn't care for any of that. They became my mirrors. When I got lost behind my masks, whether in self-importance or in self-deprecation, they would stay away. When I let go of the masks of identity, they would come around and we would enter together into ecstatic play. Eventually, I learned that it was safe to let go even of the mask of being human. Here, we could meet in a space of pure essence, and that is when they truly welcomed me into their pod.

I will never forget the day that the four Elders of the pod first swam with me cheek to cheek inseparably for an hour, making deep eye contact that entire time. It felt like an initiation into pod consciousness. I felt myself falling deeply in love with these beautiful wild dolphins, falling deeply in love with all of myself, and deeply in love with love itself. I learned about communicating from the heart. As I would enter into the state of love and join it with an intention or a picture, they would respond immediately. I felt awed and so deeply grateful for my new friends.

I learned about my attachments as well. I loved my dolphin family, and often found myself feeling more connected to their world than to my own. I would fall into bouts of great depression if a day went by and they didn't show up, and so of course they stayed away. When they did come in, they would seem to be totally ignoring me while playing around with everyone else. I finally realized they were confronting my deepest fears of separation, abandonment, jealousy, and loss, all these things that are so much part of our normal human neurosis.

I never experienced any kind of judgment from them, but always a direct reflection and feedback to whatever form of energy I was putting out. I learned more from these unconditionally loving and compassionate teachers than I ever had in any ashram or meditation retreat.

Then one day I had an encounter with a mother and baby whale, which again changed my perception of life forever. As I approached the bay for my customary swim I noticed a spout of water. My heart leaped within me. Although I had seen whales often on their migration paths through these waters, I had not seen them here so close to shore. I swam out in the general direction where I'd seen the spout, then closed my eyes and called out to them in the way I had learned to do with dolphins.

When I opened my eyes it was to see a huge humpback female directly beneath me. At first I panicked. What if she chose to surface just now? What if I got flipped around or sucked under by her immense size? Then I realized that she was very minutely aware of my frail presence, that each movement she made was very deliberate, and that she would never let harm come to me in any way. I relaxed, and we entered into a space of communion, while her baby playfully wove his way in and out, through and around us.

Suddenly I found I was no longer locked into my physical body. As I merged with the consciousness of the whale, I found myself expanding far out into the Earth, entering into her consciousness, and becoming one with her body. I was the Earth. I was Gaia, Goddess of the Earth. I could feel the vastness of her form and of her being, and it was inside me as I was inside her.

I realized there was literally no separation between us, and I realized that this was the consciousness that the whales lived in all of the time. They were the guardians and holographic reflections of the very life of Mother Earth in a way that most of us in human skin cannot begin to imagine. I felt immensely privileged to experience this glimpse of truth. Time stopped, and ecstasy filled my body in wave upon wave of understanding and joy. There has always and forever been only one of us here!

Later, as I went back to my cabin and began to write of my experience, I knew that this connection with my humpback friend would always remain and through her, my connection with the soul of the Earth. In that merging of our consciousness, a pathway opened up within me that has remained open ever afterwards. Or perhaps the pathway has always existed, but the whale taught me to access it, and to trust what I was feeling.

Kiara Windrider, MFCC, is a transpersonal psychotherapist and the author of the books, Doorway to Eternity: A Guide to Planetary Ascension; Deeksha Fire From Heaven; and Journey into Forever: Surfing 2012 and Beyond. For more information on his work, travels, and seminars, see his website, http://www.deekshafire.com or http://www.ilahinoor.com. He can be reached at: kiara@deekshafire.com

Cetacean Dreams

By Kiara Windrider

Sailing through endless oceans of starlight,
Leaping through vast gateways of time,
I dream great dreams of freedom.
Nothing is veiled from me;
All life is a mirror of the truth that I AM.
Creation unfolds,
All play is creation,
All creation is play.
From starlight I create the oceans,
From stardust I create the earth.
I dream beautiful bodies for my expression
And we move through Earth's oceans,
Circling each other
In playful connected song.
We circle the Earth,
We circle the universes.
We are the sea people.

CHAPTER FIVE

Angels of the Sea

By Michelle Gold

Several years ago, I began to have very lucid dreams with a common motif... dolphins inviting me to join them. Not only did I not have time for dolphins, I lived in Hollywood, was terrified of deep water and boats, and was absolutely broke. I did not have a clue regarding where to go or how to begin, but I knew one thing. I had to be with them.

My dreams of dolphins became more and more vivid. Families of wild dolphins beckoned me to follow them, to follow my heart. I arranged to attend a lecture by Dr. John Lilly, famous for his work with dolphins and shared my dilemma with him. He told me go to the Bahamas. Now I had a place in mind, an objective.

Within three days, I received several phone calls from people I did not even know, informing me of places I could be with the dolphins. That same day a magazine arrived and I read a two-sentence blurb about a research study with wild dolphins. Bingo! My heart pounding, I grabbed the phone and dialed, only to find out there was a one-year waiting list. I figured many other people must be having the same dolphin dreams, but I gave them my name anyway.

Anticipating a miracle, I began a three month endurance training program, swimming and treading water for hours to build up the strength required to keep up with strong ocean currents and the acrobatics of dolphins. Using my photography skills, I created a line of greeting cards and sold them to finance my vision. Each night, while in meditation, I gave a flower from my heart to the dolphins.

Then, one very exciting day, I received a call informing me that because of a cancellation it would be possible for me to go to the Bahamas. By that time I had sold exactly one thousand cards and earned just what the trip would cost.

The first time I hit the pure crystal aqua water three wild Atlantic spotted dolphins surrounded me. As one of the young males bounced his sonar, I felt a gentle breeze of electricity flowing through the core of my body, sheer bliss, pure love, and ecstasy. We made eye contact like old friends who have not seen each other in a long time. As we played, two dolphins were gracefully moving the snow-white bottom sand with their rostrums.

The encounter ended and as I watched their beautiful bodies disappear into the lucid sea, the idea that all life is connected was revealed to me as Truth, when looking down, I saw that the two dolphins had etched a perfect flower into the sand below, just like the one I had given them in my daily meditation.

A meditation teacher told me that dolphins and whales are teaching humans unconditional love. To me, they are Angels of the Sea. Perhaps they are Bodhisattvas, enlightened beings, who vow to delay their own complete enlightenment until the suffering of all other beings has ended.

I experienced the guardianship of dolphins during my second trip to the Bahamas. The water felt thick and pressurized, jellyfish were everywhere. Something felt very strange. When I looked under the ship, my heart stopped as I saw over thirty dolphins lined up under our boat with their rostrums pointed towards shore.

When we jumped excitedly into the water, the dolphins went wild, like they were aggressively trying to tell us something. The sonar was so intense it felt like whips of electricity and sounded like lyrical thunder. We got the message, picked up our anchor and headed for land, barely making it in before a formidable hurricane hurled through the very spot where we had been anchored. Once again, dolphins were our Guardian Angels, for dolphins touch and attract us in exactly the same way angels touch our hearts and fill us with the wonder of the mystery of life.

Dolphins are wonderful at bringing people together with love. An exchange of dolphin experiences was the beginning of a most beautiful relationship with my partner. Scott was involved in a near fatal motorcycle accident in 1987. Doctors told him that he might not walk or play guitar again. Time spent in Hawaii swimming with wild dolphins and whales served as inspiration and healing. Scott's music and poetry is now filled with the songs of the Angels of the Sea and the great beauty of life.

The photos I took underwater of the dolphins became my first gallery exhibition. My work in the gallery led to a beautiful friendship with Chris Carson, who directed "Dolphins: Minds in the Water," which won an Academy Award. An introduction to his mother, Meridel, led to a very special friendship and business partnership with angels at its core. Dolphin experiences, like angelic experiences, allow strangers to connect at deep and intimate levels, transforming fear and judgment into love.

Hundreds of stories exist about dolphins assisting individuals who are blind, who are in pain, who are in danger, who need tenderness and guidance. In Russia, there is a doctor who has helped women give birth in the Black Sea with the assistance of dolphins, who actually lift the babies to the surface for their first breath of air. His studies have overwhelmingly shown that each of these babies is healthier, happier, and more socially skilled, with a more developed sense of humor than babies born traditionally in hospitals.

I still cry for joy when I think of the dolphins with whom I had the great honor of spending time. I miss seeing a mother dolphin delicately caressing her baby with her fin, and seeing multiple generations of dolphins swimming freely, feeding, loving, and being. I recall their hilarious sense of humor as they played with us, and each other. I think of the wise elders whose eyes looked deeply into my soul, sharing their ancient wisdom, and the thrill as they swam up to me as we sang together underwater.

I remember the way the sun filtered through the blueness, casting veils of light, emanating off their luminous, shimmering skin, and their fins moving silently like wings. I will never forget the profound feeling as eleven dolphins swam in slow circles around me. Time stopped. Only this otherworldly luminous bliss existed as I thanked them for allowing me into their home, and for helping me light the path to following my heart. I am so very grateful to the Angels of the Sea for teaching me the beauty of the present moment.

Michele Gold, author of Angels of the Sea, is a professional illustrator, writer, photographer and musician. Her book is available at all bookstores or by calling Hay House at 800/654-5126. More information can be found on her website, http://www.angelnet.com

CHAPTER SIX

Telepathic Journey With a Manta Ray

By Dr. Vernon Woolf

The year was 1989. I was scuba diving around Molokini off the coast of Maui. Molokini is a volcanic crater with just the upper rim out of the water. All kinds of coral grow there, and it's a great place to scuba dive. We anchored the boat right next to Molokini, and then began to swim underwater around this wonderful crater to the other side. There were three people swimming with me.

We came to the crater edge and looked down into the deep, dark blue ocean. It's a little scary when you first experience that, because it slopes sharply. It looks bottomless. Just as I was feeling a little bit of anxiety, my companion pointed to a certain spot in the dark blue. Out of that spot came this huge shape. My first response was, "How far away is our boat?" I then started to focus on the shape. It turned out to be a large manta ray, which have these vast airplane wings that make them look like they're flying underwater.

My three companions immediately started to swim after this manta ray as it came up over the ridge and then began to circle the bay. I then let go, and decided to try an experiment. I lay face down in the water and said to myself, "I think I will just become the manta to really experience it." So I closed my eyes, went to my inner Place of Peace, and called up the fullest potential of the manta and just let myself become that potential. I got into what I call the harmonics of it. I moved my arms up and down two or three times at exactly the same rhythm of the manta. Instantaneously, a wave of water rushed over me, and I thought to myself, "What could be doing that?" I opened my eyes and suddenly found myself thirty or forty feet beneath the surface of the water staring into a mouth about 2 1/2 feet wide. I could hear what must've been the manta laughing. It startled me. I started to ask myself what mantas eat, when I heard a voice in my head, "Are you all right?" I instinctively looked around but there was no one else there but the manta. And then it said to me, "Are you a manta?"

I realized then that it was telepathically communicating with me, or that was my experience of it. I said, "I'm all right, but I'm not a manta, I just wanted to experience your world." And it giggled, literally. It appeared delighted with that prospect and then, took me down over the edge into this deep, dark blue. The first thing that registered, as we rapidly descended, was this incredible sense of peace.

I had never experienced such peace, and I had done quite a lot of advanced meditation at that point in my life. That was the first lesson I received from that manta. Then it took me farther down among all the dark shadows of the volcano, deep, deep down. And I realized that it wasn't afraid of anything. This was really a peaceful place for it, but a little overwhelming for me.

After a while, I asked, "Could we go where there's light and color?" Then it took me up and over a series of coral reefs that were just like flower gardens. They were magnificent. They were the very best coral reefs I've ever seen. I was just having the most delightful, peaceful time. That manta was so at home, and I could experience all this in the world of the manta.

Then all of a sudden it was swimming in the galaxy. You know how the Hubbell telescope brings back all those wonderful pictures? This manta saw all that and more in bright color just like the coral reefs. And after I realized what was happening, after I got over my astonishment at the beauty of the galaxy because it was not encompassed by sky and atmosphere and all that kind of thing, I said to the manta, " How can you, a manta that is confined to the water, know about the stars and the galaxies?" It replied, "Don't you know anything at all?"

I was a little astonished at that. That it would know everything. That it would have incredible access to every part of the universe. So we traveled there for a while. Then all of a sudden an agonizing feeling came over me. I opened my eyes immediately. The manta was still in front of me.

My companions had followed the manta back to me and were at the end of each of the manta's wings. They were just watching me and this manta face to face in a "Vulcan mind-lock" for the longest time. The third guy, who had retrieved the underwater camera from the boat, had now swum up behind us taking pictures. So now the manta was surrounded on three sides by people, which seemed to make it uncomfortable. It looked at me a little sadly and said, "I have to go now." It broke our "lock," and just swam away. That oneness, the realization of the peace the manta experiences, has never really left me.

Dr. Woolf is the author of ten books including Holodynamics. He consults individuals and businesses. He is an internationally known public speaker, an experienced trainer, seminar leader, therapist, and entrepreneur.

His specialty is improving relationships and building high performance teams through the holistic study of situational dynamics. His "Unfolding Potential" Seminars, which began in the United States, have now expanded worldwide.

During the Cold War his team created support chapters in more than 100 cities in Russia, where more than 600 trained and certified teachers were operating as part of the transformation of the Soviet Union. He has now fully recovered from the assassination attempt made in Dubna, Russia in 1997.

He is the Chairman of the Board of the International Academy of Holodynamics, and the Chairman of the Board of the Global Alliance Foundation (GAF), a non-profit organization dedicated to creating sustainable and affordable communities of the future.

GAF networks resources, raises funding and researches solutions to extreme climate changes, effective waste remediation, alternative energy sources, sustainable food production and other aspects required for communities of the future.

For more information on the work of Victor Vernon Woolf, Ph.D see his website at http://www.Holodynamics.com

CHAPTER SEVEN

A Skeptic Gets Healed

by Dr. John E. Upledger

Since my first dolphin experience in 1954, while in the U.S. Coast Guard patrolling in the Gulf of Mexico, I have had a strong instinctive desire to interact with these wonderful beings. Off and on over the next 30 years, I continued having many positive dolphin encounters. Then, in the summer of 1996, I helped start a dolphin-therapist CranioSacral Therapy (CST) program at The Upledger Institute in Grassy Key, Florida.

The format was to float a patient in about four feet of water with three CST Therapists working on them at the same time. Usually we had one therapist at the patient's head, another at the feet, and a third at the pelvis. This left one side of the patient's body free for any dolphin who desired to join the process as an equal partner. We worked together this way with dolphins for over four months with some impressive results. Their "energy" had an amazing effect on the human body.

During this time, I became very friendly with a particular dolphin named AJ. Actually, AJ initiated our relationship and I was more than happy to accommodate him. He would often lie very still in the water next to me while I was working with a patient. I could feel his energy even when we were not in physical contact with each other. His presence seemed to accelerate the healing work being done.

On one occasion a dolphin trainer, who had been observing us from the pier, suggested that I simply extend my left hand, palm down, upon the surface of the water. Within seconds AJ was under my hand. He began moving so that my hand was rubbing up and down his back. Then he put his blowhole, his breathing aperture, under my hand so that my palm covered it. Lore has it that you never touch a dolphin's blowhole because the dolphin, out of fear, might go into a frenzy.

AJ kept his blowhole under my hand for a minute or so. Then he began moving his body fore and aft again for a while before he left. During this contact, I could feel his energy running through me, and I sensed that I would be able to tap into the dolphin's vibrational energy and use it when appropriate. Indeed, I frequently do use it while working at our clinic in Palm Beach Gardens, Florida. In fact, it has become rather automatic for me now.

The following spring I flew to Edinburgh, Scotland, to conduct a symposium. There were about seventy therapists in attendance, all of whom had completed intermediate-level studies in CRT. At such symposiums, I work on patients with difficult case histories recommended by attendees. I think aloud as I evaluate and treat the patients, often inviting their own therapist to join me.

On the morning of my second day, I was working with a young boy suffering from cerebral palsy. I encountered a very strong resistance to physiological motion in his head. Working in a train-of-thought mode, I said aloud, "I'm going to apply some dolphin energy here." The therapeutic energy input increased significantly with dramatic results. Later the audio technician told me that each time I applied the "dolphin energy," the static in his recording also increased significantly.

After the symposium, I was approached by a conservatively dressed woman in her 60s. She informed me that she was a professor of physical therapy at the university in Edinburgh, and that she did not believe in such non-scientific claims as "applying dolphin energy." Then, in a rather distressed voice, she explained that, she too, had heard the static in her hearing aid, which she had been using for over twenty years. She said the static continued each time I "applied" the dolphin energy throughout the third and final day of the symposium.

About a month after returning home from Scotland, I received a letter from the skeptical professor. She told me that she still did not believe in "dolphin energy," but she also felt compelled to inform me that four days after the symposium she discovered that she no longer needed her hearing aid. She could now hear a watch ticking with what was once her deaf ear. Then she asked me to explain what had happened to her. I had no theoretical explanation, other than to say that there are many useful things you can employ but still can't explain. Among these are gravity, some electrical phenomena, and perhaps dolphin energy. Fortunately for her, believing was not a prerequisite to healing.

Dr. John E. Upledger is the author of *CranioSacral Therapy; CranioSacral Therapy II - Beyond The Dura; SomatoEmotional Release and Beyond; Your Inner Physician and You; A Brain is Born; and CranioSacral Therapy, Touchstone for Natural Healing.*

He is the President of The Upledger Institute, Inc. Dedicated to the natural enhancement of health, the Institute is recognized worldwide for its groundbreaking continuing-education programs, clinical research and therapeutic services.

Throughout his career as an osteopathic physician, Dr. Upledger has been recognized as an innovator and leading proponent in the investigation of new therapies. His development of CranioSacral Therapy in particular has earned him an international reputation. He has also served on the Alternative Medicine Program Advisory Council for the Office of Alternative Medicine at the National Institutes of Health in Washington, D.C. See more information on The Upledger Institute, Inc at http://www.upledger.com

Part Five

Light From Angelic Realms

CHAPTER ONE

Light from Angelic Realms

At this exciting period in earth history, Angelic encounters are sweeping every country and culture. Fulfilling a unique role in awakening humanity, they are inspiring people with a greater awareness of their Soul Purpose. For those who have been graced with this extraordinary communion, Angelic Inspiration has inspired a deeper sense of responsibility for the planet and a resolve to make a difference in our present planetary equation.

Patricia Diane Cota-Robles, author of *The Awakening* said, "The Company of Heaven is being revealed to us, now that more people than ever before are reaching a critical moment in their life experiences. Consequently, millions of people are asking God for Divine Intervention. Many of them are praying for the very first time. This powerful event, in unison with the millions of Lightworkers who daily invoke the Light of God, has created the greatest influx of Light the Earth has ever experienced. This Heavenly assistance will greatly empower the patterns of perfection for the New Earth, and it will accelerate our individual hopes and dreams by leaps and bounds.

In past ages, it was the rare saint, sage, or shaman who communed with the heavens. Jesus spoke on the Mount with beings from higher realms. Saints communed with angels and other Divine Beings. Joan of Arc led an army of believers on behalf of France, inspired by her encounters with Archangel Michael. Catherine of Sienna, St. Therese of Lisieux, Lucia of Fatima, Moses, Mohammad, Gautama, and others brought hope or warnings through their communication with Divine Realms.

In recent times, the children in Medjugori, Yugoslavia experienced continual visitations by Mother Mary, known by some as the 'Queen of the Angels,' over the course of many years. Countless individuals journeyed from all over the world to be a part of that sacred communion and experienced miracles while there.

In the 90's, Time Magazine made a compelling statement. Over 75% of the people in America believed in angels and many felt they had their own Guardian Angel. Since then, mystical interactions with angels and other Divine Beings have been on the rise, inspiring recipients to bring forth their unique creative expression to a world in dire need.

From this dramatic increase in divine encounters, a host of books, films, TV shows, music, and art have flooded the world. This flood of information about higher realms and Beings of Light has been working its magic upon the psyches of humanity. Today, people from all over the world are having mystical encounters, in what has become, a worldwide phenomenon unique to our time.

Everyone is capable
of some degree of personal and
spiritual transformation,
and even of imagining the possibility of
angelic intervention and miraculous healing.

--Lewis Mehl-Madrona
Author of Coyote Medicine

CHAPTER TWO

My Mission With the Angels

By Doreen Virtue, PhD

The angels are with us as a gift from our Creator,
And their aim is to establish Peace on Earth,
One person at a time.
Working wing-in-hand with the angels,
I believe that this goal is possible.

On July 15, 1995, my personal life and career was irrevocably altered by an incident that is nothing short of miraculous. I had been ignoring the angels' guidance to become a teacher of mind-body-spirit issues. So, when an angel warned me that my car was going to be stolen on that fateful July afternoon, I ignored him. After all, my habit of arguing with and ignoring the angels was deeply ingrained by then. Despite this, the angel did not abandon me in my most dire moment. As I parked, two armed men, intent on a car jacking, brandished weapons and physically accosted me. A voice spoke to me again. It was loud, distinctly male and it instructed me to scream with all my might. This time I listened, screamed loudly, and a passersby became alarmed and sent my attackers running, saving my life.

I immediately began a daily rigorous practice of receiving and deciphering my Divine Guidance. Simultaneously, I was reexamining my spiritual beliefs, along with my Western Psychological beliefs. The end result being twofold: I was guided to look at psychology from a whole new perspective, and my natural clairvoyance rapidly returned with the same clarity and strength of my childhood experiences.

After my brush with death during the car jacking, I was very humbled. The fact that an angel had KNOWN my future just shattered all of my illusions about the material world and linear time. I began actively soliciting the angels' advice on all matters. What they taught me completely reshaped my healing and therapy work. After having spent many years helping patients using traditional psychotherapy, I was compelled to incorporate my intuitive skills and angelic messages into the therapeutic process. The positive results were amazing.

Today, I use Angel Therapy with every one of my clients and in all my workshops. The angels help to heal away every seeming problem, and their healing efficacy makes all the traditional forms of healing I'd ever studied or used pale in comparison.

Doreen Virtue, PhD, a fourth-generation metaphysician who works with the angelic, elemental, and ascended-master realms in her writings and workshops, is the author of more than 20 books about angels, chakras, Crystal Children, Indigo Children, health and diet, and other mind-body-spirit issues, including the best-selling Healing with the Angels and Messages from Your Angels books/angel cards.

She holds B.A., M.A., and Ph.D. degrees in counseling psychology, was the founder and former director of WomanKind Psychiatric Hospital at Cumberland Hall Hospital in Nashville, Tennessee, and was also an administrator at Woodside Women's Hospital in the San Francisco Bay Area. Both all-women psychiatric hospitals specialized in treating women's psychological issues. Doreen also directed three outpatient psychiatric centers, including an adolescent drug and alcohol abuse center. For more information on Doreen and her amazing work, see http://www.angeltherapy.com

CHAPTER THREE

A Visit From a Dreamtime Friend

By Ann West, PhD

It was a warm Indian morning, with the cool mountain air gently blowing through the room. I was lying on my bed, caressed by the breeze. I couldn't tell if I was awake or on the edge of a lucid dream. My senses told me that I was falling backwards down a spiraling tunnel of white light. I could hear waves crashing against a shore close by. I saw what looked like white foaming surf, billowing, getting larger and larger, until I realized that I was looking at a white effervescent cloud formation. I was being pulled into the clouds as if by an invisible thread attached to my solar plexus.

As I entered into the clouds they parted and I was standing in a space with no visible boundaries. I turned to my left and found a most beautiful angelic being, tall and regal, standing next to me. He had blond wavy hair down to his shoulders and his eyes were as noble as two royal jewels, emitting the semblance of dignity and benevolence. He wore a long, flowing white gown with a hooded cloak attached to it. I could see the tops of his wings appearing above his shoulders and gently cascading down his back, almost reaching the hem of his gown.

We stood side by side in silence for a moment as I experienced a deep reverence and awe. I was filled with a sense of peace and love. In front of us was a podium that came chest high, made from transparent, luminescent fiber. Resting on it was a large brown book, the largest I had ever seen. As I looked deeply into the eyes of this beautiful being, I knew intuitively that he was the Archangel Michael. I was in the presence of an exalted being filled with compassion and kindness for humanity. A knowingness emerged from within me that we were not strangers.

Then, without uttering a word, we started to communicate telepathically. He said, "This book that we are looking at is called the Akashic Records. It has been in existence from the beginning of time, and everyone in the universe has a book of records. In fact every living thing has a record of every moment of their existence. Everything you have ever said, done or thought is kept in the Akashic Records for all time." Without a moment's delay, he turned to the large book and it opened automatically.

I glanced at the book and now it seemed as if I were looking through a window into a turquoise sky with big, puffy, white clouds floating by. Instantaneously, I was not looking at a book with paper pages that you turn. Instead, the picture I saw started changing as if I were looking at a movie. A vision of me, sitting on my bed in Los Angeles, appeared before us. I knew exactly what day it was. I had been very sad and confused that day and I had gone into my bedroom feeling despondent because of the lack of depth and real communication in my relationship with my husband. I was experiencing an intense sense of loneliness and misery.

This was not a new problem, for I had quite often felt alone in the relationship. It had started way before I even married him, but I had been in denial. He wanted a beautiful woman and I wanted security and a lifestyle of comfort. We were both out of integrity with each other and ourselves. Neither of us married for true love, but rather out of our insecurities. The hardest part of it all was that I had two young children and found myself completely dependent on my husband financially. As I sat on the bed that day, I cried, devastated at being trapped in my satin-lined prison.

What had attracted me into the marriage, the financial security, was the exact thing that had stopped me from going out into the world and creating my own freedom. I had compromised myself by agreeing to marry him, being driven more by my childhood fears of poverty and lack of security and being afraid for my future.

The archangel and I continued to watch the recorded visions, feelings and thoughts of that day when I sat on the bed crying. I knew that the only way out of this was probably divorce, but I also did not feel that I had the courage or strength to go through such a major life change.

He said, "We want you to know that there is a family of teachers on the planet at this time. They are the 'light workers' of the earth and they are of the Christ-light consciousness, the Buddha consciousness and you are most definitely one of them, Ann. However, you have much work ahead of you before you actually realize what I am saying is true, and it will take a great deal of courage and strength to do what you have to do. It is now time for your awakening, and you have heard your wake-up call, which brought you to India. You have had much deciphering to do because of the distraction your childhood created. You chose to come in this life with certain emotional handicaps as a child, but that was simply because you knew before coming in that the challenges of your poor lifestyle and your alcoholic father would add wisdom, strength, and compassion to your personality that no other situation could offer. We want you to know that you are very capable of doing what you came to earth to do."

I was entranced by his words, and they rang as truth in my heat. I knew I would remember everything with ease. He went on. "The Law of Magnetic Attraction," is the first law. It is very simple to understand when you realize that you are constantly attracting what is in your life like magnets draw metal. Every situation in your life has been brought to you by the power of your own mind. As I stood next to this beautiful angelic being, I was completely taken by his presence and the profound teachings that he was sharing. I absorbed every word like a sponge.

I looked at the pitiful sight of myself still on the bed, completely engulfed with confusion and tortured by this emotional crisis. I felt concern for the future of Ann and as I spoke to Archangel Michael, I was completely detached from my physical self. "What will happen to her?" I asked with a great deal of compassion yet detachment. What happened next occurred instantaneously. As I looked into his eyes that were filled with love and compassion, he said, "That is up to you."

In that very same moment, I was no longer in his physical presence but was lying in a cold sweat on my bed in the Himalaya Mountains. I sat bolt upright and burst into tears, knowing that what I'd experienced wasn't just a simple dream that could be pushed aside and forgotten. It gave me the strength to make the life decisions that were important to make, which eventually led me to true love and a very happy family life.

When Scottish born Ann West awoke one morning it was the beginning of an extraordinary journey that has taken Ann from Malibu to India, the San Juan Islands, Kauai, Ibiza and Glastonbury. Following her spiritual awakening she turned away from her cosmopolitan lifestyle to study and then to teach. She has hosted talk radio shows, coerced the US Navy to cancel military exercises, become a Doctor of Metaphysical Science, received her PhD in Psychological Studies and written a book about her experiences in India called From The Source. In 2008, she released her debut album, Confidante. See more about Ann at http://www.annwest.co.uk

CHAPTER FOUR

One Angel's Story

By Aurora Juliana Ariel

One day I was heading over the Pali Hwy on the island of Oahu, intent upon getting to a World Healing Service. During these meetings, Angels and other Divine Beings were invoked for the blessing and healing of humanity as we addressed specific conditions in the world. Being a devotee of this spiritual healing work over many years, I never missed a service. It was a profound weekly experience that I was dedicated and committed to.

The sun had begun to set, casting a rosy glow over the lush green jungle growth that trailed over the cliffs. Embedded with gorgeous flowers, it was an awe-inspiring sight with the turquoise ocean in the distance. Normally I would have loved to stop and take in the view at the overlook, but I was intent on arriving on time.

Looking forward to yet another powerful evening, my mind was going over all the possible world conditions we could address, when an amazing story started running through my mind. It had distinct intonations and phrases that were unique and definitely not my own. Pausing to grasp the situation I became aware of an angel who was intently delivering his story to me. As I listened, I found it quite incredible and very interesting. It felt like it was meant to be a children's story. When I realized that, I was thinking, "Oh my God, how am I going to remember this?" but I couldn't stop driving. I was so committed to being on time for these weekly services.

The story continued and was quite brilliant and exciting. I had already received two children's books through divine inspiration, so was quite open to incorporating this story into the collection. As the Angel spoke, I was setting a mental intention to remember everything, but once I had attended the service, I realized I had forgotten everything.

I was dismayed and somewhat disappointed in myself. I mean, how often does one have an angelic visitation and one of such import? I felt ashamed. Did arriving on time at one World Healing Service really mean that much more than a precious picture book for the children of the world written by an Angel? This compelled an in depth self-exploration and discovery over the next days, but sadly enough, that precious story was gone.

A year and a half later, the same Angel returned and began delivering his story to me. I was so incredibly grateful, I immediately stopped everything, ran and got a pen and wrote down every word.

What I love about the story is that it has a unique style and expression that is distinctly different than my own. It is his personal story about his journey to earth and the special gift he brought the people who loved the angels.

Though this experience happened many years ago, I've kept the story safe for that perfect time when it could be released as a children's picture book. I've since met the perfect, classically trained visionary artist to do the artwork for my children's books. His story follows. Someday, children all over the world will be reading, *One Angel's Story*.

CHAPTER FIVE

Commissioned By The Heavens

By Marius Michael-George

"I paint angels because they are an intrinsic part of
my own nature and in the course of daily life
I am always surrounded by people I believe
are angels in human form."

I had just finished my classical art training when I received my
first 'Commission from the Heavens.' I was hired to paint Archangel
Twin Rays for a book. Over the next year, I had incredible experiences
as the different archangels overshadowed me as I worked. For hours I
would be enveloped in their aura and energy. This project opened me up
to the angelic realms and began my mission as a visionary artist.

There's been an unfolding destiny and magic around my work.
First, I had to get the training I needed, and then for years I did my
spiritual work and purification through the violet flame, which has
continued for 26 years. I made myself available and now the Heavens
are commissioning me to bring forth their art, and each experience is
unique.

When I'm painting, I'm transported into another realm, a different
dimension where I see and hear things, though I am never really able to
capture what is in that other realm because colors and light are so brilliant and different than what I can create here with the tools available.
A huge difference, but I try to extract the essence and do my best with
what is available and then I add on special effects with the computer.
From all these Divine Experiences, my art studio has become a fortress
of light. Set high in the mountains, when I step into the room, it is like

entering the higher realms.

The vibration from all these paintings and the work I've done here has completely changed the physical field to a divine energy that allows me to be in a timeless place as I work. Every one of my paintings is an angel story. This is pretty much what I do. I record angel stories in paint and the paintings really speak for themselves. They are portals into the angelic realm that put the viewer into direct contact with the angels represented and in many instances people have their own personal experiences with angels as a result. The paintings also anchor the special vibration and presence of the being, which then permeates the home or temple it is placed in.

I remember this one lady that was taking art classes with me and she was working on reproducing one of my angel images, the Angel of Miracles. At one point, while all the other students were painting or drawing, she just sat there motionless, looking intensely at the painting. I asked her if she was OK and she told me in a whisper that the angel was talking to her and at one point came out of the painting and blessed her with the wand.

For me almost every day has an angel story because they are very much part of daily life, beginning with the people of my close circle which are all, I think, angels in human form and a constant wonderful inspiration, and then the angels on the "other side" which are always around in great numbers and very much part of orchestrating wonderful synchronicities, blessings, inspirations, revelations, ideas and many other elements of this magical daily reality.

The most tangibly interactive part of my experiences with the angels is taking place when I work, because of course it directly involves their presence, which is usually the main subject of the paintings I create. So they part the veil, clock time stops and we get to play. I call my work "play" because that's what it really is and there are times when my hand and brush are gliding effortlessly along light pathways that materialize over the painting surface, or a blank canvas becomes superimposed with a very clear vision that I can follow and execute pretty fast, so in this way being able to bypass the very slow and time consuming process of experimenting with ideas for composition, color scheme, values, figures, anatomy, costumes, backgrounds, etc.

Other times I receive floating images and different options I can choose from and compose in the traditional way but in a mode of being super charged with un-stoppable creativity and inspiration which keeps me completely focused on the work and sometimes without any need for taking breaks for 10-12 hours straight.

The most tangible and wonderfully detailed stories about those realms are my paintings for anyone who wants to get the real scoop. All that you need to do is spend time looking at and being with the painting and then a doorway can open. You can be transported to those realms. You can talk to that master or angel and amazing things can happen. These are portals into that Being's causal body and into the higher realms.

As we open to these realms, we are infused with ideas, visions, and inspirations. This is the work of the Angels and Masters. They are working hand in hand on earth, orchestrating the wonderful things that are continually happening in our lives.

Marius Michael-George is a classically trained visionary artist and art teacher who specializes in Sacred Art. He is a native of Eastern Europe born in Bucharest, Romania and presently works at his art studio in Paradise Valley, Montana.

Scanning the unseen through the "eyes of the soul," Marius creates images that become portals into other realms and invite the viewer to participate in a spiritual experience. Angels, Faeries, Saints and Ascended Masters seem to feel at home in his studio and whether in ethereal bodies or physical form, they are the main protagonists of his compositions.

Marius studied painting with one of the most prestigious masters of classical art in the U.S., Frank Mason, at the Art Students League in New York City and afterwards he was trained in the system of classical realism at Atelier LeSueur and Atelier Lack in Minneapolis.

His original oil paintings and murals are found in public and private collections across North and South America and Europe and all artwork is published internationally as prints and cards. For more information or to purchase his beautiful art see: http://www.MariusFineArt.com

Journey Into the Fires of Montana

By Aurora Juliana Ariel

In the summer of 2000, I was traveling with my Beloved (now best friend) and two sons in an RV through many spectacular sites in the western U.S. and Canada. At one point, more than 60 fires were blazing out of control in the northwest, most of them in Montana where we were heading. We considered turning around but the energy was so strong to continue the journey, all we could do was drive on.

Though I had initiated what became a six-month adventure through western US and Canada, I often wondered how I would be able to keep on track with my work as we traveled. I was in the midst of creating the logo for the healing system I had created, TheQuest™, and was ready to work on the brochure, business cards, and stationary. I had wondered as we set off on this journey if this trip would take me off course, and had felt concerned but then, miracles started happening and I was entranced by the beauty of the regions we visited and the amazing experiences we had at each place.

As we traveled north, we arrived at the foot of the Teton Mountains, just as the sun was setting over the spectacular snow capped peaks. As I stepped from the RV, Violet hues mixed with gold bathing me in an exquisite mixture of beauty and light.

Amidst this glorious scene, there were three fires blazing in sight and we were told the road into Yellowstone National Park was closed because of fires that were out of control. As I was falling to sleep that night, a Divine Presence enveloped me with an exquisite peace. A gentle woman's voice said, "You must go north, there is an important meeting up there." I wondered, "How?" as I drifted into a deep sleep. The fires were raging and the road was closed....

The next morning, to our surprise, the skies were clear, the fires were under control and the road into Yellowstone was open. As we drove through the park, the ravages of uncontrolled fires had left their mark everywhere around us. Lands were smoldering, helicopters were flying overhead with water buckets, and firemen were containing fires.

Entering Montana, the smoke was so thick it was almost impossible to see. The RV could only go at a slow pace. Finally arriving at a hot springs, I remembered that a visionary artist, Marius Michael-George, whose beautiful work I had seen on the web, lived near by. I was inspired to call him, and a meeting was set up for the next day.

Stepping into Marius's world of visionary art the next morning was an amazing experience. As I entered his art studio I was stunned to see a large painting of an angel on a mountain on the far wall, the exact image I had been seeing for my logo, which would speak to the freedom one could realize through TheQuest™. I could not believe my eyes! In this remote cabin in the wilderness of Montana, large ornate gold frames filled the walls with spectacular paintings. It was like stepping into a master's workshop back in the Renaissance period.

A creative synergy followed as Marius created my logos, while his wife at the time did the graphic arts for the brochure, business cards, and stationary. This powerful and timely meeting was one of many sacred adventures during the journey that had taken us into the heart of the fires of Montana.

Six months later, as my travels came to an end and I arrived back home on the Island of Maui, I was amazed how Divinely Orchestrated our journey had been and how much I had accomplished.

CHAPTER SEVEN

The White Seraphim

By Alana Ciri

I was feeling that motherly concern that many mothers have experienced when they 'know' their children are in danger. Through various phone calls over the summer from my ex-husband, who had summer visitation with my children, I had realized that things were not right. I didn't know the extent of it, but I felt absolutely sure that my children were in trouble.

For weeks I had attempted to get my husband to put the children on the plane home to me, but instead, I would find a raging, seemingly insane person on the other line who would not allow me to speak to my children. Sometimes I would receive calls in the middle of the night with my ex screaming obscenities and false accusations at me. Then, he would drag my children out of bed and force them to tell me they didn't want to come home, with him raving in the background. They would be crying so hard, my heart would break. I did not know what was going on. Had my ex gone insane?

Calling the police in Hawaii, I received no help. Weeks were going by and I was becoming frantic. Finally my ex husband promised to put the children on a flight home but made me drive seven hours to a different city to pick them up. Arriving to get them on my birthday of all days, I was devastated when they never got off the plane.

Summoning up all the strength I could muster, I convinced airlines to let me fly with little money and soon I was on the plane to save my children. By that point, I was very emotional and feeling somewhat shaky. I was overwrought and deeply concerned about my children. I didn't have a clue if they were ok or not. I began crying and continued crying silently the whole way to Hawaii.

Along the way I began to notice a strong energy coming from the empty window seat beside me. Looking closer, I saw an incredibly powerful tall Angel in white. Seraphim was the word that entered my mind. He never interacted with me or even looked in my direction. He simply sat there, radiating a calm strength that was very comforting the whole way across the ocean. It gave me a feeling of safety in spite of my emotional state and concern for my children's welfare.

This unexpected Divine Escort was what I really needed at the time, because what I was facing with so little money and resources, was very scary. I didn't know what I would find when I got to Hawaii. My children were being harmed, I was sure, and I had to save them, but how? I felt alone in the world, facing something beyond my capacity to deal with. The Seraphim stayed with me the whole six-hour flight, which really helped me to stay calm though I felt like my heart was breaking and my mind felt tight with fear.

I arrived at the home with a police escort, who were there to help me retrieve my children under my Child Custody Agreement. I was devastated to find my three children living in a complete wreck, with clothes and belongings strewn everywhere. They had been left all alone, and didn't know where their father was. His absence was a relief. It gave me an edge, allowing me time to round up all their belongings and get them safely into the car without being rained with abuse. Before I had finished rounding up all their possessions, my ex arrived and became estremely angry and abusive. He seemed demented and reeked of alcohol. As he ranted and raved in the driveway, screaming out disgusting things about me to the two policemen, they began siding with him and became mean and degrading to me as well, despite his obvious condition and that he was violating child custody laws.

I felt alone in a very scary situation. I seemed to be the only one who understood what was going on and that my children were in danger and needed rescuing. They had even seen the interior of the home. I've never been able to understand that. My children were in danger and yet, these men were becoming increasingly rude to me. By some miracle, despite the great unkindness of these two policemen and the drunken condition of my ranting and raving ex, I got my children safely out of there. But, they were so traumatized by their summer visit with him and all they had witnessed it broke my heart. Seeing my children like that was almost too much to bear.

It was heartbreaking to hear my children's stories, how their summer months had been filled with their father being drunk, binging and suicidal, and how he had driven them numerous times intoxicated, while the car swerved recklessly down the road. This had scared them to the point where they had begun walking miles into town to do his errands for him, so that they would not have to drive with him.

These were small children. They also tried to fill his alcohol bottles with water in a desperate attempt to stop the scary nightmare they were in, but like most children when they are being abused, they never called me to tell me what was going on. Our inner connection and the strange phone calls I had begun receiving were the only way I knew something was wrong.

Thanks to a beautiful angel woman friend, my children and I had a safe shelter for a couple of days, and the airlines too were very helpful in giving me good rates to get the children and I back home, though the whole ordeal left us broke for quite sometime.

The hardest thing was the degree that my children were traumatized. They were in shock when I found them. It took quite a while to get them back to normal. The cost of alcoholism is great, especially upon our children. The repercussions can last a lifetime.

Somehow, I was given the strength to get to my children, even though I didn't have the money. Each step of the way I was met with angels, whether human or divine. I truly believe I got my children out of there in time. Had they stayed, they could have lost their lives in a horrible accident.

I will always remember how, at a time when I felt all alone in the world, facing something that was almost too huge to handle, a Seraphim came to help me. I am still in awe when I think of it. A mother's heart and prayers for her children were heard, honored, and answered! That God sent me an escort on such a terrifying and uncertain journey, amazes me to this day, and showed me without a doubt, that we are not alone. God is with us and our cries for help are heard.

Part Six

Divine Intervention

CHAPTER ONE

Extraordinary Divine Encounters

The Time of the Awakening is upon us.
It is a promise that is being birthed within our hearts.
It is a Vision that sings in our Souls. It is our longing for a better life,
for a safe future that is our legacy to the precious children of the world.

Like a spectacular fireworks display across a brilliant sky, or an Aurora Borealis shining it's brilliant emanation into the night, Divine Encounters are lighting a fire in humanity. They are quickening the masses, creating a ripple of change within the human psyche. They are lifting people up into higher realms and nobler realities, giving them a glimpse of the eternal. They are reminding the souls of Earth that they are on a sojourn here. They are on a planet that is in dire need of loving care and attention, but they come from ethereal realms. Their true home is in Worlds of Light where beauty, majesty and grace reign supreme.

These Encounters with the Divine help us remember who we are and the higher archetypes we are on earth to inspire. It is an exciting time, where a once unique experience is now happening all over the planet.

The stories that follow serve to bring real this very inspiring phenomenon. The magic of these stories is that they are true-life encounters that speak eloquently of a Universal Presence that is ever working towards a greater good for humanity, while being intimately involved in the minute details of our lives. These experiences have taken the Violet Person beyond traditional beliefs in God into a personal relationship with the Divine.

CHAPTER TWO

Dark Night of the Spirit

In 1996, I lost everything. It was as if a big wrecking ball came in without warning and smashed my world to smithereens. I was in the most intense period of my life. It was a full on Dark Night of the Spirit, which I've been told is beyond a Dark Night of the Soul experience.

After years of living opulently, supporting my family with ease, and working on exciting projects while earning my BA, MA, and PhD in psychology, my wonderful lifestyle had come to a roaring halt within months. Finally, I was facing homelessness.

It all started when a director sabotaged my global project right when my husband and I were separating. Through his business troubles and failings over many years, he had literally cleaned me out financially while I had striven to support him in every way and give him endless loans that taxed my credit cards and were never paid.

The sad movie of my over generosity and unclear boundaries on top of a host of other unexpected events had literally translated into my being evicted at Christmas with three of my four beautiful children. We were being forced out of our palatial home and in just a few days, we would have nowhere to go. This made me wonder about homeless people and how they came to be that way. If I could have everything change so drastically in a matter of months bringing me to the brink of homelessness, what had happened to them?

I told my daughter, "I've got to move you to safety, because I don't know what's going to happen. I've lost everything and the boys and I might end up living in my car." It was very scary. She was upset, because she was going to college and working, and it was hard for young people to make it on their own on Oahu. Thankfully, everything came together for her quickly, with a great place to live with her girl-friends that she could afford.

I had tried to stay on in the house that the owners were now putting up for sale, offering my expensive jewelry, Chinese rugs, and paintings in exchange for rent while I got back on my feet, but to no avail. After two years of paying high rent faithfully on time and keeping their home spotless, they closed their hearts to my children and me, and were pushing us out with the intent of keeping the home empty while selling it. That didn't make sense, but they didn't care.

Now the hours were ticking away and move out day was coming fast. In a couple days, that next Saturday, two friends were coming at noon to help me pack, but I didn't know what would happen after that. Even though my ex had flown in to help and gave me $1000, I knew it was not enough to get the boys and I to a safe place, but I didn't know what to do. I didn't have anyone to turn to in the world. I had always had to make it on my own.

A few more stressful things added into the mix and I was at the breaking point, falling under the weight of this immense experience, when an unexpected thing happened. As I sat quietly feeling like my mind was going to crack under the strain, I began smelling incense. The next thing I knew, a tall ethereal figure in a saffron robe, stepped through the veil before me. He reached out and placed his hand firmly on my upper arm, telling me to be at peace. He would take care of everything. I recognized him from pictures I had seen. It was the Indian Sage, Yogananda.

This luminous being cared! That felt amazing, but everything was so intense with the seven major situations I was handling all at once, it took hours for me to move completely into peace. So much was happening all at once, great losses, betrayal, severe financial challenges and more, but soon I began to feel the burdens lifting.

Saturday came and I was preparing to pack everything, when the phone rang. It was 10 am, two hours before my friends were coming to help. A realtor friend of an artist from the Big Island, who had said he'd rent a place with me, was on the line. She wanted to show me a house and asked if I wanted to see it... right then. I said yes and jumped in my car, drove over the Pali Highway and arrived at the place thirty minutes later, which was at the end of Manoa Valley.

As I stepped into the spacious home with its large windows looking out at a stream running through the rain forest, I noticed the sound of water flowing. I was entranced. It was such a magical setting. After a quick tour of the four-bedroom home, the realtor turned to me and said, "Do you like it?" I said, "Yes!" and immediately she threw me the keys and began trotting out the door. Turning back for one quick second she said, "You can move in now and then start paying on the 1st." I stood there in shock. I had never heard such a thing. Days with free rent? No deposit or credit check? It was incredible. To add a final touch to the miracle, my share of the rent would only be one thousand dollars a month, the exact sum my ex had given me. I got on the phone and called him and said, "Order two trucks, I have a home."

In the days that followed, all my challenges seemed to melt away as I was led into my New Life. Miraculously, one by one, my situations cleared up and my life took a happy turn for the better. My ex stepped up to support us, telling me he was going to cover my rent each month until I got back on my feet. Finally the nightmare was over.

I wondered at the gift Yogananda had brought when I didn't know much about him, had never read his book, or had been his disciple. Curious to find out more about this amazing being, I bought his book, *Autobiography of Yogi*, and was amazed by the life he had lived. His focus had been on Self Realization, a practice he had brought to the west from India. He had worked many years while on earth, helping others awaken to the Glorious Self within. It was such a similar path as I had been on. A great mystery surrounded his passing. According to reports, his body did not begin decomposing for 22 days!

It was then I remembered that years before, when I was a teen, my mother had taken me to his Lakeside Shrine in Pacific Palisades, where she was studying Kriya Yoga. After that, I was inspired to go there on my own, not to attend any services, but to just sit beside the lake in deep contemplation. Perhaps more than I knew had been transferred to me in those quiet hours.

A Divine Dispensation

I had been recovering from my Dark Night ordeal at the beautiful home in Manoa when another extraordinary experience graced my life. While meditating, my Inner Self appeared in radiant form and guided me on a journey. We came to a luminous world and entered a large cathedral of light that had a massive interior. I followed her down the aisle to what seemed like an altar. Before us, two of the most magnificent beings I've ever seen, sat on ornate, throne-like chairs. Telepathically,

I was told they were Alpha and Omega, representatives of the Father Mother God.

Then the Illumined Beings spoke. They said, "We have watched your extraordinary progress through your Dark Night of the Spirit passage. We have seen what you have been doing with your Inner Work, and how it has helped you make it through that diffiuclt time. We believe it will bring tremendous assistance to the people of the Earth. Because of this, we are gifting you a Dispensation to continue developing your work." At the time, I didn't know what a 'dispensation' was, but I was soon to find out. The far-reaching possibilities of my work were transferred to my mind in that moment in living color. I had experienced victory upon victory through my Dark Night. Each catastrophe hit hard, but then drove me inward where I used what eventually became TheQuest™ to heal the patterns causing all the problems.

An astrologer had wondered how I could traverse such a devastating time with such ease. She said, "You're experiencing a double astrological whammy that wipes out people for years. What are you doing to stay so calm?" I had shared about my life's work, and how it was helping restore me each time I fell under the weight of my immense experiences. Now I saw this passage had been my 'final exams.' I had made it through victoriously and had proved a way for others. Now I was being given assistance from Divine Realms to further develop my work. The celestial beings had given me a glimpse of my Destiny. I now saw the profound nature of my life's work and what it could mean to humanity.

Soon I was transported into a New Life. I met a beautiful beloved and moved to Maui to be with him. We found a gorgeous villa we named the Temple Shanti Aloha, where I was able to do my most landmark work in the psyche. People would somehow find me and I would help them unlock the puzzles of their life from within. I witnessed many miracles from the work, which helped prove my theories and perfect what became a full Counseling Theory and Healing Practice.

To this day I sit in wonder at what happened to me. At my darkest hours, I had been lifted up. And then, once I had made it through to the other side of the Dark Night, I received the Divine Dispensation that completely changed my life. I had been standing in the rubble of my destroyed life and within months, I had been gifted love and a beautiful palacial villa to live in, where I was completely supported to further develop my life's work.

CHAPTER THREE

Miracles at Delphi

A few months later in April 1997, I arrived at the ancient site of Delphi in Greece with my new beloved. Around 200 people were milling around, chattering noisily. I was inspired to sit in front of the main temple, which I found out later was the Temple of Apollo, the place where the Oracles of Delphi brought illumination and guidance to heads of nations and other important people.

I was drawn into a deep meditation, and immediately, a huge presence rose up before me, her arms outstretched over the entire site. I recognized her as Pallas Athena, the presiding Goddess of this ancient period of history and someone I had come to know years before in my own spiritual journey.

She spoke to me of an ancient unfed flame that once burned within this temple and said it was a Flame of Truth that even now continues to burn, though it is invisible. She told me, "Every person who visits this site receives a small replica of this flame in his or her heart. The ruined temple represents a message to visiting souls, that no matter what they've been through, no matter how worn or decayed their bodies have become, there is still a living flame within them."

Amazed by this encounter, I opened my eyes to find everyone at the site kneeling before the Temple with deep reverence. As I made my way with my Beloved through the ruins and began to ascend the stairs, a man grabbed my arm and said, "Who are you? I've been here every day for a week and nothing has happened. What did you do?" I smiled but could not speak. I was in awe myself.

At the top of the stairs, a boy and his family were just arriving. He looked over the edge down at the site and said, "I've waited so long to be here!" I stopped in my tracks. What a profound statement for a child to make. I stopped to talk with the eleven-year-old boy who turned out to be quite extraordinary.

Later that afternoon, we climbed another ancient site of Apollo nearby. Immediately a huge waterfall of highly charged energy came down over my partner, sliding down my arm and the right side of my body, but never touching me. The electric male energy was reserved for him alone.

As we climbed up past the amphitheatre, I began to get glimpses of an ancient past when Twin Souls had worked together to create conscious community there, and saw how some of the 'Vestal Virgins' who were Oracles of Delphi at the time, had actually been married to their Twin Flames. I began drinking in the essence of these relationships, which touched a chord deep in my being. This was a Sacred Tryst, a bond that was very special. They were sacred partnerships in service to life, shared destinies that are now rare on earth and which, my Beloved and I had been blessed with. Today this blessing continues, even though the nature of our relationship has changed and we are now 'best friends,' we still continue to create healing inspired music together and support each other's highest destiny in every way. It is a love that is rare and which never dies.

The energy continued to flood my Beloved's being beside me as we traversed the mountainside of ancient ruins and entered the Olympic Field. We stopped at the far end of the field and sat on one of the stone bleachers, sharing about our experience, wondering at the amazing energy that was still flowing over him, and how both of us had been blessed, me with a feminine energy under the guidance of Pallas Athena, he with a male energy from Apollo. After a full forty-five minutes, the energy stopped and we descended the site in a similar awe as we had felt from the Temple of Apollo experience with Pallaa Athena.

After spending the night in the town of Delphi near by, we were preparing to depart when Pallas appeared to me again and told me I had to return to the Temple of Apollo, and that she had a gift for me. Obedient, I returned to the first site, noticing a big bus filled with tourists arriving just as I was descending the long stairway. As I walked down the steps, I felt Pallas's presence with me. She said, "Walk slower." Every few steps, she would remind me to slow down, until finally near the bottom, I realized I had stepped into a body I had worn in ancient times. It was a feminine body, quite a lot older, taller, and bigger boned. I was wearing a long dress with a belt and had jewelry on my arms and a pendant around my neck.

As I began walking towards the temple, I looked back and saw a strange sight. The whole busload of tourists was halfway down the stairs, held in place by an invisible hand. Not being able to go farther and not knowing what to do, they all stopped and began taking pictures of the site.

As I came to the temple I noticed that there was not a single person on the grounds, except for the two of us. This was strange, when the day before, the site had been filled with hundreds of people. Immediately Pallas told me to come into the temple, something that is absolutely against the law in Greece with the penalty of jail. Obediently, I climbed up into the temple and knelt before her in the forbidden zone.

Pallas was in her Glory again. A Radiant Divine Being, she reconsecrated me as a Vestal Virgin (of the Virgin Consciousness she explained), saying I had once been an Oracle of Delphi. She gifted me with a small invisible Flame of Truth and asked me to carry it throughout the world, placing it on altars everywhere, which I have faithfully done.

As the anointing concluded, I heard a shrill sound ringing out through the site. Opening my eyes, I realized the guardian had seen me and was now walking towards me. Swiftly I moved backwards and slipped down from the temple. My Beloved took my arm and quietly we walked past the Guardian to the stairway leading out of the site while somehow, he could not speak or detain me.

Looking up, I saw the busload of people still standing half way up the stairs. They looked as if they were frozen in motion. Amazingly, they had been this way for at least twenty minutes or more. As my foot touched the bottom step, the people were released. They became animated and began descending the stairs towards me. The hold on them had been lifted and they were now free to enter the site. It was hard to believe that all this had really happened, but my Beloved was there as a witness. It was a very unexpected, incredibly glorious sacred experience, and one I will always treasure.

CHAPTER FOUR

Roses from Mother Mary

Years had passed and I had made great strides in perfecting TheQuest™. People would somehow find me and would have miraculous healings. One day, a new client walked into the room, distraught. Her eyes told the story of immense suffering. It was her first session. I said a prayer to help calm her, when Mother Mary stepped through the veil. I watched, amazed, as she poured a cascade of magenta colored roses over my client.

Many years before, fourteen to be exact, I had had an incredible experience with Mother Mary, but had not seen her before or since. Now she was standing over my traumatized client administering a special healing to her. I found it amazing that my Jewish client was being ministered to by one of the premier archetypal icons of the Christian era.

My client closed her eyes and entered a deep meditation, while the room filled with so much light, it was hard to stay conscious. I kept being drawn deep into the center of my being and then would struggle to become fully conscious, so that I could be there for my client when she came out of her meditation, but it was hard. The light was so strong, I could barely keep my eyes open. I kept trying to swim my way back up to the surface to no avail. Immediately, I would be drawn back down again.

Finally, after what seemed a long time, my client emerged one half hour later, her eyes sparkling and radiant. Excitedly she said, "Mother Mary came to me and held me. She helped me take strands of darkness out of me. This is the most peace I have ever experienced in my life."

I was amazed. For a new client, paying a high hourly price, to go into a deep meditation and stay there for a long time was incredible. I had never experienced that before. That she also had been raised in the Jewish tradition and now had consciously received this powerful healing from Mother Mary was truly astounding.

I then took her through TheQuest™ Counseling and that was equally amazing, for we traversed a deep wound that had created a pattern of abuse in her life. This had translated to her being abused by her ex-husband, teenage son, and boyfriend all at the same time, after a long history of abuse beginning in her early childhood. It was a miracle this woman had survived with such an open loving heart. It was a lot to deal with, and I really had never heard of a worse childhood.

The next day I arose to another glorious day on Maui. The sun was sparkling through my bedroom window, the ocean a deep turquoise blue in the distance. I was meditating at a beautiful altar I had created in my bedroom, when all of a sudden the scent of roses filled the room. Then, a swirling mist of light appeared and turned into Mother Mary. Her eyes were glowing with such love, I felt myself melting. She said she had come to sponsor TheQuest™ in the world and that she would be bringing people for healing who had Great Missions, but who were entangled in their karma and patterns. After that, the only people who seemed to ever find me were these type souls that later I realized were Violet People.

For a long time, she spoke about TheQuest™ and the work ahead, how it would touch the world in a profound way and make a difference to many people on Earth. She said many souls were waiting for TheQuest™. It was an essential key to their freedom and victory. Their destinies depended on it. As she spoke, I saw visions of what she was sharing and the many lives that would be healed. I was amazed that she had come to help me bring my life's work to the world. After she departed, the scent of roses remained for a long time, though there were no roses in my garden or in the surrounding properties, and I never smelled them in my home again. I was in a state of ecstasy for hours, feeling a profound gratitude and awe. Since then, Mother Mary has been present at every session, working silently with each soul on deep inner levels, and sharing sacred wisdom and profound insights personal to each one.

In June 2000, Mother Mary inspired me to set up the Institute of Advanced Healing, a Universal Healing Ministry dedicated to healing lives throughout the world, through the Principles and Practice of TheQuest™. Today, many people have received this healing.

The Rose Temple of Divine Love

In early October 2001, when the world was in shock from 9/11, I began having the most amazing and glorious experiences at the Rose Temple of Divine Love. I had been guided to the foot of Mount Shasta for the winter to write. Enveloped in the solitude and majestic beauty of that mountain, I soon fell in love. Marveling, I wondered, "Can you fall in love with a mountain?" Each day I drank in the incredible energies that radiated from Mount Shasta and felt a sense of peace and protection, as if a vast masculine power was holding me in his strong embrace.

When I had first arrived in Shasta, I received a Divine Message telling me I was about to be prepared for a 'release' from the Heavens. I wondered what it would be, writing, a sacred song? I didn't know. In that moment, a white energy began spiraling up from my feet to my crown, enveloping me in a cocoon of light that continued for two months.

Wrapped in this Divine Energy and spending much time in solitude, I traversed the scary nightmare of September 11, holding in a place of deep peace. While others felt shattered, depressed, and lost, I was witnessing light from the Heavens pouring into my being daily, wrapping me in an exquisite white light.

The days had grown colder. Each night, after writing, I looked forward to soaking in a hot bath surrounded with rose candles. One night, as I lay in the large bath tub, Mother Mary appeared to me, inviting me to the Temple of Divine Love. Immediately I was transported to a glorious Temple in the Heavens, where I found myself bathing in a healing pool of Rose Light, while Mother Mary spoke to me about the Healing Power of Love.

No sooner was I in my candlelit bath, Mother Mary would appear and take me to the healing pool in her Temple. Each night she would instruct me on the healing properties of the Rose Essence while a deep and hidden pain would emerge from inside of me, like a dark mass of energy, and be transformed. Through the Rose Light, I was being healed of all my misinterpretations about love gathered from the painful experiences of my past.

After two weeks, the powerful healings at the Rose Temple of Divine Love were complete. Over the next days, Divine Ones took turns delivering messages on the Healing Power of Love to me, which I was inspired to record. Each sacred message contained a healing that was having a powerful effect on me. I was being transformed by Love through this gift for humanity from the Heavens. And so, the mission was complete. The Divine Ones had released their offering to the world at a time when people all over the planet shuddered in fear from the aftermath of 9/11, once again a confirmation that we are not alone, and that we are loved.

A Rose Borealis over Shasta

Winter had arrived and there was snow on the ground, which was exciting for a Maui Girl. I spent my days writing by a window that looked out at beautiful Mount Shasta. During that time visionary artist, Marius Michael-George came for a visit. When he showed me the incredible paintings he had done in the year since our meeting, I could not believe my eyes. Each one was a perfect match for the children's picture books I had written. It was then I realized our work was not only inspired from the same realms, it was meant to go together.

One painting was of a beautiful angel. As I looked at the picture, I was amazed. This was the angel who had come to me with his story some years before, that was to become the children's picture book, *One Angel's Story*. When I mentioned this to Marius, he said it was rare to find a picture that would match a character in a book.

The meeting with Marius was so electric, I could barely sleep over the next days. It was as powerful, spectacular, and purposeful as our first meeting the year before in Montana. As if to confirm the Divine Purpose behind this meeting and a continuation of the Rose Energy I had been gifted since I stepped foot in Shasta, we were drawn outside one evening to see the sky filled with the incredible rose rays of light of an Aurora Borealis. Rare to be seen that far south, this spectacular array of rose energy touched us as no other experience could. I felt infinitely blessed by our creative connection and sacred tryst with the Heavens, a synergy that was destined to bring many beautiful works of art to the world.

As Marius drove away the next day, brilliant rainbows filled the sky, drawing me outside. It was as if elemental life were rejoicing at our meeting. Electric and powerful, these rainbows were different than any I had ever seen. Rare for such a dry desert region, it was a further blessing and confirmation of the beautiful sponsorship from the Heavens and the releases that were being prepared to come through us to bless humanity.

CHAPTER SIX

Lady of the Golden Light

By Robin Miller

I was about six years old and I was not happy. My parents had many fights. It was a very painful and turbulent family life. I remember being in bed one night crying myself to sleep. I didn't want to be there. I began crying, "Take me home, I want to go home." I knew that earth wasn't my home. For me, it had been a descent into hell.

It was dark in the room and all of a sudden a Golden Light started appearing at the end of my bed. It began swirling and twirling, getting brighter and brighter until a woman was standing in front of me. She had a beautiful loving smile on her face and was looking at me with incredible love. It was one of those things you never forget. The Love that was emanating from her was something that I had never experienced in my troubled childhood.

Light filled the room and she was calling me. I remember she spoke to me, not with her mouth but with her thoughts, with her mind. She said, "Oh Robin, one day you will know and understand why you are here, why you have chosen to come here. You have a mission. One day you will know and understand that. It is not time to come home yet."

In her presence, the Love that I was feeling was so all encompassing, so fulfilling. All of a sudden she started disappearing. I remember saying, "No, take me with you. Don't leave!" and I started crying. She immediately reappeared by the side of my bed, touched my forehead, and I fell right to sleep.

Robin Miller is an extraordinary composer whose angelic music makes the heaven realms accessible to the earthbound and transports us to a tranquil world free of worry and struggles. He has recorded albums with various artists for labels such as A&M, MCA, and RCA. Proficient on guitar, keyboards, bass, and mandolin, Robin loves to incorporate his versatility through rock & roll, blues, new age, and many other types of music.

In 1993, Robin received the prestigious Arizona Entertainment Award for New Age Artist of the Year. In 1995, Robin performed on the NBC nationally syndicated talk show, THE OTHER SIDE.

Other performances included shows with well-known celebrities such as medium and healer James Van Praagh, who has been seen on LARRY KING LIVE, OPRAH, and UNSOLVED MYSTERIES and who now uses Robin's music on several of his meditation tapes.

Robin has also appeared with world-renowned psychic Sylvia Browne and toured with her for two years. Sylvia has said that, "Robin's music comes directly from the angels."

Currently living in Sedona, Arizona, he is continuously creating new music and performing locally. Robin is available for concerts, tours, group functions, and seminars. Find out more about Robin and his heavenly music, which is available to purchase at http://www.robinmillermusic.com

CHAPTER SEVEN

Surrendering to My Magnificence

By Trish Regan

For several years my husband, Doug and I had received divine messages that our work was going to be changing. We were going to touch more people. We were holding about a dozen spiritually focused dolphin seminars a year, which we limited to eight participants each, so we were touching a relatively small group of people at the time. We were excited about the new work, but didn't have a clue what we would be doing.

Then I began receiving the book, *Essential Joy, The Art of Balance*, which came to me in a vision, followed by a flood of information over the next ten months. I thought, "This is the work we are meant to bring out into the world," but when I began to write more information for the book, I encountered a deep sense of unworthiness. I was afraid that I wouldn't be able to talk about it eloquently to an audience, that the information wouldn't flow easily and that I would be humiliated.

These unexpected feelings catalyzed an even deeper pain for me because I knew we had been given a gift, but how could I bring it forward into the world if I didn't have the confidence? I began to panic and be fearful about our financial security. The new work was just beginning to come in, while our dolphin work was slowing down after 9/11. Finally we found a healer who cleared cellular memories within the body. Doug and I began to prepare for this healing. We felt we needed to surrender everything in our lives, each other, our families, our work, the dolphins, and our beautiful home in Hawaii, to clear the way for our next step in our spiritual work. As we did this inner piece, we both deepened our commitment to follow Spirit unfailingly.

After the healing, I went into yet another deep and dark place. The Healer had warned me that might happen, as she saw there was one more piece for me to do. I was laying on my bed, listening to beautiful meditative music. All of a sudden I was drawn out of my body beyond the earth plane, out into the cosmos, and beyond the universe, beyond anything that I knew. I was drawn to a space where I met with a circle of Light Beings in an unknown dimension. Some of them were Ascended Masters I recognized and some were Beings I had never known before.

I found myself in the center of the circle looking through a transparent floor where I could see the universe below in three-dimensional reality. I prostrated myself, surrendering the deepest part of my heart, being and soul. I told the Beings of Light, "If I am to do this work, I need your help. I can't do this alone." As I finished, they invited me to be a part of the circle and to join energetic hands with them. Immediately I became one of these beautiful Light Beings. Once I had gotten used to being in that energy of oneness, they asked me to individuate out again and to lie on a solid amethyst table in the center of the circle.

They took a star of energy and put it into my third eye. I could feel my third eye opening and I could also feel my crown chakra opening very wide at the same time. They began sending a beautiful energy into my body. The only word I can use to describe it is Grace. As it entered my body, I felt so taken care of, so guided in such a safe and beautiful space. Then they created an oblong shaped light from three-dimensional reality, as we know it, which came up from under the table into my body and filled it with the energy of creation. Then from above my body they brought another oblong shaped white light into my body, which came from the Source, God Goddess, All That Is.

The Light energies blended and melded within my body, becoming an exquisite, beautiful, powerful energy. The Light Beings then asked me to become transparent so I could radiate this Light. I became transparent and I could see this union of spirit and matter beginning to shine forth from within me. Then they told me my purpose is to be a bridge for Spirit, to bring Spirit into matter.

While that was occurring I began to feel pain in the left side of my neck. I went into that area in my neck and saw it as a small wooden box with two huge locks on it. I asked the Beings of Light to help me open the locks and they did. Inside the box was a small circular faceted diamond. They told me that it was a diamond of Truth and that if I became the diamond I would radiate Light and melt the box. In doing that, I would be powerful enough to do just about anything. I became the diamond of Truth and started radiating the Light. I could see the Light melting the box until it was almost gone. I still felt a little bit of pain and remembered what the healer had said about there being one more level I had to go to, that there was one more little thing that I needed to do in my healing. In that moment, I let it go and surrendered. As soon as I did that, I knew I had reached the core of my being. I had finally surrendered everything.

Immediately, it all came together and I became illuminated with the knowledge of the totality of the new work. I saw it in its entirety. I knew then that this experience had been an initiation and that by surrendering to that deepest level of trust in myself, the Universe and these Beings of Light, I would be able to bring forth this work to the world. This absolutely changed my life. It took away all my fear. I felt capable of bringing forth this truth and sharing the divine energy.

By surrendering the human conditioning, with all its attachments and fears, I had gone deep into the core truth of my being, becoming my True Self. In that moment, I had become the essence of my book and new life's work, *Essential Joy*. I had surrendered to my Magnificent Self and I had learned to allow that Self to bring forth the messages of the Divine Ones and to bless others with their wisdom and grace.

Trish Regan, Visionary Writer and Intuitive Soul Reader, is author of the book series Essential Joy: Finding It, Keeping It, Sharing It. She has been spiritually aware for all her life and has been on a dedicated path of Light and spiritual expansion for over thirty-four years.

She has been married in spiritual partnership to her husband, Doug since 1992. They travel internationally, bringing workshops such as Essential Joy, Sacred Partnership, Dolphin Essence Experience, Empowering Magnificence and Be the Vision to many Seekers of Light and bring to their visionary work a deep connection with the dolphins, whales and many Beings of Light.

See more about their amazing dolphin and whale tours, events, and products at http://www.dolphinspiritofhawaii.com and www.essentialjoy.net

Part Seven

Miraculous Recoveries & Cures

CHAPTER ONE

Miraculous Healings

By some inner mystic Presence,
I was told to live and to love, to laugh and to be glad.
I was told to be still and know of the One Almighty Power,
in and through all.
I was told to let that Power work through and in me.
I believed that voice and I received my Good.
I am healed - The joy of Life.

--Ernest Holmes
Science of Mind Textbook

Stories of miraculous recoveries and cures are filling the planet, inspiring humanity to go beyond their once limited beliefs. Individuals across the earth have had extraordinary healings, miraculous cures, and received great learning and growth from illnesses that transformed their lives.

Pioneering doctor, Bernie Siegal, author of *Peace Love, Healing, Body Mind Connection and the Path to Self Healing* said, "It took me many years to learn that our ability to mobilize our healing capacity means that survival statistics do not apply to individuals. Individuals who change their response to their illness can exceed expectations or achieve results doctors consider miraculous. When talking to these exceptional patients, the words love, faith, living in the moment, forgiveness, and hope come up again and again. The inner peace these people have acquired on a psycho-spiritual level leads to healing and often to a cure as well. Self-healers are all the same. The results they achieve are no coincidence. Every doctor can share anecdotes about these people, but few doctors understand what they have witnessed. We must begin to acknowledge that these miraculous healings are scientific and can be taught to others thereby creating more anecdotes and eventually a scientific understanding of these events."

Healers throughout time have spoken of Divine Energies that flowed through them to affect powerful cures. Today, many healers have been trained in ancient traditions, while others are leading doctors who are pioneers in their fields. A whole new world of possibility has opened up through our understanding of quantum physics. We are part of an energetic field that is highly transmutable. As consciousness shifts, not only can it change our personal lives, but it can also cause a major shift on our planet.

In the words of James Redfield, Author of *The Celestine Prophecy*, "A new spiritual awareness is emerging in human culture. Human beings are essentially spiritual beings slowly awakening from the mistaken idea that we are material beings living in a material world. We are made up of atoms, which are much more mysterious than we ever thought, consisting of so-called elementary particles of minuscule size separated by mostly empty space. What most physicists are understanding of course, is that these particles, rather than being material are actually fields (patterns) of energy. At our core, we humans are not made of matter at all, at least not in the ordinary sense. We consist of a most fascinating and mysterious energy that is capable of shifting and changing dramatically. How else can we explain the numerous documented cases of wounds healing and tumors disappearing suddenly in our bodies - and not in days or weeks, but instantaneously."

Storytelling throughout time has been an inspiration to the weary masses, reminding us that life is a profound adventure. In the following stories, we explore profound healings that awakened souls and transformed lives.

CHAPTER TWO

My Healing Journey

In 1991, I was standing in the driveway of my newly rented home in Hawaii, when a large Hawaiian Chinese man came over and greeted me. He introduced himself as Grandmaster Kimo Pang, head of Shaolin Internal Systems, a martial arts school in Honolulu and Portland. With piercing eyes that immediately intrigued me, he said he had been drawn by the healing music that was always coming from my home, and we began talking. In that moment, a connection was formed that would change my life.

He had come to Hawaii to bury his father and was staying across the street with his protégé. I had just returned to Kailua after being away for two years. I had taken flight from Hawaii, the place I loved living the most in the world, to escape a painful relationship.

That relationship had changed without warning, but in the beginning, it had been a spectacular experience. I felt grateful and blessed every day, believing I had found my Twin Soul. After a year of experiencing the most transcendent love while long distance dating, we were in a committed relationship, when he turned cold and cruel without warning, and then physically violent. Six months later, shattered and broken-hearted, I prepared to leave, but somehow the bond was so strong I could not break away. It would be another one and a half years before I could leave, but by then I would be severely ill from all the abuse.

Up until that time, I had never been around abuse and did not know anything about it, so I really did not have the tools to deal with it effectively. I thought our healthy, spiritual lifestyle would be enough. I was told I could stop the violence right away by calling the police when it happened, and this seemed to help, but then the abuse became psychological, something I was equally clueless about.

Being of a spiritual persuasion and someone who had studied and applied some of the most advanced systems on the planet, I became a master at spiritual bypass. Not listening to my heart or tending to my inner wounds finally took its toll. I suffered two heart attacks within six months, and became so weak I barely had energy to walk to the kitchen to get a drink of water. I was shocked to find he didn't care. This gave me the strength to leave him. As I was preparing for my departure amidst heart pains and fatigue, I found out I had an incurable heart condition that could quickly debilitate me to death. The cyle of abuse had taken it's toll.

Within a month, a natural remedy helped increase my energy so that I had the strength to pack and move, and my stained glass business in Kailua picked up, bringing in the needed funds to move my children and I from Hawaii. However, that meant leaving someone I loved with all my heart, but who had hurt me so much. Arriving to my new home on the mainland, I cried myself to sleep each night for two months, and then one day I found myself smiling. I couldn't believe it. I had thought I would never be happy again. Losing such a beautiful love in such a devastating way had been so painful.

For the next two years, a miraculous doorway to healing my condition opened up through an Institute that was thirty miles from my new home. Focused on healing my heart, I was drawn to trainings by doctors who were pioneers in the field of alternative medicine and holistic health visiting the center. This training included NET (Neuro-Emotional technique), TBM (Total Body Modification), Stress Release Therapies, Biokinesiology (The inter-relationship of emotions and disease), Personality Traits and Their Relationship to Disease, Touch for Health, Zone Therapy, and more.

By the time this cycle completed, I had a new career as a Holistic Health Practitioner and had been able to keep my body from debilitating by applying these advanced healing modalities on myself, but they did not affect a complete cure. My healing journey was meant to continue. I returned to Hawaii and had just settled in when I met Grandmaster Pang.

About two days had passed since our meeting when he came to see me. He said he had received visions of the future where I was helping people all over the world. He explained he was a Kahuna (Hawaiian Healer), and that he was meant to pass his lineage to me. This was out of the ordinary, because normally the Kahuna succession passed to a family member, but he said I was Soul Family and that it was meant for me.

In the following days, Grandmaster Pang began to train me in ancient Hawaiian Huna Healing Arts, allowing me to experience them for myself. The Ho'oponopono was a profound experience. You are taken back to the roots of all the pain you have accumulated in your life. At a very deep inner level, you work to release the aka cords (negative ties) that connect you to others and cause you to lose your power, sense of self, and esteem. You take the accumulation of painful memories, weights, burdens and hardships you have carried through time, and which cause stress and illness, and cast them into a white fire, where they are consumed.

The mind believes they are dissolved, just like a computer believes it has disposed of the trash when you empty it, even though it is still in the computer. The mind works the same way. It believes the painful past is healed because it has witnessed it burn in the fire. This is very powerful work.

Through the next years, each time Grandmaster Pang returned to Hawaii he would give me the next piece, working on me as he trained me. I would immediately find my healing abilities at a whole new level. I began traversing 'uncharted' realms of the psyche in my clients and myself, gaining more insights and tools to heal the wounds that keep us all burdened and in a limited expression.

On my birthday in 1993, Grandmaster Pang initiated me as a Kahuna. After that, I was compelled to continue my Quest for Truth and delving deep into the psyche. To gain further knowledge and tools, I entered B.A., M.A., and Ph.D programs where I mastered many of the cutting edge Counseling Theories and Practices from the last century. These included Gestalt, NLP, Person Centered Counseling, Reality Therapy, Behavioral Therapy, Psychosynthesis, and others. I then went on to do my most landmark research and work in the psyche, made many exciting discoveries, and developed TheQuest™.

It was through TheQuest™ that I was finally able to heal my heart, by going to the causes behind my heart condition. I had to trace not only the deep pain from my relational experiences, as well as patterns of self-denial through spiritually bypassing my feelings, but also get to the core of why I would draw in abuse. This led me to the Martyr Pattern that I have since found embedded in most every client. This pattern has left its legacy of suffering upon our world. I found it responsible for all the travail humanity is currently undergoing and included more information about this pattern in book one, *Earth 2012: The Ultimate Quest.*

Today I am free of that heart condition and the patterns and pain that created it. I've also freed myself from countless other wounds, and continue to work to heal the cause of suffering within me as each new challenge arises. This is a powerful Self Mastery Path, where we address our life issues at the deepest levels and affect a complete healing of a specific patterning in each session.

I have worked so diligently to remove the weights and burdens I've taken on from this earthly life that affect our happiness, health, and cause aging, that I now live in my youthful, joyous, passionate self most of the time.

Through years of working in the psyche, I discovered that the Authentic Self is our Divine Birthright and source of peace, happiness, and fulfillment, not the outer things we think bring us joy. When we experience harmony with others, our Authentic Self is activated and we enter that amazing grace we witness early on in a relationship.

When I was abused, my Shadow Self with all her pain was activated. With this activation came my opportunity to heal her. I learned that this is how challenging people serve us. Unconscious actions from their Wounded Self help activate our wounds. That is when a great healing can take place, but we need the right knowledge, comprehensive understanding, and tools.

My illness drew me into a new frontier that had, to date, been largely untapped. The pain I was feeling from the struggles in my life compelled me to seek a way out. They were the catalyst that birthed my soul purpose. I became a pioneer, delving deeply into the inner world of the soul to find out life's most compelling questions, and developed a way to eliminate the cause of suffering from within, which helped forge my Destiny.

Learning to heal issues quickly and the patterns that had created them became a Life Mastery Path that has helped me through countless challenges. One of my greatest joys is passing this Self Mastery Technology to my students and the world.

The greatest gift was in learning that my abuser had gifted me more than any other person in this life. If he had not played such a severe role for me, I would not have contracted that illness. Without the heartbreak and illness, I would never have embarked upon a Healing Path nor had the knowledge and attainment I've gained today. I had suffered the worst and made it through victoriously, with many gifts to share and ended up with a sacred offering for humanity in TheQuest™.

CHAPTER THREE

Over the Cliff and Still Alive

By Mirra Rose

My brand new sports car sped down the road. Glimmering in the light, it was fast, beautiful and sleek, and I was very proud of it. A mother and her six-year-old son were driving with me to Wisconsin. We had been enjoying the countryside, when she pointed to something on the right. I looked, and the next thing I knew, the road had curved and we were heading over the side of a cliff.

As we sailed into the air, I was lifted up out of my body by my angels and enveloped in an amazing peace. There was no fear, only a feeling of being protected. Looking out the windshield, the sun, green grass and blue sky were all blending together as the car was rolling. The colors were gorgeous.

Then the car hit bottom, flipped over, and kept rolling for many feet through a fence into some trees. Instinctively, I knew we were all right. I crawled out of the jagged remnant of the car window, through splinters of broken glass. Looking back, I could not believe my eyes. The car was completely destroyed with nothing left but the frame, and I wasn't even hurt!

I saw my friend trying to open her door, but it was locked. Three strong men arrived and began trying to pry the door open to no avail. As if in trance, I walked around the car, pulled the barbed wire out of the way, and effortlessly opened the door. The men could not believe what they were seeing or that we had survived!

For three days I remained in this incredible bliss, feeling grateful for that experience of being in my higher self and with the angels. It was as if I had died and was now living 'out of time.' I was assessing my life from a soul awareness I hadn't accessed before. I knew everything was perfect and was free of concerns. I knew that what should have happened was that we should have all died. It was such a huge miracle. I felt sure it was part of an amazing plan.

It was then I was shown that I had braided two future lives into this lifetime and that what had taken place was intention rather than being an accident. It had been arranged by myself and by the two other souls who participated in it. We had gotten together at that particular time in order to have that experience.

I was shown how I had a particular agenda set for myself in this lifetime and that this accident allowed me to change that. Being near death, I was in a higher state of consciousness that allowed me to make a decision to braid the possibilities and potentials for what I would accomplish in two future lives into this one life. I needed to be in that state of consciousness to do it. So that is what happened. It was a magnificent experience for all of us because we learned so much from it. It was a miracle of Grace.

Mirra Rose is an internationally acclaimed spiritual teacher and healer who has been sharing her gifts world-wide for over thirty years, touching thousands of people with her loving Presence. Her primary mission is the empowerment of individuals to attain Divine Consciousness through a direct connection with the Soul. See http://www.MirraRose.us

CHAPTER FOUR

Surrendering to Spirit

By Lee Shapiro

I was in Argentina and Chile in 1993 on an expedition kayaking on the Monza River, which had never been run at this flood stage level before. It had only been run two or three times before at low water. So, it was particularly challenging because no one knew what it was like at this stage. With the river running between steep canyon walls, I knew that if we ran into trouble a helicopter wouldn't be able to get in to save us. There would be no way out.

We arrived in the morning on the first section in which there were three waterfalls. The first one was about eight feet, the second one was about ten feet and the third one was about twenty-five feet. Having scouted them earlier, we had determined it was possible to traverse them. The first one looked like the most difficult one in terms of the water flow.

We knew we had to find a place in the waterfall where most of the water was flushing through, otherwise the water circulates back on itself and we could get stuck there. There were twelve of us and most of the guys with me didn't want to do it, but a few of us were so enthusiastic we persuaded them to take the 'leap.'

One guy did it first and he was fine. I went next. When I came over the waterfall it sucked me back in. I was trapped upside down in the kayak. I tried rolling on my right side, but couldn't get my paddle to the surface. Then I tried rolling on the other side and I couldn't get my paddle to the surface that way either, so I tried the other side again. At that point I was running out of air, so I crawled out of my boat, tweaking my knee, and tried to swim up to the surface. The water continued to pound on me the whole time.

I could see the sunlight pretty clear above me, but I couldn't get there. The thought came, "This is it. This is how I die." I knew that my wife would be really upset if I didn't come back. I was frantic. I called out, "God, let me live for Joyce!" And in that moment, I knew that Spirit heard me. So I started looking around for Richard Dreyfus because I had seen the movie, *Always*, where Richard Dreyfus comes as an angel to save Holly Hunter out of the water. But I never did see him.

Finally I just let go. I gave up resisting and stopped struggling. Then without warning, the water pushed me down and circulated me into an eddy. To my amazement, my boat appeared beside me. I was free. Breathing huge gulps of air, I was extremely grateful that I was alive, and not only that, to see my kayak, because to go over the next two waterfalls would be pretty hairy without it.

Though it was a harrowing experience and one I will never forget, it gave me a deeper trust in Spirit, for without this Divine Intervention, I would not be here to tell the story.

An extraordinarily talented artist, Lee Shapiro's fascination with Zen Buddhism and eastern philosophy is evidenced in the flow and spontaneity of his works. By combining vibrant color with powerful gesture, his dancers are dramatic and expressive. These energies and feelings emerge in all of his subjects, be it landscapes, florals, or wildlife.

Lee's paintings are displayed in prominent galleries across the country. He is internationally renowned as the illustrator of the best-selling children's classic, There's No Such Place as Far Away, by Richard Bach.

To see and purchase his beautiful paintings and prints, go to his website at: http://www.hleeshapiro.com

CHAPTER FIVE

Ho'oponopono

By Dr. Joe Vitale

Two years ago, I heard about a therapist in Hawaii who cured a complete ward of criminally insane patients without ever seeing any of them. The psychologist would study an inmate's chart and then look within himself to see how he created that person's illness. As he improved himself, the patient improved.

When I first heard this story, I thought it was an urban legend. How could anyone heal anyone else by healing himself? How could even the best self-improvement master cure the criminally insane? It didn't make any sense. It wasn't logical, so I dismissed the story. However, I heard it again a year later. The therapist had used a Hawaiian healing process called Ho'oponopono. I had never heard of it, yet I couldn't let it leave my mind. If the story was at all true, I had to know more.

I had always understood "total responsibility" to mean that I am responsible for what I think and do. Beyond that, it's out of my hands. I think that most people think of total responsibility that way. We're responsible for what we do, not what anyone else does, but that's wrong.

The Hawaiian therapist who healed those mentally ill people would teach me an advanced new perspective about total responsibility. His name is Dr. Ihaleakala Hew Len. We probably spent an hour talking on our first phone call. I asked him to tell me the complete story of his work as a therapist.

He explained that he had worked at Hawaii State Hospital for four years. That ward where they kept the criminally insane was dangerous. Psychologists quit on a monthly basis. The staff called in sick a lot or simply quit. People would walk through that ward with their backs against the wall, afraid of being attacked by patients. It was not a pleasant place to live, work, or visit.

Dr. Len told me that he never saw patients. He agreed to have an office and to review their files. While he looked at those files, he would work on himself. As he worked on himself, patients began to heal. After a few months, patients that had to be shackled were being allowed to walk freely, he told me. Others who had to be heavily medicated were getting off their medications. And those who had no chance of ever being released were being freed. I was in awe.

"Not only that," he went on, "but the staff began to enjoy coming to work. Absenteeism and turnover disappeared. We ended up with more staff than we needed because patients were being released, and all the staff was showing up to work. Today, that ward is closed." This is where I had to ask the million dollar question: "What were you doing within yourself that caused those people to change?"

"'I was simply healing the part of me that created them," he said. I didn't understand. Dr. Len explained that total responsibility for your life means that everything in your life, simply because it is in your life, is your responsibility. In a literal sense the entire world is your creation.

Whew. This is tough to swallow. Being responsible for what I say or do is one thing. Being responsible for what everyone in my life says or does is quite another. Yet, the truth is this: if you take complete responsibility for your life, then everything you see, hear, taste, touch, or in any way experience is your responsibility because it is in your life. This means that terrorist activity, the president, the economy or anything you experience and don't like, is up for you to heal. They don't exist, in a manner of speaking, except as projections from inside you. The problem isn't with them, it's with you, and to change them, you have to change you.

I know this is tough to grasp, let alone accept or actually live. Blame is far easier than total responsibility, but as I spoke with Dr. Len, I began to realize that healing for him and the practice of Ho'oponopono means loving your self. He teaches, "If you want to improve your life, you have to heal your life. If you want to cure anyone, even a mentally ill criminal you do it by healing you."

I asked Dr. Len how he went about healing himself. What was he doing, exactly, when he looked at those patients' file? "I just kept saying, 'I'm sorry' and 'I love you' over and over again," he explained.

"That's it? I asked. He replied, "That's it."

Turns out that loving yourself is the greatest way to improve yourself, and as you improve yourself, you improve your world. Let me give you a quick example of how this works. One day, someone sent me an email that upset me. In the past I would have handled it by working on my emotional hot buttons or by trying to reason with the person who sent the nasty message.

This time, I decided to try Dr. Len's method. I kept silently saying, 'I'm sorry' and 'I love you,' though I didn't say it to anyone in particular. I was simply evoking the spirit of love to heal within me what was creating the outer circumstance. Within an hour I got an e-mail from the same person. He apologized for his previous message. Keep in mind that I didn't take any outward action to get that apology. I didn't even write him back. Yet, by saying 'I love you,' I somehow healed within me what was creating him.

I later attended a Ho'oponopono workshop run by Dr. Len. He's now 70 years old, considered a grandfatherly shaman, and is somewhat reclusive. He praised my book, *The Attractor Factor*. He told me that as I improve myself, my book's vibration will raise, and everyone will feel it when they read it. In short, as I improve, my readers will improve. 'What about the books that are already sold and out there?" I asked.

"They aren't out there," he explained, once again blowing my mind with his mystic wisdom. They are still in you." In short, there is no out there. It would take a whole book to explain this advanced technique with the depth it deserves. Suffice to say that whenever you want to improve anything in your life, there's only one place to look: inside you. When you look, do it with love."

Dr. Joe Vitale, is the president of the Hypnotic Marketing Institute and author of numerous best selling books too numerous to name including The Attractor Factor, Life's Missing Instruction Manual, The Key, and Zero Limits. He has a doctoral degree in Metaphysical Science, is a Certified Hypnotherapist and Chun Kung Healer. Joe has been in eleven movies, including the blockbuster "The Secret" and the recent one, "The Compass."

He's been on Larry King and Donny Deutsch's TV shows. He created a Miracles Coaching program and helps people achieve their dreams by understanding the deeper aspects of the Law of Attraction and the Law of Right Action. He's also recorded many audio programs, including "The Missing Secret" and the new one, "The Secret to Attracting Money." This man was once homeless but today is a bestselling author who believes in magic and miracles. You can see more information at http://www.ZeroLimits.info and http://www.JoeVitale.com

CHAPTER SIX

From Suffering To Soaring
How I Transcended AIDS

by Richard N. Schooping

I am Richard N. Schooping and I have Transcended AIDS. I am now a living example that we are more than AIDS, fear, death, limitation, and suffering. Today I am sharing that we may, from the depth of any misery, follow the light of our heart home. All we need do is pause, observe, and listen.

Here in my 41st winter let me share my story. I was officially diagnosed HIV+ in 1994 during the last months of my third husband's life. At that time I discovered I had 444 T-Cells. I was incredibly stressed after my previous suffering and losses so having a low t-cell count should not have been unexpected. But this information about how the immune system may be suppressed in times of high stress was not shared with me, only the fact that I was now dying like my lover and the two before him. Though I did not realize at the time all is a gift when we observe and experience without attachment, even situations which seem negative like HIV and AIDS.

I had already lost two lovers and my best friend to AIDS in less than five years and I was a wreck. I experienced a nervous breakdown while with my third lover, and afterwards I was not the same. I was overloaded with the years of suffering. This breakdown was a gift in that it released an incredible amount of stored energy, but a by-product was that it fried much of my circuitry. One cannot imagine the depth of loss and extreme heartache experienced with losing three lovers, husbands, or wives, when losing only one seems more than the body, a life, or a heart can handle. I lost three husbands to AIDS in eight years and I was only 27.

To further explain the fracture of my consciousness I was also, during these losses, the lead-singer in a straight world. I was straight and gay. During the suffering and passing of my first two husbands I was not out to my friends. I was the lead-singer in local bands perceived as a straight man. It was maddening. I was two different people. What was heavy is that when I was with my straight friends I became so good at acting like them that I forgot who I was until I was in my car driving to see my dying lover in the hospital

Here I was in my early 20's, broken and going mad. I slept in hospital chairs for so many days that I lost count. I have been a mother, a father, a brother, a lover, a fighter, a priest, a nurse, you name it I have been it. I have changed innumerable adult diapers and performed indescribable services of love for one who is incapable. I will say that every experience I experienced, be it of joy or horror revealed a new piece of life.

In 1995 I moved back home to live with my parents (again) after losing my third lover, most of my belongings (again), and my home (again). I vividly recall lying in bed, curtains drawn, lights off, and praying to God, "Please let me die. I can't take this. I want to come home." I sat in that room for about two weeks depressed and disconnected until one day I wondered if it was sunny beyond the closed curtains. I got up, opened the windows and the window of my heart, and marched on.

In 1996 I began to dramatically slow and show signs of illness. I experienced intense bleeding facial skin dermatitis and large boils on my forehead and back. I realized later that I was incredibly toxic and this was the body's way of releasing the toxicity. I had no clue then, so I sought out help. The one thing my then and current lover Cal and I knew to do was to see an infectious disease doctor. Due to my deteriorating health in late 1996 I started the medications for AIDS. After three weeks of experiencing horrible side effects on these drugs I stopped taking the Cocktail: the prescribed combination of nuclear drugs.

Around 1998 I still had painful and visible rashes and persistent allergies, but also started debilitating with stress-induced migraines that rendered me immobile upon their occurrence.

Over the next few years I learned to live with my body, its limitations, and the parade of illnesses. I was enjoying my jobs and musical projects as best I could and loving life with my golden angel Cal. I was slowly healing my wounded past just through living. I was not on medications or seeing a doctor. I was sleeping more and more, still fading yet still managing until… My life turned from just barely normal, from living with Advanced HIV Disease to having AIDS.

In 2003 I was diagnosed full-blown AIDS (having less than 200 T-cells). I think I had 157 t-cells, this count measured after I experienced an extensive snowboarding injury in 2001 that put me in a soft-body cast and rendered me bed-ridden for months. I could not stand on my own or let alone walk without assistance.

Cal became everything to me. The pain and atrophy I experienced cannot be expressed. Bones were shattered and beyond surgical repair. I was skin and bones unable to lift my feet off the ground. All muscles atrophied. I lay in bed unable to do anything for months. This utterly stopped my life, and from within this cocoon I began to observe and realize who I am.

This snowboarding injury compounded my already damaged immune system. I was now spiritually and physically broken. From 2003 through 2005 I developed colon lesions and Aggressive Dysplasia: A pre-cancerous abnormality of the cell, which multiplied and metastasized from having no immune system. I required multiple operations over a two-year span to remove these lesions and growths, each operation and anesthetic weakening my already severely damaged immune system and mind.

I was but a skeleton in misery in perpetual pain. The storm intensified. Even more agonizing was that I also experienced Fistulas, infected colon lesions that create a puss that slowly eats through the colon and muscle walls and tissue, and then bursts out through the skin. This was agonizing pain. I brought a pillow everywhere I went, even upon returning to work. I could not drive for months. I worked as long as I could until another fistula developed which forced me to take another leave of absence in which I lost my job and went on disability.

In 2004 I was barely alive. After losing three lovers, the snowboarding injury, colon surgeries, fistulas, constant allergies, depression, the unending stress that I would die soon, and whatever other myriad illnesses I incurred during, there was little left. Cal was more than worried. He told me that when he looked into my eyes there was no light. I was dying. I was distant. I was drained. I did not care. I did not have the energy to care. The creative and vibrant man he had married was not there and had been replaced with a limp and drained thing. I agreed to whatever Cal wanted so I started AIDS medications again. I assumed I was going to die and wanted him to be at peace with the situation. I also developed an aggressive skin cancer on my forehead, which required four plastic surgeries for removal and to reduce scarring. This was another blow to my barely functioning immune system and sanity. I required interior and exterior stitches and the removal of a 2" diameter area of tissue down to my skull. At this point my life was pain. I was never at ease for fear of the next misery to endure and the ever looming and impending death of AIDS. The procession of storms was relentless. There was never reprieve.

Somewhere in late 2005 after two years of meditation and being a vegan/raw foodist for three years I began to experience what I refer to as The Rocket Ride. Everything I had been began speeding up and spreading out into more. I started to expand into more than what I had known myself to be, and at a rapid pace. I will say that during my injuries I was slowly becoming more of an observer. Seeing that my body just could not handle the pain a larger aspect of me began drifting in and remaining to keep me sane. It felt like I was having a continuous word-less conversation with a mysterious comforter. This comforter was somehow conveying that everything was fine and that all that I was experiencing was for my benefit.

During the time of The Rocket Ride I would sit down in meditation and then stand expanded and new, with new knowing or new unknowing. I began to observe and absolve core and root beliefs in my consciousness. I had harmonized the surface layers of my consciousness in meditation and was now reaching the center of my being. I began to experientially experience and become what I had only previously intellectually known. I realized being more than gay; being more than a man, being more than a body, and these realizations literally blew my mind. The space that was occupied by these absolved gargantuan beliefs was now occupied by my awareness. When the belief was realized I was then the space in which the belief resided.

I found that this was not about physically healing AIDS (the symptoms), it was about curing the consciousness of suffering that became AIDS. January 26, 2006 I stopped the medications for AIDS for a final time. Then in August of 2007 I was hospitalized with double pneumonia. I had very high fevers and chills for a week prior and lost

15 pounds in a few days but this was different. I was now free. I knew that I was more, and though I was told that I would probably die I was out of the hospital in five days.

Today I am alive and well. After almost 20 years of mental anguish and physical suffering through losing three lovers, my best friend, and my own inexpressible journey through cancer, depression, AIDS, sexuality and mortality confusion, guilt, and more, I realized that I am more than AIDS. I realized that I/we are more than any thing. I realized that it is not AIDS we are to address for a cure it is AIDS Consciousness. AIDS Consciousness being a combination of limiting beliefs and crippling fears of which we cling to that cause our suffering, that cause what we today refer to and know as AIDS. I now realize that each suffering was a blow to my ego that essentially destroyed layer upon layer of who I thought I was, revealing more of the love that we are through my suffering. Each suffering afforded me a unique perspective to realize more of the love we are. There was never a time to heal so I unknowingly expanded as I observed, absolved, and purified my consciousness.

I finally relaxed in the knowing that there is no right or wrong to our life experience, only growth. Through my journey, I grew through and beyond AIDS like a sapling breeching the shadowed lower-layer of woods. This is analogous to our limited understandings growing (or expanding) beyond the shadowed layer of ego, the limited idea we have of ourselves.

"Know Thy Self. The Kingdom of Heaven is within. Be Still, and Know that I am GOD. Be Here Now." Those that have and do realize 'the more' leave pointers to the eternal love that we are through simple, and yet oh so powerful quotes such as these. We are to know ourselves to know the more that we are. Not until we fully embrace who we currently are do we open up to know more of the love we are. We need to balance our current energetic before we join (or realize) into larger harmonies of GOD, harmonies that are more than AIDS.

Concerning life, we create our individualized experience as our awareness observes through filters and structures within our consciousness. We have created these layers (or veils) as we have evolved, and evolve into wholeness. Through limited beliefs I experienced a limited existence and now I am here and I have transcended this limited path, for there is no path, only being. When we realize the prismatic play of mind (the mirrors, mansions, reflections, etc.), we can transcend. We are evolving intelligence to learn what to next unlearn, or disbelieve.

When we experience the ever-changing flow of forms from a heart of gratitude and non-judgment, we surrender our limitations and become unlimited. When we realize our fears we are fearless. When we embrace our lives we are here. When we realize all that we are there is no more karma, polarity, cause and effect… we are free. We have exited the loop or hoop of illusory time.

In my book "From Suffering to Soaring; Through GOD I Transcended AIDS," I discuss my personal suffering in detail and illumine and simplify aspects of all that we are. One needs to realize that no matter the level of misery there is always a way beyond the current experience of suffering, even when suffering with AIDS because we are more. Let this message be a lamp unto the world.

Today I am free of AIDS, or AIDS Consciousness. How paradoxical it is that when we surrender things we value, we experience things more deeply. When we are not afraid or paranoid of losing them we can enjoy them fully. Life has bloomed. I have bloomed and now everything is bright and pure. All is simple and a joy to experience.

Now I am here writing words and melodies of love. I am being. I am profoundly humbled to be in an over 13-year relationship with my lover Cal who has expressed and expresses such kindness, selflessness, and love to me and to the world that it renders me speechless. I am honored to share this journey and to offer simplifications for our current understandings and insights into the love that we are. I am fearless knowing that fear is an illusion created when we attach to only a fragment of an experience before realizing the love inherent, the love we are.

When we are love we only know love, no matter if walking through a field of flowers or field of warring armies. I am free of death, for we are beyond death. Death is a belief within the infinity that we are. Pure consciousness is not alive or dead, it IS. I am free of mind-created suffering. I am at peace in knowing more.

When we transcend or realize, our intellectual understanding shifts from learned experience to experiential being. We are not associating ourselves with existing volumes of collected beliefs and stories. We are the space from whence they derived, realized through the purification of our consciousness.

It is my honor to have shared my journey from illusion to illumination with you. Let this glimpse into my suffering and my transcendence offer a new way for us to know AIDS, suffering, and any challenge in our life experience.

Richard N. Schooping is a Holistic Health Consultant, Author, Speaker, Singer, and Songwriter. He currently resides in Michigan with his partner Calvin. He is vibrant, creating, employed, and healthy. Richard can be reached via email at: richardschooping@gmail.com.

Visit http://www.richardschooping.com to order Richard's book, "From Suffering to Soaring; Through GOD I Transcended AIDS" from which this story was inspired.

Other products of love and inspiration are also available and you can also schedule a Shareapy Session© with Richard. Let us individually or in group join physically, by phone, through video chat or chat, or through email consultation, creating a sacred space and share and balance our lives. Let us together realize the more that we are.

CHAPTER SEVEN

Through The Light

By Mellen-Thomas Benedict

In 1982 I died from terminal cancer. The condition I had was inoperable, and any kind of chemotherapy they could give me would just have made me more of a vegetable. I was given six to eight months to live.

I had been an information freak in the 1970's, and I had become increasingly despondent over the nuclear crisis, the ecology crisis, and so forth. So, since I did not have a spiritual basis, I began to believe that nature had made a mistake, and that we were probably a cancerous organism on the planet.

I saw no way that we could get out from all the problems we had created for ourselves and the planet. I perceived all humans as cancer, and that is what I got. That is what killed me.

Be careful what your worldview is, it can feed back on you. I had a seriously negative one. That is what led me into my death. I tried all sorts of alternative healing methods, but nothing helped.

So I determined that this was really just between God and me. I had never really faced God before, or even dealt with God. I was not into any kind of spirituality at the time, but I began a journey into learning about spirituality and alternative healing. I set out to do all the reading I could and bone up on the subject, because I did not want to be surprised on the other side.

I started reading on various religions and philosophiies. They were all very interesting, and gave hope that there was something on the other side. I ended up in hospice care.

The Light of God

I remember waking up one morning at home about 4:30 AM, and I just knew that this was it. This was the day I was going to die. So I called a few friends and said goodbye. I woke up my hospice caretaker and told her. I had a private agreement with her that she would leave my dead body alone for six hours, since I had read that all kinds of interesting things happen when you die. I went back to sleep.

The next thing I remember is the beginning of a typical near-death experience. Suddenly I was fully aware and I was standing up, but my body was in the bed. There was this darkness around me. Being out of my body was even more vivid than my ordinary experience. It was so expansive that I could see every room in the house, I could see the top of the house, I could see around the house, I could see under the house.

There was this Light shining. I turned toward the Light. The Light was very similar to what many other people have described in their near-death experiences. It was so magnificent. It is tangible. You can feel it. It is alluring. You want to go to it like you would want to go to your ideal mother's or father's arms.

As I began to move toward the Light, I knew intuitively that if I went to the Light, I would be dead. So as I was moving toward the Light I said, "Please wait a minute, just hold on a second here. I want to think about this. I would like to talk to you before I go." To my surprise, the entire experience halted at that point. You are in control of your life after your death experience. You are not on a roller coaster ride.

So my request was honored and I had some conversations with the Light. The Light kept changing into different figures, like Jesus, Buddha, Krishna, mandalas, archetypal images and signs. I asked the Light, "What is going on here? Please, Light, clarify yourself for me. I really want to know the reality of the situation." I cannot really say the exact words, because it was sort of telepathy.

The Light responded. The information transferred to me was that during your life after death experience your beliefs shape the kind of feedback you are getting before the Light. If you were a Buddhist or Catholic or Fundamentalist, you get a feedback loop of your own stuff. You have a chance to look at it and examine it, but most people do not. As the Light revealed itself to me, I became aware that what I was really seeing was our Higher Self Matrix.

We all have a Higher Self, or an Over Soul part of our being. It revealed itself to me in its truest energy form. The only way I can really describe it is that the being of the Higher Self is more like a conduit. It did not look like that, but it is a direct connection to the Source that each and every one of us has. We are directly connected to the Source. So the Light was showing me the Higher Self Matrix. I was not committed to one particular religion. So that is what was being fed back to me during my life after death experience in the many images that were appearing.

As I asked the Light to keep explaining, I understood what the Higher Self Matrix is. We have a grid around the planet where all the Higher Selves are connected. This is like a great company, a next subtle level of energy around us, the spirit level, you might say. Then, after a couple of minutes, I asked for more clarification. I really wanted to know what the universe is about, and I was ready to go at that time. I said "I am ready, take me."

Then the Light turned into the most beautiful thing that I have ever seen: a mandala of human souls on this planet. Now I came to this with my negative view of people and what was happening on the planet. So as I asked the Light to keep clarifying for me, I saw in this magnificent mandala how beautiful we all are in our essence, our core. We are the most beautiful creations.

The human soul, the human matrix that we all make together is absolutely fantastic, elegant, exotic, everything. I just cannot say enough about how it changed my opinion of human beings in that instant. I said, "Oh, God, I did not know how beautiful we are." At any level, high or low, in whatever shape you are in, you are the most beautiful creation, you are.

The revelations coming from the Light seemed to go on and on. Then I asked the Light, "Does this mean that Mankind will be saved?" Then, like a trumpet blast with a shower of spiraling lights, the Great Light spoke, saying, "Remember this and never forget. You save, redeem and heal yourself. You always have. You always will. You were created with the power to do so from before the beginning of the world."

In that instant I realized even more. I realized that WE HAVE ALREADY BEEN SAVED, and we saved ourselves because we were designed to self-correct like the rest of God's universe. This is what the Second Coming is about. I thanked the Light of God with all my heart.

The best thing I could come up with was these simple words of total appreciation: "Oh dear God, dear Universe, dear Great Self, I Love My Life."

The Light seemed to breathe me in even more deeply. It was as if the Light was completely absorbing me. The Love Light is, to this day, indescribable. I entered into another realm, more profound than the last, and became aware of something more, much more. It was an enormous stream of Light, vast and full, deep in the Heart of Life. I asked what this was.

The Light responded, "This is the RIVER OF LIFE. Drink of this manna water to your heart's content." So I did. I took one big drink and then another. To drink of Life Itself! I was in ecstasy. Then the Light said, "You have a desire." The Light knew all about me, everything past, present and future. "Yes!" I whispered.

I asked to see the rest of the Universe, beyond our solar system, beyond all human illusion. The Light then told me that I could go with the Stream. I did, and was carried through the Light at the end of the tunnel. I felt and heard a series of very soft sonic booms. What a rush!

The Void of Nothingness

Suddenly I seemed to be rocketing away from the planet on this Stream of Life. I saw the earth fly away. The solar system, in all its splendor, whizzed by and disappeared. At faster than light speed, I flew through the center of the galaxy, absorbing more knowledge as I went. I learned that this galaxy, and all of the Universe, is bursting with many different varieties of LIFE. I saw many worlds. The good news is that we are not alone in this Universe!

As I rode this stream of consciousness through the center of the galaxy, the stream was expanding in awesome fractal waves of energy. The super clusters of galaxies with all their ancient wisdom flew by.

At first I thought I was going somewhere, actually traveling. But then I realized that, as the stream was expanding, my own consciousness was also expanding to take in everything in the Universe! All creation passed by me. It was an unimaginable wonder! I truly was a Wonder Child, a babe in Wonderland! At this point, I found myself in a profound stillness, beyond all silence. I could see or perceive FOREVER, beyond Infinity. I was in the Void.

I was in pre-creation, before the Big Bang. I had crossed over the beginning of time, the First Word, the First vibration. I was in the Eye of Creation. I felt as if I was touching the Face of God. It was not a religious feeling. Simply I was at one with Absolute Life and Consciousness. When I say that I could see or perceive forever, I mean that I could experience all of creation generating itself. It was without beginning and without end. That's a mind expanding thought, isn't it?

Scientists perceive the Big Bang as a single event, which created the Universe. I saw during my life after death experience that the Big Bang is only one of an infinite number of Big Bangs creating Universes endlessly and simultaneously. The only images that even come close in human terms would be those created by super computers using fractal geometry equations.

The ancients knew of this. They said God had periodically created new Universes by breathing out, and recreated other Universes by breathing in. These epochs were called Yugas. Modern science called this the Big Bang. I was in absolute, pure consciousness. I could see or perceive all the Big Bangs or Yugas creating and recreating themselves. Instantly I entered into them all simultaneously. I saw that each and every little piece of creation has the power to create. It is very difficult to try to explain this. I am still speechless about this.

It took me years after I returned from my near-death experience to assimilate any words at all for the Void experience. I can tell you this now, the Void is less than nothing, yet more than everything that is! The Void is absolute zero, chaos forming all possibilities. It is Absolute Consciousness, much more than even Universal Intelligence.

The Void is the vacuum or nothingness between all physical manifestations, the SPACE between atoms and their components. Modern science has begun to study this space between everything. They call it Zero point. Whenever they try to measure it, their instruments go off the scale, or to infinity, so to speak. They have no way, as of yet, to measure infinity accurately. There is more of the zero space in your own body and the Universe than anything else!

What mystics call the Void is not a void. It is so full of energy, a different kind of energy that has created everything that we are. Everything since the Big Bang is vibration, from the First Word, which is the first vibration. The biblical "I am" really has a question mark after it. "I am—What am I?" So creation is God exploring God's Self through every way imaginable, in an ongoing, infinite exploration through every one of us. I began to see during my near-death experience that everything that is, is the Self, literally, your Self, my Self. Everything is the Great Self. That is why God knows even when a leaf falls. That is possible because wherever you are is the center of the universe. Wherever any atom is, that is the center of the universe. There is God in that, and God in the Void.

As I was exploring the Void and all the Yugas or creations, I was completely out of time and space as we know it. In this expanded state, I discovered that creation is about Absolute Pure Consciousness, or God, coming into the Experience of Life as we know it. The Void itself is devoid of experience. It is pre-life, before the first vibration. Godhead is about more than Life and Death. Therefore, there is even more than Life and Death to experience in the Universe!

When I realized this I was finished with the Void, and wanted to return to this creation, or Yuga. It just seemed like the natural thing to do. Then I suddenly came back through the second Light, or the Big Bang, hearing several more velvet booms. I rode the stream of consciousness back through all of creation, and what a ride it was! The super clusters of galaxies came through me with even more insights. I passed through the center of our galaxy, which is a black hole. Black holes are the great processors or recyclers of the Universe.

Do you know what is on the other side of a Black Hole? We are, our galaxy, which has been reprocessed from another Universe. In its total energy configuration, the galaxy looked like a fantastic city of lights. All energy this side of the Big Bang is light. Every sub atom, atom, star, planet, even consciousness itself is made of light and has a frequency and/or particle. Light is living stuff. Everything is made of light, even stones. So everything is alive. Everything is made from the Light of God. Everything is very intelligent.

As I rode the stream on and on, I could eventually see a huge Light coming. I knew it was the First Light, the higher Self Light Matrix of our solar system. Then the entire solar system appeared in the Light, accompanied by one of those velvet booms.

I could see all the energy that this solar system generates, and it is an incredible light show! I could hear the Music of the Spheres. Our solar system, as do all celestial bodies, generates a unique matrix of light, sound and vibratory energies. Advanced civilizations from other star systems can spot life as we know it in the universe by the vibratory or energy matrix imprint. It is child's play. The earth's Wonder child (human beings) make an abundance of sound right now, like children playing in the backyard of the universe.

There Is No Death

The Light explained to me that there is no death. We are immortal beings. We have already been alive forever! I realized that we are part of a natural living system that recycles itself endlessly. was never told that I had to come back. I just knew that I would. It was only natural, from what I had seen during my life after death experience.

I don't know how long I was with the Light, in human time. But there came a moment when I realized that all my questions had been answered and my return was near. When I say that all my questions were answered on the other side, I mean to say just that. All my questions have been answered.

Every human has a different life and set of questions to explore. Some of our questions are Universal, but each of us is exploring this thing we call Life in our own unique way. So is every other form of life, from mountains to every leaf on every tree. And that is very important to the rest of us in this Universe, because it all contributes to the Big Picture, the fullness of Life. We are literally God exploring God's Self in an infinite Dance of Life. Your uniqueness enhances all of Life.

As I began my return to the life cycle, it never crossed my mind, nor was I told that I would return to the same body. It just did not matter. I had complete trust in the Light and the Life process. As the stream merged with the great Light, I asked never to forget the revelations and the feelings of what I had learned on the other side. There was a "Yes." It felt like a kiss to my soul. Then I was taken back through the Light into the vibratory realm again. The whole process reversed, with even more information being given to me.

I came back home, and I was given lessons from my near-death experience on the mechanics of reincarnation. I was given answers to all those little questions I had, "How does this work? How does that work?" I knew that I would be reincarnated.

The earth is a great processor of energy, and individual consciousness evolves out of that into each one of us. I thought of myself as a human for the first time, and I was happy to be that. From what I have seen, I would be happy to be an atom in this universe. An atom. So to be the human part of God... this is the most fantastic blessing. It is a blessing beyond our wildest estimation of what a blessing can be. For each and every one of us to be the human part of this experience is awesome, and magnificent. Each and every one of us, no matter where we are, screwed up or not, is a blessing to the planet, right where we are.

I went through the reincarnation process expecting to be a baby somewhere. But I was given a lesson on how individual identity and consciousness evolve. I was so surprised when I opened my eyes. I do not know why, because I understood it, but it was still such a surprise to be back in this body, back in my room with someone looking over me crying her eyes out. It was my hospice caretaker. She had given up an hour and a half after finding me dead. My body was stiff and inflexible. She went into the other room. Then I awakened and saw the light outside. I tried to get up to go to it, but I fell out of the bed. She heard a loud "clunk," ran in and found me on the floor.

When I recovered, I was very surprised and yet very awed about what had happened to me during my near-death experience. At first, all the memory of the trip that I have now was not there. I kept slipping out of this world and kept asking, "Am I alive?" This world seemed more like a dream than that one.

Within three days I was feeling normal again, clearer, yet different than I had ever felt in my life. My memory of my near-death experience came back later. I could see nothing wrong with any human being I had ever seen. Before that I was really judgmental. I thought a lot of people were really screwed up, in fact I thought that everybody was screwed up but me. But I got clear on all that.

About three months later a friend said I should get tested, so I went and got the scans and so forth. I really felt good, so I was afraid of getting bad news.

I remember the doctor at the clinic looking at the before and after scans, saying, "Well, there is nothing here now." I said, "Really, it must be a miracle." He said, "No, these things happen. They are called spontaneous remission." He acted very unimpressed, but here was a miracle, and I was impressed, even if no one else was.

Lessons Learned

The Great Mystery of life has little to do with intelligence. The universe is not an intellectual process. The intellect is helpful, but our hearts are the wiser part of us. Since my return I have experienced the Light spontaneously, and I have learned how to get to that space almost any time in my meditation. You can also do this. You do not have to die first. You are wired for it already.

The body is the most magnificent Light being there is. The body is a universe of incredible Light. Spirit is not pushing us to dissolve this body. We don't need to commune with God, God is communing with us in every moment.

I was given a tour of all the heavens that have been created, the Nirvanas, the Happy Hunting Grounds, all of them. I went through them. These are thought form creations that we have created. We don't really go to heaven. Whatever we created, we leave a part of ourselves there. It is real, but it is not all of the soul.

During my near-death experience I also had a descent into what you might call Hell, and it was very surprising. I did not see Satan or evil. My descent into Hell took me into each person's customized human misery, ignorance, and darkness of not knowing. It seemed like a miserable eternity, but each of the millions of souls around me had a little star of light always available, though no one seemed to pay attention to it. They were so consumed with their own grief, trauma and misery. But, after what seemed an eternity, I started calling out to that Light, like a child calling to a parent for help.

Then the Light opened up and formed a tunnel that came right to me and insulated me from all that fear and pain. That is what Hell really is. So what we are doing is learning to hold hands, to come together. The doors of Hell are open now. We are going to link up, hold hands, and walk out of Hell together. The Light came to me and turned into a huge golden angel. I said, "Are you the angel of death?" It expressed to me that it was my Over Soul, my Higher Self Matrix, a super ancient part of ourselves. Then I was taken to the Light.

Soon our science will quantify spirit. We are coming up with devices now that are sensitive to subtle energy or spirit energy. Physicists use these atomic colliders to smash atoms to see what they are made of. They have got it down to quarks and charm, and all that.

Well, one day they are going to come down to the little thing that holds it all together, and they are going to have to call that... God. We are just beginning to understand that we are creating too, as we go along.

As I saw forever, I came to a realm during my near-death experience in which there is a point where we pass all knowledge and begin creating the next fractal, the next level. We have that power to create as we explore, and that is God expanding itself through us. Stop trying to become God. God is becoming you. Here.

I asked God, "What is the best religion on the planet? Which one is right?" And God said, with great love: "I don't care." That was incredible grace. When Godhead said, "I don't care," I immediately understood that it is for us to care about. It is important, because we are the caring beings. It matters to us and that is where it is important. What you have is the energy equation in spirituality. Ultimate Godhead does not care if you are Protestant, Buddhist, or whatever. It is all a blooming facet of the whole. I wish that all religions would realize it and let each other be. It is not the end of each religion, but we are talking about the same God. Live and let live. Each has a different view. And it all adds up to the big picture. It is all important.

I went over to the other side during my near-death experience with a lot of fears about toxic waste, nuclear missiles, the population explosion, the rainforest. I came back loving every single problem. I love nuclear waste. I love the mushroom cloud. This is the holiest mandala that we have manifested to date, as an archetype. It, more than any religion or philosophy on earth, brought us together all of a sudden, to a new level of consciousness. Knowing that maybe we can blow up the planet fifty times, or 500 times, we finally realize that maybe we are all here together now.

For a period they had to keep setting off more bombs to get it in to us. Then we started saying, "we do not need this any more." Now we are actually in a safer world than we have ever been in, and it is going to get safer. So I came back from my near-death experience loving toxic waste, because it brought us together. These things are so big. As Peter Russell might say, these problems are now "soul size." Do we have soul size answers" YES!

The clearing of the rain forest will slow down, and in fifty years there will be more trees on the planet than in a long time. If you are into ecology, go for it. You are that part of the system that is becoming aware. Go for it with all your might, but do not be depressed. It is part of a larger thing.

Earth is in the process of domesticating itself. It is never again going to be as wild a place as it once was. There will be great wild places, reserves where nature thrives. Gardening and reserves will be the thing in the future. Population increase is getting very close to the optimal range of energy to cause a shift in consciousness. That shift in consciousness will change politics, money, energy.

After dying, going through my near-death experience and coming back, I really respect life and death. In our DNA experiments we may have opened the door to a great secret. Soon we will be able to live as long as we want to live in this body.

After living 150 years or so, there will be an intuitive soul sense that you will want to change channels. Living forever in one body is not as creative as reincarnation, as transferring energy in this fantastic vortex of energy that we are in. We are actually going to see the wisdom of life and death, and enjoy it. As it is now, we have already been alive forever.

Mellen-Thomas is the author of Journey to the Light and Back, and Hitchiker's Guide to the Other Side. Since his near death experience, he has maintained his direct access to Universal Intelligence, and returns to the light at will, enabling him to be a bridge between science and spirit.

He has been involved in research programs on near death experiences and has developed new technologies for health and wellness. With humility, insight, and depth of feeling he shares his experience and insights.

He brings back from his near death experience a message of hope and inspiration for humanity, delivered with a joy and clarity that is refreshing. His depth of feeling and passion for life is a gift to be shared. For more information see http: www.Mellen-Thomas.com

Part Eight

Miracles of TheQuest™

CHAPTER ONE

Birth of TheQuest™

For years, my focus was on mastering spiritual practices in the hope of attaining the highest adeptship, but while I reached incredible heights in consciousness, my emotions played havoc in my world. I could not control them. And no matter how much I wrestled with patterns and personality traits, I could not free myself from them. Neither could I end the recycling of painful relationships, financial constraints, and personal hardships.

While I was living all the highest spiritual formulas for success in positive thinking, daily affirmations, meditation, and healthy diet, my life kept coming unraveled. What I built I lost. What I attained spiritually disappeared in moments of frustration or anger. Though I held the highest ideal for my relationships, they would consistently be so much less than my visions and dreams. Heartbreak seemed to be the reward of an exemplary spiritual life, rather than happiness and success. I could not understand this. Wasn't I doing everything right?

Seeking to stay in my "higher consciousness" through the severely painful relationship I wrote about in *My Journey of Healing* story in Miraculous Recoveries and Cures, I had become a master at spiritual bypass. When, without warning, I had two heart attacks within six months and was told I had an incurable heart condition that could quickly debilitate me to death, my life was forever changed. I had received my wake up call. My spiritual practices and higher state of consciousness were not enough.

Mortally challenged, I began to look deep into myself to find answers. As I shared, this led me into the psyche where I discovered heartbreak was the cause of my illness. Through that journey, I gained an understanding of the inter-relationship between emotions and disease. Going deeper still, I found the patterns behind the challenging conditions I had faced and why I had drawn in a relationship that had been so heartbreaking. This helped me understand the challenges I had encountered in life and how my subconscious patterns had created everything of a dire nature I had ever gone through.

I also learned the value of listening to my feelings and supporting myself when going through something difficult, attention that I would have naturally offered to one of my children, a client, or a friend, but somehow had left myself out of the equation.

My greatest discovery was finding the Authentic Self at the core of my being, not something bad, dark or evil. In each session, I would discover this Self beyond every pattern and human emotion. Instantly, I would be filled with love, understanding, wisdom, and compassion. I could finally see myself in my true state, a powerful spiritual being having a limited human experience.

I began to have a more conscious relationship with this part of me, who many times appeared in my inner sight as a radiant woman emanating light. I learned that her intention was to fulfill my every dream, vision and desire, but to receive her gifts, I had to clear the way in my subconscious. I also had to release control. As I did this, I became more 'enlightened' and free.

I became an adept at resolving my issues quickly and healing their underlying patterns. I was a Master Alchemist moving from upset to peace quickly, shortening the time of misery I would have gone through by dramatic degrees. I was freeing myself from every painful condition that appeared in my life. Increment-by-increment, the human patterning was dissolving as I cleared the way for my Authentic Self to manifest her vision in my life.

By healing my patterns, I found I was also clearing my family lineage with its history of pain. Finally, I understood why the planet looks the way it does, why so often we fail to bring our Enlightened Self into the equation. The world keeps reflecting the inner wound of humanity, while the Authentic Self remains lost beneath this programming.

Everyone on earth is run by subconscious patterns to a lesser or greater degree. To get off this endless track and manifest a higher vision, we need to address the inner causes of our life dilemmas. When we release ourselves from suffering, our victory ripples through the collective helping others break free. We are all connected in the Circle of Life. Our healing helps to heal the psyche of humanity and literally changes the world from within.

So many times, I've risen like a phoenix from the ashes of devastation and despair. Through the hardest experiences, I learned how to restore myself quickly, and return to my Authentic Self. These challenges also translated into years of delving deeply into the psyche, where I made many landmark discoveries. Through this pioneering work, I developed my Counseling Theory and Practice, TheQuest™. The mastery I gained on my personal trek became TheQuest™ Life Mastery Path I teach today under the Institute of Advanced Healing.

My son, Aradeus also become adept at TheQuest™. As I shared in book one, *Earth 2012: The Ultimate Quest*, I trained him over a year and a half, where we gave each other back to back sessions each week. He was the one who inspired me to distill TheQuest™ into a seven-step process that could be taught to others. This totally resonated with my vision of handing this knowledge to the layperson, instead of just to practitioners, as is normally done.

Aradeus and I began holding a weekly Teen Forum and gave classes at local high schools in Aspen, taking the kids and their teachers through the Seven Steps. I was amazed to find they loved it! I was also holding a weekly Healing Circle and watching people's lives change. This was very heartening. It showed me that anyone can use TheQuest™ to do their own self healing process. A complete Healing System had been born.

By training Aradeus, I began developing TheQuest™ Master Counselor and Spiritual Leadership Training. Today it is a two-year certification course that can also be done as an accelerated one-year program. It is an exciting journey with my students, where I pass my knowledge to them in a way that is experiential. As they encounter life difficulties, I give them essential information to help them understand what is really going on at deeper levels. Then we do TheQuest™ Counseling to clear the way.

Step by step, session upon session, they extricate themselves from painful conditions. They gain Self Mastery by applying TheQuest™ in self-counseling sessions as their issues arise, an important part of the program. Upon graduation, they are not only masters of their psychology, but they have an exemplary skill as a Counselor and Life Coach that can help others. They then have the opportunity to transfer this knowledge to their community by setting up a chapter of the Institute there.

TheQuest™ Healing System provides a missing piece to rehab and addiction programs, prison reform, youth at risk programs, and to many afflictions humanity is facing today. Excited by the ramifications of transferring this healing system to others, I designed the program so that anyone can take it no matter how busy they are or where they are living in the world, though at this time, the transfer comes directly from me. It is a very in depth experience and something that I can only pass to seven students at a time.

In the future, TheQuest™ University will pass this Healing System to many others who will then take it to their communities around the world. I see counselors from different programs mastering this technology and rapidly changing their clients' lives. I see it being taught as a college course and in high schools.

TheQuest™ brings the missing link at a time when humanity must awaken and take its place as a wise steward of the earth. It is a key to finding our Lost Identity, for it awakens us to the Authentic Self that lives at the core of our being. We then remember our true heritage, our Lineage of Light beyond the human programming.

Through my own arduous journey, I proved a way of Self Mastery that is empowering and life changing. No matter what circumstances we were born with, or how ingrained our patterns or addictions are, we can take back the scepter of power and change our life.

This is the Path of the Initiate. By mastering our psychology, we become Adepts in the New Millennium. Our inner focus and healing work has a rippling affect, touching lives throughout the world. By transforming our life, the world is transformed around us. By living more often in our Authentic Self, we anchor Heaven on Earth in our own life experience, and pave the way for Eden to manifest its glory on Earth.

CHAPTER TWO

Out Of the Darkness Into The Light

Over the years I've continually seen miracles with the TheQuest™ in my life and the lives of my friends, family, and clients. So many, that it has compelled me to bring this technology to the world. At my darkest hours, it has been my saving grace, allowing me to transcend the most challenging situations and to emerge unscathed from the most devastating circumstances. This story is about one of those times and about someone very close to me who I love with all my heart that I had to let go of. Not an easy thing to do, when it is your child.

I had spent years on a roller coaster watching in anguish as my eldest son's life and sanity unraveled from substance abuse. This broke my heart and caused so much stress that there were times I could barely handle it. Sometimes the weight was unbearable. Of course, guiding him to a substance free life was an impossible quest. I finally realized that we must heal ourselves and that can only happen when we are ready. No one can compel us to do anything!

Things finally accelerated to where I thought I would lose him. The use of drugs and alcohol had taken their toll and he had become delusional, depressed, and suicidal. After three days straight on drugs without sleeping or eating, violence erupted in a fight with his girlfriend.

So much was revealed as his girlfriend poured out her painful story, my daughter and I listening silently by the speakerphone, tears flowing from our eyes. I was devastated to learn the dark places my son had entered over the past year caused by prescription and other drugs he had been misusing. I finally had to face that he was not well and this was so hard, because he is so talented and exceptional in every way.

She was brokenhearted that things had escalated between them into harsh words and violence. She loved him very much. She spoke of how she had beem living in dread that at any moment, he would die of an overdose, and how morning after morning she would come to his window and look in, scared that she would find him dead.

As she shared, my daughter and I had the same premonition at the same moment. We saw my son standing over his girlfriend in remorse. He had accidentally taken her life and then took his own life. We sat there in shock. He had already gone three days without sleeping and eating, overdosing the Percocet his doctor had him on. He was not in his right mind. Violence had already taken place. It could easily happen again.

When we realized we had both seen the same vision, we immediately moved into action to 'save their lives.' This culminated in reporting the 'fight' to the police, and his subsequent arrest. With the arrest, came a ray of hope dependent on the courts remanding him to rehab and into psychiatric care he had avoided to that time. We were relieved.

Now there was a chance he would get help, but then something unexpected happened. A backlash of anger, outrage, and blame was thrown at us from his grandmother, uncle, and father. Even though he lived with his grandmother and uncle (on his father's side), they seemed to be in complete denial about his rapidly deteriorating condition, how violent and angry he was becoming from the drugs, and his substance abuse. Lives were in danger, but they couldn't see that.

Enter A Dark Night

In the days that followed, I felt sure I was going to 'lose him.' Everything had taken its toll. His girlfriend had shared how he had been increasingly morose and suicidal from the prescription drugs, and his already damaged liver had been enlarging in pain with each substance abuse. I knew he was on his way out, but there was no way for me to reach him. He had cut me off.

TheQuest™ helped me release the trauma and fear. This brought me back into my proactive self quickly. In an inspired moment, I wrote an appeal to the court, asking that they please help him by remanding him to rehab, telling them I felt his death was imminent and that the arrest was my son's last ray of hope. I also shared what an incredible person he is. As I wrote, my heart felt like it was being ripped open and seared with intense pain, and this anguish poured into the letter. I wouldn't know till much later, what a powerful effect it had on its readers.

In the midst of this devastating experience, my daughter was rushed to the hospital with a tonsil abscess that alarmed the doctors so much they put her on 'watch.' If the infection moved to her lungs she would die. And then I learned my mother's cancer had returned. As if that were not enough, the stock market was crashing and a major investor in my company took a hit, delaying important funds that were greatly needed for my company. Without them, I didn't know how I would be able to keep on track, bringing my work to the world. I was just months into the launch with my first book and solo music CD. Now it looked like I was being stopped in my tracks.

In that moment, the glorious future I had been envisioning where I was reaching people across the earth with this body of knowledge became uncertain, and I had to wonder if I would be able to fulfill the Destiny I was born to and which I have worked towards all my life.

As the stock market was plummeting, people around me were falling under the weight, frightened or in despair. I could feel everything they were going through to such an immense degree, it was almost unbearable. With the added stress of the planet's financial world coming undone, my only resort was to retreat into silence and do my Self Counseling with TheQuest™.

Over a couple weeks, I had three profound sessions, emerging with such clarity and peace that I was amazed how positive and proactive I felt each day in the midst of such personal and planetary crises. It was an incredible feat to be this peaceful, artfully making my way through so many devastating experiences all at once.

This Dark Night gave me the ability to see the level of mastery I had gained through TheQuest™. Each session brought me to the realization that the immense challenges in my life had been the most powerful catalysts, especially my experiences with my son.

I'd spent years striving to assist my son in his plight, knowing TheQuest™ could make a great difference in his life, but though he had access to these tools, he had rarely availed himself of them. Instead, he had been in the grip of ever challenging circumstances, overcome at times with anxiety, depression, and other mental problems caused by years of substance abuse, dwelling continually in victimhood, and continuing to make life choices that took him further and further into darkness, while I stood by in despair. At these gravest times, TheQuest™ had been my saving grace. The revelations in my sessions helped me realize that he is in the driver's seat and I really have no control over his life and choices. This helped me to let go increment by increment and became an essential key to reclaiming my own inner peace.

A Way Out

The horrendous experiences I've had to endure over so many years with my son, literally drove me to find a way out of the misery, heartbreak, and pain. Through each self-counseling with TheQuest™, I was able to restore myself quickly from the immense stress the worry, fear, and concern caused.

During one excruciatingly painful period in 1999, my son had entered a drug-induced psychosis for months ending up in suicide watch in jail after being arrested for attacking someone. This experience drove me to the brink of a nervous breakdown, but once again TheQuest™ saved me. Here I was going through the worst of what people have to endure and was restoring myself so fast, people around me were amazed. They'd see the anguish, grief, and despair. They knew I was on the edge and then, I'd emerge from my session clear, calm, and directed, making wise decisions that would help the situation or at least, help me to endure it.

An Extraordinary Meeting

In the midst of the latest Dark Night, an extraordinary thing took place that dramatically changed my perspective about my son's plight that had caused so much pain. After my session, I sat under the stars and spoke to my son's soul before I went to sleep. I released his life into Divine Hands, knowing that I must let go, because there was nothing more I could do. He had been released from jail with his trial pending and saw me as an adversary now.

His future was uncertain, hanging in the balance. I knew I could hear at any moment that he had lost his life through suicide, a drug or alcohol overdose, or through liver failure. There was only one ray of hope and that was if he was sent to rehab and I had come to realize, it was in Divine Hands, not mine.

In the middle of the night, I was awakened to an unexpected experience. My son's soul was standing before me, shining with a peaceful radiance. He took my hand and began speaking to me. He said, "No matter what happens, I am ok. I am always in peace. You need to understand that my earth experience is like putting on clothing that I wear for awhile, but these clothes are not who I am. Eventually I will tire of them and return to my Real Self. They give me an experience that I can learn from. The darkness I've entered has helped me traverse a realm that I am exploring that is not part of my True Nature. It is what I've come here to experience, even though you have seen a greater potential for me. This allows me to grow and expand my knowledge and understanding of aspects of the dark side of earthly life. But nothing I go through, nothing I encounter, no matter how dark the depths I traverse or the degree of darkness that overcomes me will be forever. When I leave this earth, I will be restored. I will enter a place of healing and I will study and review my life and all that I went through. I will go over every experience and gain insights and understanding that no other trek could have afforded me."

I wondered, "Does this mean my son is going to die?"

He smiled at me. I realized then, that his True Self had been speaking to me. I saw how often I had been sad, because I had believed he was losing, ruining, or destroying this Self. I was in awe. The Creative Genius that had inspired me so often and which I loved so much was still intact. No harm or ruin had come to him!

A Love That Never Dies

My son's loving nature and exceptional intelligence had made him special and unique. Even though the past 16 years had been interspersed with drug abuse, accidents, arrests, alcoholism, drug induced psychosis, and subsequent mental problems, there had been so many times when we cruised together like eagles, loving being together and sharing deeply about the mysteries of life. We had delved deeply into healing arts and played in multimedia projects. We shared a love that is profound, that transcends time, and spans lifetimes.

This was the person I knew and loved, not the tortured, angry and abusive one who would spew his wrath at me. This was the alliance I believed in and knew was rare to find on this earth. This was the soul connection that had graced my life despite the times he had turned on me and accused me of horrendous crimes that never took place from his drug or alcohol induced delusions.

Though this anger and abuse only took place once a year in the beginning, these episodes had increased in the past two years to such a great degree I knew I was losing him. But, despite all this, his True Self would emerge at times from the darkness. Then he would meet me in this amazing Love we've always shared, the true reality that has always existed between us. At those times he would speak of the power of our connection and that I was the most important person to him in this life, his greatest mentor, teacher, and ally, and the person he's learned the most from. The love and understanding between us would be profound. Each time I would have renewed faith that he would be ok, but then the dark cycle would begin all over again.

To watch his True Nature replaced by a person who was angry, demented, suicidal, and abusing drugs had been too much to bear. Now, from this amazing encounter, I was seeing how many times I had bought into these earthly dramas, alarmed that he would be completely taken over, convinced that if it continued he would die young, and knowing that I would not be able to handle it. It would ruin my life and I would never be able to recover.

He smiled at me and said, "You know how strong our Love is. This love will always be. It is our special bond. No matter what happens, you need to remember, I am eternal. This is but one life in a span of lifetimes, each with their unique experience and learning opportunities. I will always return to who I am. That will never be lost because it is the core of my being and everything else is just experiences I cloth myself with to learn."

I found myself relaxing, but still fully aware this could mean he would die soon. My mind did not want to go there. It was too horrific to imagine. I would not be able to handle it. I would be devastated, feel great despair and regret. I would always feel there was something more I should have done or that I had not done enough. I would have let him down. Because I had seen what great potential he had, I would always feel his death and demise was not right. He had been meant for so much more, a great destiny to fulfill. His death would be too great a loss.

He continued, "You will never lose me. Our love is too strong. We will always be close. This is one moment in an eternity of time." Tears poured from my eyes as his love penetrated my being and for a time I basked in the truth I had always known, that we share a unique bond, a special love that has never been ruined no matter what we've gone through and no matter how many illusions about me have flooded his mind or how horrendously he has treated me, it was never destroyed.

Healing

I became aware of a pervading sadness that had permeated my life and how strongly it had infected me below my conscious awareness. I had caught glimpses of this Sad Soul at times, as had others. In fleeting moments I would look in the mirror and catch sight of her. Beyond my lighthearted personality was this deep secret. I was a sorrowful soul who had barely been able to make it through all I had endured.

I saw her standing before me. She carried a weight that was too much to bear. Her body was bent over and she was in dark colored rags, impoverished by all the strain and strife these experiences had etched upon her life. She had not been able to feel a true happiness all the years my son was undergoing his trials. Instead, she had been in constant fear, alarm, worry, and concern for him. Each sad event had left her troubled and broken hearted. She had also been infected by the suffering of others who had been close to her and by the immense suffering on earth.

This dark element in my psyche had kept me from being truly happy or having an authentic smile from deep in my soul. How could I be happy when my son was suffering and in danger, and when so many people close to me and across the world were in pain? How could I live in a transcendent peaceful reality when they were struggling under such dire circumstances? It was a cross I had been born to carry and with it, a strain that was hard to bear. This part of me could barely handle the suffering in the world on top of all the suffering of my loved ones. It was too much and I had barely made it through. How could I find happiness on a planet when all this was going on? It had finally taken its toll.

He drew closer. "Trust in our love and know that everything I've gone through has been my choice. It is important for me. Remember who I really am and will always be. It is the same with everyone. Each person has this authentic reality they will return to in time. Therefore, you do not need to take on the burden of what they are passing through. You can live in your Authentic Reality as you have been doing, and shine that light upon the world, for this has been a great strength to me. Through everything I've passed through, your strength, your ability to be your Authentic Self most of the time has helped me immensely. I could go deeper and deeper into the darkness knowing I was connected to you and that you were holding in the Light. This gave me the ability to venture deep into the dark side of my nature knowing I would never get completely lost, because you were always there showing me the Authentic Reality that is my innate truth."

He continued, "Because you were in my life, I could never lose myself, even though I lost touch with my True Self so many times. You know this is true, because no matter what I've gone through and no matter how dark I've become or deranged, I have had lucid times where we have communed as we are doing now. I am the part that you've held to, believed in, known was there, no matter how scary things became. You never stopped believing in me for you knew the truth, you know who I really am, and you have never lost sight of me. Because of your strength, because you've held for me through everything, I had an anchor to the light. Because you could see the Real Me, you helped me know it was there."

A shift in perception began taking place within me as his perspective illuminated my mind. I turned to the inner woman, knowing it was time for her to be healed. I could not continue to bring my work out to the world and be the shining light he had acknowledged when she was inside me feeling this way. At last I had found her and now it was time to release her from her pain.

I saw how she had stayed fixated on my son's demise and this had broken her heart. She looked like the pictures of the saints with a sword piercing her heart. Now she was seeing the Truth. She saw that his Eternal Self was unharmed and knew he would come through unscathed, no matter what he went through, no matter how great the darkness, no matter how much it looked like he had lost his soul.

A huge relief rippled through me as she began to lighten. Finally she was ready to transform. She had gained so much from her horren-dous life experiences. She had sought the cause of suffering and found a cure. She had proved this in her own life and in many others, and now she was bringing TheQuest™ technology to the world. If she had not undergone so much, she wouldn't have had such a fire to accomplish all she had or possibly even cared that there was so much suffering in the world.

I emerged from the experience secure in the knowledge that my son and I share a Love that will never die, because it is our truth. Even if he dies young, I can see that we will eventually meet again in the higher realms, once we are back 'home,' and that all will be right between us. We will be restored from the ravages of this earthly life and our bond will continue secure. Nothing that can happen in this world can change that. This has brought me great peace.

Letting Go

I've now let go to an amazing degree, knowing that my son is in Divine Hands. There is a divine part of him that lives forever in a reality beyond this earthly experience, that is always there for him and that he can forever rely on for the Truth.

I cannot deny him his earthly experience, even though I've want-ed so much more for him. Who am I to say what his life should look like? After all, it is as he said, only one out of many lifetimes. Through millennia of time, we grow and learn from our experiences. Each one is unique and important, each essential on our soul evolutionary path for a particular learning. They may seem wrong, but are they really? Maybe everything is always working towards our greater good and we can never lose who we truly are.

The next month I experienced what I suspect others go through when a loved one passes on. You long with all your heart to be with them, to experience the love, the bond, and affection that now is lost to you. I realized, "I'm grieving!" I had lost him, as I know him. He had shut me out and continued on his path in denial about everything. I felt like what everyone else must feel, when they lose a loved one. You hope that it won't be too long until you meet up with them in Heaven... but now I have an inner peace knowing that will happen someday.

I emerged from this experience with a new sense of lightness in my heart. Happiness returned I thought I had lost. I was finally free from the stress filled rollercoaster ride I had lived for too many years. My attention was redirected on bringing out my life's work and taking care of myself rather than everyone else. The biggest miracle of all was that, against all odds, I was able to complete the writing of this book.

One day, I had the most amazing awareness. I realized that what my son had done by cutting off contact with me, was really an Act of Love. It had freed me from more rounds of suffering. It was harsh and sad for me, but it was protecting me from having to witness more of his demise. In that moment, I felt his Presence with me. He was looking at me with so much Love. I felt it enter my heart. It was strong. Nothing we had been through had ever ruined it and nothing can. In Eternity, our bond has never faltered. This is a love that never dies.

A couple months later, I received a call from the Prosecuting Attorney about my son's case. My letter had greatly impacted the public defender, who saw how much I love my son and how desperate I was that he get help. He inspired my son to plea bargain and showed the PA my letter. This inspired her to help, by giving him a year of outpatient rehab, NA meetings, an anger management course, and probation where they would drug test to help keep him on track. For the first time in many years, there was a ray of light!

I could hardly believe my letter had such an impact that the PA was calling me herself. I could tell she was very pleased with the outcome and the role she had played. I expressed my gratitude that she had given him a chance to heal his life, and told her what a beautiful and amazing person my son is. She concluded with, "God bless you."

A blessed light rained over me and I felt there was hope for the first time in years, a chance that he could overcome the substance abuse. In the following days, an inner awareness showed me the future had been altered. A power triad had formed when my daughter, his girlfriend, and I had aligned in support of his soul. In that moment, everything had changed. A new future path had formed and he was now walking on it. Despite the greatest odds and adversity, my son's life was extended. What he does with it, will be up to him, but at least my daughter and I are at peace, knowing we reached out at a moment of great danger, and pulled him back from the jaws of death. Please join me in sending him Light and Healing,... and holding the Highest Vision for him!

CHAPTER THREE

Redemption

I had cruised in absolute bliss for some time, immersing myself in writing this book and feeling empowered and freer than I had ever been from my last healing with the situation with my son, when a new episode began that would call me into another deep and profound change.

It began with a series of emails from a female student from Israel who I will call M. M had recently visited her home country after a year in TheQuest™ Master Counselor and Spiritual Leadership program. She had made great changes as she did the work and had written a glowing testimonial of how TheQuest™ had changed her life. Session upon session, she was becoming free of old programming that had caused a lot of distress and unhappiness, especially in her relationship.

As she reentered the US, she was interrogated by Immigration for six hours while her boyfriend worried on the other side, not knowing what was happening. She didn't have the right paperwork, something I had in the past said she must have, but she hadn't listened. Now she and her boyfriend were blaming me, as I had been the one working on her Visa under the Institute of Advanced Healing so she could be in the US to receive this training.

We found out they had denied her, but for some reason, they had botched up the Institute's new address and we had never received the letter. Instead of taking responsibility for her own actions and waiting to find out the true reason for the denial, she and her boyfriend launched a host of false accusations and character assassinations. This was a hit financially for the Institute and myself at a time when I was relying on this income to support me while launching my life's work.

As the drama accelerated, I went deep in my inner process. Session upon session, I used TheQuest™ to heal my sense of hurt and betrayal, and kept emerging clear and directed, which helped me to write loving emails to help resolve the situation, but they stayed locked in their position. I had just been editing the story by Joe Vitale on Ho'oponopono (see the section on Miraculous Recoveries and Cures), a Hawaiian ritual of forgiveness that Kahuna, Grandmaster Pang, had trained me in. This is a very powerful ritual of release that helps clear negative energies, cuts the aka cords that keep people in negative dynamics, and helps make things right. The Kahunas teach that everything we encounter in life is a reflection of what is going on inside of us. Therefore, our challenges are our responsibility, no matter who out there seems to be doing it to us. This had become the premise of my life's work.

Redemption Through Suffering

That night, I began seeing how all the people who had been hurtful in my life had been a reflection of a part of me that was being mean to myself. I was working with an Inner Aspect that was ready to step into a New Life of greater abundance, happiness, and fulfillment. She was standing in the darkness looking out through a doorway to this new pathway and she was in great pain. She had lived forever this way, being loving and kind while others crucified her. She was punishing herself in this way to 'redeem' herself for her past transgressions. I traced these and found the self-judgments she had carried from all the times she had unconsciously hurt others or made mistakes. This had added up to a huge loss of self-esteem, and had literally transformed a blessed life into a nightmare so many times in my past. Now I had found the part of me that was carrying this pattern, who was enforcing a path of suffering, and who was implementing it with all the strategic success of a military general.

I began traversing the past, seeing each person who had harmed me. People who had stolen from me, lied to me, taken from me without being able to give, men who had abused me, fathers and others who had abandoned me, friends who had turned on me, assassinating my character and turning others against me. As I faced each person and reviewed the painful past I said, "I forgive you. I am sorry. And, I forgive myself." This is Ho'oponopono. A way of taking responsibility for what we draw into our life, and then releasing, letting go, thereby 'cleaning' our past.

I kept feeling freer and freer as the hours passed. Finally I lay down in my bed ready to go to sleep, seeking to find anyone I had missed, and there was more. I woke up the next morning and the Ho'oponopono continued. Interspersed with this forgiveness work I was having huge realizations. I was really getting how each harmful person was a reflection of a part of me, and how I had drawn these situations in to punish myself. I returned to TheQuest™ inner process to work with the Inner Aspect in charge. She was reviewing her life history and seeing how much she had abused herself. She had created grave challenges where she had been heartbroken and cast out. Friends had turned their backs on her and people had treated her so unkindly, while she had been so loving and a true friend to them.

She was seeing how her idea of redemption through suffering had caused her so much heartbreak and pain, and how she had become that idealized martyr that some religions think is the highest offering we can give to God to redeem ourselves. And she was seeing that this was not true, for living such a harsh existence at times had taken her away from the qualities she knew were God, like love, harmony, peace, happiness, beauty, and abundance.

There was also an upside. Through many hardships in my life, I had learned to be good to myself, to be my True Friend, and session upon session, I had used TheQuest™ to heal my past and release myself from patterns that created suffering, never realizing I had forged a way to redeem myself. This was Ho'oponopono, True Forgiveness of Self.

I marveled at how this present horrific experience was serving me, as other challenges had. How the worst people in my life have given me the greatest growth and learning, and if it had not been for them, I would never have found this Path of Redemption, nor been able to free myself of this legacy of pain. Now I was uncovering a crucial piece in my life history, a deep core wounding I never knew was there. This had played out through so many scenarios and people that it is an absolute miracle my pure heart and loving nature stayed intact.

TheQuest™ had over the years restored me from these hits, cleared the deep sorrow and pain they created, and removed the stains from my soul. As I had done this work, I kept feeling younger and lighter, until I never looked my age again. I had learned to dwell in the part of me that is always joyous, alive, and passionate about life, who loves deeply and is a true friend to others and to myself. I had forged a way of freedom that I was sharing with many. My experiences had all served a grand purpose.

Redemption Through Healing

Now I was with the woman in black standing at the open doorway. The New Life looked awesome, a radiant vision of abundance, opulence, and peace. Quite a stark difference from the times of financial constraint and misery she had known.

I longed to step through the doorway and leave this momentum of pain behind, but she was not ready. She wanted to talk to me and so I listened. She said, "I have lived like this forever, for I am in all humanity. I am in women who have suffered greatly in this world, been denied their rightful place and freedom to be all that they are. I have been at the heart of indigenous cultures whose ancient heritage was wiped from the earth until they rose up with all their might to reclaim and restore it. I have been the innocent child who is abused by the father she loves, breaking her trust in men and creating a lifetime of painful relationships. I have been the child who was beaten and who became a violent abuser to reclaim their power. I have been the sorrowful soul who has covered over their pain with substance abuse, the millions who suffered genocide, who have been trampled under and misused. I am the one who suffers and must keep suffering to redeem myself. So my legacy has been written into all the world religions as the path I must take to be redeemed. But now, I am tired of suffering. I am tired of this history of pain. I am tired of being small, manipulated, and used. I am tired of being cast out and made wrong when that is not the truth. I am tired of having every good thing I create destroyed. I am tired of illness, poverty, and strife. I can no longer live this way."

I looked on with great compassion, seeing the many histories and people she spoke of in a living movie that wrenched my heart and tightened my stomach. I felt it all as if it had been me, every last history. And then she smiled with a radiant purity and took my hand. "I needed to show you," she said. "I needed you to know the truth. This is a world of suffering and this is why. It is not that God has willed it so, or that we are prisoners in a hell created for sinners. We have been lost in a wilderness of beliefs that make it so, that create the very reality we would escape from, and we never knew way. Humanity doesn't understand why, but you must tell them. You've come through all of this so that you could show them the way out."

Tears of joy streamed from her eyes as she took my hand. "Now we can ascend this sad movie, for it is time. You've learned enough through this arduous trek. Now it is time to live the Abundant Life that is the Divine Intention for you and every soul on earth. From that new vantage point, you will illuminate the way for others."

She was transforming before my eyes from the sorrowful woman in black to a radiantly beautiful, shining woman who was now stepping through the doorway into her New Life. I sighed with relief, knowing how huge this was. It was one of the most powerful, landmark moments in my life.

I reflected on the cruel behavior of my student and how she had served me to claim this victory today. I saw how everything of a dire nature in this life had turned me to the Light and how each horrendous experience had driven me back to my Self, that bastion of light and love within me. Could the worst people in my life really have been my Saviors helping redeem me from a painful past? Each had highlighted a dark history that had been set in motion by false beliefs so that I could set myself free. All the good people in my life had just left me as I was, whereas the mean people had catalyzed my deep inner work, and that had resulted in victory upon victory. I saw then that they had been the ones who had helped move me into fulfilling my Destiny of bringing TheQuest™ to the world. I was amazed.

A huge wave of relief passed over me and I shuddered from deep within, as the change took place inside of me. I was being redeemed in the only way that is True Redemption, restoring the Shadow Aspects back to their Divine Nature. Standing in that bastion of peace, I can honestly say, I've come home.

I saw my Inner Aspect standing in the citadel of True Authentic Power, wielding a Scepter of Truth that represented all the knowledge she had gained. A golden pathway opened up before her. It felt warm beneath her bare feet. She was in a luminescent long white flowing dress and her heart radiated love out to the world. She smiled from deep in her soul and radiated pure love from her being. She had released herself and was free. I watched this happy scene, as opulent pictures formed around her. This was the Abundant Life, a place of safety and peace where true fulfillment could be found. This was a way in which she could drink in the best of life and also walk a pure and saintly path. This was the true meaning of redemption. As the soul is restored, it becomes pure like snow and I had found the way.

CHAPTER FOUR

TheQuest™ Session That Saved Three Lives

By Kaitlyn Keyt

I had been consciously and physically raising my Vibrations for over a year. One morning as I was getting dressed, I literally heard a voice say, "Today is the day you are ready to heal some major obstacles that are needed to clear, so you may move forward on your purposeful path." I went out into the day expecting just that to happen.

Sure enough, as I walked up to the New Age Retailer booth at the International New Age Trade Show in Denver, Kathy, the editor of their trade magazine introduced me to Aurora saying, "I don't know why but I am suppose to introduce you two. I feel very strong about this. There is an important reason you two are supposed to know each other."

Immediately Aurora and I began to share about our work. When I heard about TheQuest™ I had a strong feeling I needed to experience it while Aurora was excited about my VibesUp Energy Raising Tools. So, off we went to do a trade.

About 2 months prior to meeting Aurora I was at an event where I had someone read my aura and then take a look at my palm. He said, "Oh! There's a fatal car accident!" looking at the lines on my hand, and than gulped and tried to change the subject.

I said, "I haven't been in an accident."

"It hasn't happened yet?" he replied. He looked disturbed.

In the days that followed, I kept trying to get that experience out of my head, but now I know I needed to get it out of something much deeper than just my conscious thoughts.

My session with Aurora was not only life changing, within hours it literally saved 3 lives! I prepared myself for the session by placing a couple of my VibesUP cylinders on the front and back of my heart area. I know that stuck energy moves faster when it is in a higher vibration, and this was the basis of my work, to create products that would quickly raise people's energy.

Aurora was incredibly skillful as she walked me through her process. We went to the root of some core wounds and patterns that kept me attracting more of the same hurtful experiences. Then something amazing happened. As the wounded feminine part of me was being healed, the wounded male aspect that had been in the dynamic with her came into my awareness, ready to be healed as well.

I had for some time been aware of the importance of healing the wounded feminine we all carry, that suppressed intuitive side of us that has been dormant for far too long. Yet I was not aware of the 'wounded' masculine, which is the logical side of our brain. I was amazed as both came forward to be healed and than merged together as a team bringing their powerfully positive sides actively into my awareness. I felt this amazing connection of the two and a renewed whole self.

That night I was driving with my precious family. As the light turned green, I headed into the intersection, but 1/3 of the way through stopped for no reason. A feeling had come over me to stop, which normally would have been overridden by an analytical response from my 'male side,' a pattern I had had for years. It was amazing that 'all of me' was ok with following this inner feeling and holding still in the beginning part of the intersection in the middle of traffic!

Without warning and before I could think about what I was doing and why, a speeding car zoomed through their red light and missed my car by a few feet. Had I not stopped, we would have been t-boned at a very high speed. I sighed in relief, realizing immediately that my beautiful 12 yr. old son would have taken the brunt and most likely would have been killed by the impact because of the speed of the other car. I knew in that moment that I had literally changed my life course in my session earlier that day with Aurora, a lesson in my path I no longer needed to experience, because I had gone to the root and healed it. My rational mind was no longer in total control. Room had been made for my intuitive feminine self just in time.

I remembered then, that I had also been forewarned a year earlier that a fatal accident was showing up in my astrology. It was something I had to be very careful of, and yet I would have met this fate had I not been guided to meet Aurora and have TheQuest™ session, which altered my future before it could take place. When I look at my son, I am so relieved and feel so much gratitude that Kathy listened to her inner guidance to introduce me to Aurora, and for Aurora's help in shifting my destiny that day.

Aurora's life work is so important! I believe it is not just our conscious thinking that attracts events and circumstances into our lives. Healing the root of the old wounds that continue to send out signals attracting back more painful lessons and anchoring us to a life of suffering is vitally important at this time. We are currently in an experience of Body Mind and Spirit. They all affect each other. Raising the Vibrations of our physical bodies and environment is my work and I believe this helps us to attract the perfect healers and synchronicity on our path like I did that day with Aurora.

We are constantly being dragged down by our vibration-polluted airwaves, water, and food, so raising our vibrations is important. When our vibration is high, our healings and conscious work can be far more powerful and effective, helping us journey back to our True Glorious Self.

Kaitlyn Keyt, Founder of VibesUP, speaks internationally on rising above outdated fear based belief systems and joyfully stepping into the Higher Self. In her words, "Our thoughts, emotions, and our beliefs affect our Vibration and what we attract into our lives. Great News! Nature can absolutely help on our Journey of uplifting and healing our lives and our planet."

Kaitlyn has created a fun and powerful line of over 30 natural Vibrational Therapy products. From Vibe Bracelets that tune you into 18 specific energies to Vibrational Therapy Teddy Bears. Her favorite is the Divine Soles, earth energy shoe inserts, which instantly balance chakras and take you back to your natural state of being, helping you see above the fog of your artificial environment and creating space for a smoother healing journey.

For more information see http://www.VibesUP.com. For discounts and special sales, put in code # 216.

CHAPTER FIVE

Doorway To a Cure

When one of my sons was five, the doctor told me he had a serious growth hormone deficiency that could severely stunt his growth. It became a serious dilemma when the insurance company would not pay for the daily growth hormone shots he needed to reach his normal height. The cost was way beyond my ability as a single mother, at $40,000 a year. So, it was a very challenging situation, but I was determined to find a cure.

As with everything I've faced in life, I take my dilemmas to a deeper level. I also use natural healing methods to cure every illness, and had great success with everything my four children contracted over the years. They rarely needed a doctor except for check ups because of the healthy foods, environment, and way of life I raised them in. My natural healing methods quickly cured serious conditions like bronchitis and high fevers, but this was a huge challenge way beyond my ability. My son's body was not producing enough growth hormone to bring him to a mature height and this was out of my league, or so I thought.

One day I felt inspired to take him through TheQuest™ and to my amazement, an extraordinary history was revealed. I was focusing on why he was not growing. What was this block to growth? Immediately, we tapped into an Inner Aspect who was holding a core belief, "I don't want to grow old." The Aspect took us back into a journey through four distinct past lives all with a similar history where my son had died in his early 20's or in his late teens. He described these lives with an incredible clarity, including his name, age, and the regions he lived in, all of which were foreign countries he had never heard of or knew anything about. Even his names were in foreign languages.

His descriptions of the time periods, what was going on there, and what the homes looked liked were uncannily accurate and extremely interesting. In each scenario, he had been swept into his country's drama and had ended up dying young because of war. In this life, his soul was scared to grow old, because he did not want to die young again. So, this deep-seated fear had literally formed a physical condition that was keeping him from physically 'growing up.' Finding the Inner Aspect that was holding this belief system, we were able to heal the pattern.

Subconscious patterns affect our physical reality. At the core of these patterns are the beliefs we took on from misinterpreting our life experiences. These form the patterns that are behind our life challenges. They etch their imprint upon our physical world and body. At the heart of every illness are patterns that are calling to be addressed and healed for the last time, so the conditions they create will stop reoccurring. This then changes our future. We no longer need to go through the challenging experiences our beliefs and their patterns dictate. We can transform them and step free.

Within three weeks of this session, the doctor called with unexpected news. He said, "I don't know why and I am not going to ask, but out of all of my clients, your son is the only one the insurance company has approved for treatment!" I was stunned!

We had cleared the way and now my son was able to receive the treatment he needed. A miracle had occurred from our reprogramming his subconscious. Consequently, the insurance company paid hundreds of thousands of dollars over the next years and my son grew to his normal height. We even had a second miracle after that. A time came when we no longer had insurance and were in the same situation where I could not afford the medicine. The Company was notified about our situation and provided my son with the Growth Hormone for free.

I truly believe that if we had not done this inner work and reprogrammed this belief system in my son, none of this would have taken place, and he would have been relegated to a very different life. Also, years later he entered the Air Force, but scored so high on their test (96 out of 100), he got a higher job and never had to go to war. I have often wondered if our work determined this higher destiny path. We had healed the Inner Aspect who had been set on a course to die young. Had we altered that fate with just one session?

I continue to see miracles from this work that defy reality and yet, when you understand the inner working of the psyche and its power in our outer world, it all makes sense.

CHAPTER SIX

Fat Crippled Orphan Boy With Glasses

Author, James O'brien, PhD spoke of the phenomena of how people become tarnished by life's hardships in his book, *Silver People*. He described how Silver People once were Golden People, but life challenges and painful childhoods changed them to silver. He wrote, "My earliest childhood memory is kissing the cool, smooth forehead of my mother, who had died a few minutes earlier. That's the kind of memories Silver People have. Our hearts tarnish and turn cold when exposed to the tragedies of life. We envy Gold People. Your hearts ignite when you enter the fires of pleasure or pain. So even your bad memories keep you warm."

At the time he was writing *Silver People*, Dr. O'brien had a series of TheQuest™ sessions with me that allowed him to heal many facets of his "silver personality." In one of these landmark sessions, he uncovered the core wound that had turned him from a Golden Child into a Silver Person. His powerful healing is a testimony that Silver People can be healed and transformed, that we don't need to be shut down to where we can't feel, live in pain, or continue the patterns of our past. There is a way out, a light at the end of the tunnel. Even though we may feel wounded, tarnished, ruined or destroyed, we can be restored and emerge unscathed from the worst circumstances.

Dr. O'brien has now passed on, leaving a beautiful legacy of knowledge behind him. He had experienced such profound changes with TheQuest™, he was inspired to share the following story about one of our sessions together. In his words…

My first session… "Wow! Aurora is such a beautiful and magnetic woman! I'll just concentrate and look into her beautiful eyes, and try not to notice the rest of her."

At first, Aurora and I talk about my trust in her and her expertise, and also my fear that I might lose my creative 'edge' if I heal and transform some of my negatively judged parts, whose traumas are important to the book I'm writing called *Silver People*.

I decide to trust that the process will not turn me into 'a boring bland guy from Des Moines,' and go forward, trusting Aurora's guidance. We pray and ask for the help of Mother Mary and all concerned divine beings. I mention including my own Divine Self.

In the session, I identify my 'Fat Crippled Orphan Boy With Glasses,' as the cause of the background sadness and lack of confidence I feel many times. Then I recite a poem about him and how I've judged and not accepted this part of me. Here is the poem.

Fat Crippled Orphan Boy With Glasses

I remember
Waking up each morning
In the boys dormitory
Everyone still sleeping
Except me

Pressing trembling hands together
Fingers flat against fingers
Happiness flooding through me
Thinking, I'm not a fat boy anymore
Only to discover
Sadly to discover
That I still was
What I still was
Fat crippled orphan boy with glasses

Even now I feel him
Wandering deep inside me
Crying deep inside me
Lonely deep inside me
Waiting for me to love him
Still I do not love him

When will I ever love him
Fat crippled orphan boy with glasses

As the years continue passing
Many wives and lovers dancing
Just to share their love and passion
Trying to love that orphan boy

But he waits for me to love him
Knowing that I can't forget him
Though he knows I can't forgive him
For the shame he brought upon me
And the love he drove away

Still he waits for me to love him
Knowing I can barely love him
Waiting patiently for me to say
I love you now
Come with me now
Fat crippled orphan boy with glasses

We discover that my Golden Boy Period ended and my fat period began after my Dad's death when I was 11, and ended at 16, after I was adopted at 15. So "Jimmy", this part of me, was trying to comfort himself with food and get some notice as a bigger guy who had value for that! Since then, Jimmy has been trying to protect me by discouraging me from doing things or going after what I want, so I won't be hurt by failure or rejection by people. He says "hold back, don't ask anyone for anything, don't love or trust all the way with anyone, you can rely only on yourself."

Prayers of Self Forgiveness help me to release my judgment of Jimmy and to have compassion for what I went through and why I went through this period. I find that Jimmy's purpose in my life was to teach me how to rise above such challenges and still be a happy, loving person; to be able to have compassion for people with challenges; and to be able to have many people relate to this story and learn this lesson as I bring it out in my book, *Silver People* and other things I do.

Understanding how important and essential this life passage was for me, I thank Jimmy, who now transforms from the fat, crippled orphan boy, whose job was now over, to the Golden Boy again. I do feel that a major shift has occurred inside me. I haven't noticed that sad/not good enough feeling since. I can easily visualize that golden glow now, and it feels great!

CHAPTER SEVEN

More Miracles With TheQuest™

In the following personal accounts, the miraculous healing theme continues. Through TheQuest™, lives were healed and circumstances transformed. I share them here, because I feel it is important that we understand that no matter what we are facing, the deeper patterns behind our struggles can be healed, and the challenges we face can be transformed. There is an innate part of us that is ever working for our higher good. The more we allow it to manifest its intention in our lives, the more we can live in Heaven on Earth in our own life experience.

- 1 -

My Relationship Was Doomed For Failure

My experience with TheQuest™ has been amazing. I had been doing sessions for about 6 months and I was very changed and, life had changed tremendously too. My relationship with my partner, which is my business partner and my life partner, turned from a dysfunctional relationship, fighting daily, lacking communication, not satisfying and very unhappy to a communicative and more enjoyable loving relationship. My stress levels were reduced about 50% and my business became more successful. I felt more ready to have my baby.

The most amazing session I remember, though each one is amazing since each one solves another "mystery" that was keeping me unhappy, was at the beginning when I realized daily fighting with my partner is not normal.

We used to fight every single day and not once, but two to four times a day. After telling my partner about the session and how I realized I fight with him because fighting was what I used to see my parents do most of the time, most of my life, we realized that his parents used to do the same thing, fight with each other every day.

Both of us were keeping our parents' pattern alive in us. In that moment, we decided we were not going to be like them. We were going to solve our problems by communicating and discussing without fighting. Since then we fight maybe once a week if that. That's after 3 years of only fighting, and many times a day.

Aurora has changed my life. TheQuest™ is something I want to continue to be a part of. I want to help people like Aurora helped me, to show how they can change their lives, resolve their issues in less than an hour, teach them how to do this in their own life, and that's the reason I'm learning to be a Master Counselor. *–Michal Cohen, 2 Year Student in TheQuest™ Master Counselor and Spiritual Leadership Training*

-2-

I Have My Life Back

After years of being in and out of therapy I had changed my life very little but after four of TheQuest™ counseling sessions with Aurora I was a new person. I had come to the first session a Skeptic, but by the time we were done I was totally amazed by the amount of healing that took place.

I had been hitting my head against the wall not getting any movement in my years of therapy. Traditional therapy had only scratched the surface, whereas TheQuest™ dove right into the root of the issue, uncovered the truth, and healed that aspect of my inner self.

The sessions have been the most powerful events in my life. I'm finally free of the unhealthy part of myself that was holding me back for years. I never thought transformation like this was truly possible. I'm no longer a victim of the past and my emotional traumas have been set free. I have my life back! I've made more progress in a few of TheQuest™ sessions with Dr Ariel than I have in years of therapy. *--Lance Koberlein, Programmer, Real Estate Broker, Entrepreneur, Denver, Colorado*

- 3 -

A Miraculous Cure

I had a physical deformity from the time I was a little girl. By continually aggravating the condition through a very active and full life, it became a life long affliction. By 25 years old I had to stop running, a great passion in my life! I also loved to ski, hike, and bike, but my knees would get so sore that my lifestyle was greatly hindered.

During TheQuest™ Life Mastery Training Course in Aspen, I had the opportunity to work with Dr. Ariel. In my session we traced a pattern back to my early childhood where I had suffered severe abuse. This was something I had not remembered and yet, in the session I could see how it had affected my whole life. As we unlocked and healed the pattern, I felt a tremendous release.

The very next day I was working out at the Aspen Club gym when looking in the mirror, I noticed my legs were straight. My trainer came over and could hardly believe his eyes. My deformity was healed! --*Diane Argenzio, Estate Manager, Aspen, Colorado*

- 4 -

Transcending a Pattern

TheQuest™ session with Dr. Ariel was like an exorcism, casting a demon out of my being that was like a leach, sucking the life force out of me, and preventing me from being who I am. After one session, I am a completely different person. I feel differently. My attitude has changed. I definitely have transcended my pattern. I am a whole new being! --*Bruce Travis, Author, Real Estate Broker, Wailea, Hawaii*

- 5 -

Hopelessness Gives Way to Happiness

I had been feeling very sad, almost hopeless for quite awhile, which is very unlike my Nature, and within 24 hours of TheQuest™

counseling session with Aurora, it just lifted! Nothing outwardly changed and yet, I felt happy inside. I had a peace with where I was at. It was huge.

Aurora's healing gifts are very powerful! The energy that had been suppressed inside me came forward and new projects began moving and many new creative ideas were bursting forth. I felt freer than I had felt in many years, happier, and filled with a quiet confidence that had been battered for so long and now was emerging from an ancient cocoon with new shimmering wings with which to soar.

Aurora Juliana Ariel is a rare radiant treasure. Her magnificent alchemical gifts embraced and guided me in a manner filled with so much love and compassion, I felt free, my most profound self validated to emerge and shine.

To experience Aurora's powerful healing work is to sit in the center of an exquisite circle of angels, supporting your soul's deepest wish to transform and live the most exceptional, magical life you were born to live. *--Michele Gold, Author of 'Angels of the Sea', Artist and Musician*

- 6 -

I'm A New Person

After 20 years of being intimately involved in the human potential movement, reading endless material, attending every conference I could, listening to speakers, reading their books, and applying their principles, I was never taken to the places I was told they would take me. They just didn't hold up and I would soon be back into my old patterns without knowing why things were not working for me. Then I met Aurora and started receiving TheQuest™ sessions.

Right away, after the 1st session, I realized there was a deeper place I needed to go to resolve the issues in my life. I learned the importance of finding the root of the problem instead of adopting a philosophy that sounds great but which doesn't eliminate the effect things have had on my life.

My life has changed considerably with the elimination of stress, eliminating guilt and frustration, and knowing I can be completely honest with myself, and those around me. My self-esteem has been restored to a new high. Each day I look forward to meeting new people, making friends, creating relationships, and enjoying new and exciting experiences. I have a new outlook on life that has never been there before, and I am free to achieve my goals and aspirations. I am so grateful for this life changing experience of TheQuest™! --*Bill Mollring, Business Owner*

- 7 -

An Unruly Class of Teens Loved TheQuest™

I met Dr. Aurora Ariel about two years ago and became interested in her work. I asked if she would be willing to meet with my high school class and give them a 90-minute rendition of what she shares with others in her work with TheQuest™.

I have to admit that I was a bit skeptical how this would play out to a group of 20 or so usually somewhat inattentive high school students. She came and met with two of my classes. Both classes were surprisingly attentive and interested in what she presented. All of the students participated, as we were taken through TheQuest™, and many shared their process. I also followed along with the class in the exercise she had designed for that day and was amazed at the insights that were provided to me in so brief a period of time.

After the class had ended, several students stayed after class to speak with her further to find out what more they could learn about her work and to thank her for what they had experienced in that short period of time. The fact that she held everyone's attention with something that was somewhat foreign to all of these students and she had all the class thank her as she left for the day and others asking for more, told me that she was on the right track with the work she has dedicated her life to.

I have not met with or seen Aurora in nearly a year since those classes, but I am sure she has accomplished much with her work and will have many good revelations to share with anyone lucky enough to be a part of her teachings or her work. Her method of going inside one's self and healing past issues or gaining self-realizations is really quite amazingly simple, yet very valuable. Like finding a key to a hidden treasure. --*Brad Onsgard, Aspen Police Department, APD-SRO for the Aspen School District*

Part Nine

The Healing Power Music

CHAPTER ONE

The Healing Power of Music

Today, more than ever, music is changing the landscape of human consciousness. Transcendent and otherworldly, its powerful influence has the ability to change the frequency of the planet and affect the consciousness of humankind for good or ill.

Music has always worked its magic upon the psyche of the world throughout time. It has lifted people up into lofty heights, swayed the masses in reform, and it has also inspired the descent and departure of morality, as individuals worldwide have ventured into the 'Dark Side,' especially in our time. Seen from this vantage point, the power of music cannot be denied. Whether it is used for the upliftment or denigration of humanity, it continues to weave its spell upon our world.

For years I've studied the powerful influence music and media have on the consciousness of humanity and how it has affected the evolution of our planet. The power of media should not be underestimated. It can change thinking quickly and infuse a world with mindsets and philosophies of a beneficial or destructive nature. It can sway the masses and cause great upheaval or advancement. Thus, the responsibility is great. Musicians, as with all producers and transmitters of media, bear an extraordinary responsibility as vehicles of a powerful expression that can alter the way of life of a planet.

Daily, millions of people are affected by sound frequencies transmitted on our airwaves. The dark element on the planet is on the rise and many people are in its grip, while the light element continues to provide healing and respite from the increasing Dark Night. It's like a Grand Opera playing out where light and dark war for the souls of humanity through music that is healing or destructive.

While healing music is soothing a weary humanity and inspiring noble ideas and actions, many people have fallen under the destructive influence of music, not understanding their delicate psyche can easily be tuned to either positive or negative depending on what they are listening to. One must continually ask, "Where is this music coming from? Is it from a higher inspiration or is it the voice of a wounded soul pouring out its pain upon the world and infecting people with its misery? Is it having a beneficial effect on me or is it dragging me down or confusing me with uncomfortable messages? How do I feel when I listen to it? Is it inspiring and empowering me, or is it harmful?"

Sadly, many musicians today are unaware of the power they wield as they infect themselves and humanity with musical vibrations they naively think are harmless. In future time, musicians will have a higher code of ethics. They will understand that conscious media has a profound healing influence and can transform lives. They will lend their musical talent to the upliftment of people in their time.

Similarly, people in the future will understand they are delicate instruments being 'tuned' by sound, color, images, messages, and light to certain frequencies that are having a powerful impact on them. This knowledge will help them naturally choose the higher ones by being careful what they listen to, just as people today have become aware of what is healthful for the body and what is not. Eventually, humanity will choose to partake of only positive and supportive media that is uplifting and inspiring and this will be reflected in a harmonious and peaceful society.

Understanding that Conscious Media can profoundly affect the consciousness of the planet by facilitating positive change in the psyche of humanity, my commitment has been to translate my knowledge into transformational multimedia productions that are assisting the upliftment and advancement of humanity at this crucial time on the planet, through my company, AEOS.

Today, many talented multimedia-activists have come to a similar awareness, resulting in a dramatic increase in healing inspired music and media worldwide.

While destructive music continues to pound the psyches of humanity, the increase in healing music is the Divine Hand that is restoring people at this critical point in time. It is as if a Master Musician is fine-tuning the delicate fabric of the human psyche with music from Higher Spheres. This is inspiring spectacular musical compositions, noble artistic endeavors, and creative achievements in Awakening Souls worldwide as the Global Renaissance expands its borders.

Like a vast Angelic Presence, music is cradling people in its arms and lifting souls from their weary plights, lending its hand to the Awakening. Transcendent stories abound and I share some miraculous ones in the following chapters. Though they, like many others in this book, defy imagination, transcendent experiences have always been the keynote of the greatest compositions throughout time and many great composers have spoken of the 'Music of the Spheres' that graced them with its Illumined Presence.

CHAPTER TWO

Rivers of Life: Music Of the Angels

By Christopher Connolly

In 1993, a series of compositions began to flow forth with an incredible ease that astounded me. Up until then, it would take me four to five months to compose a song. Sitting at the piano that first time, I was amazed when a whole song came to me in one sitting. I had never experienced that before, and the magic continued. As soon as I had mastered each new song, another would come to me in this same way, until I had a whole album of songs.

During that time, I had an incredible experience. I was playing some of my new songs feeling somewhat bored. Finally, I looked up and lamented, "I need a new song!" Immediately one flowed forth. Another time, I was playing the piano when a beautiful new song began coming to me. I was lifted up into an ecstasy unimaginable. At one point, I felt a presence behind me. I continued playing until the full song had come in. Then I turned and was amazed to see not a person, but an ethereal form of light. It was my first encounter with an Angel. In that instant I understood. This was Music From the Angels.

As the album was being prepared for release, I felt shy to stand out before the world with a statement that powerful but Aurora, who was producing the album, was adamant that we honor from whence this healing music was from. Then Time Magazine came out with a statement on their cover about how 75% of people in America believe in angels. I let go of my position and the album was named, *Rivers of Life, Music of the Angels*.

When we released the album in a test market under Aurora's previous company, AngelFire Music, there was a tremendous and unexpected response. People were healed. Grown men were crying when they listened to it. A woman played the album twenty-four hours a day for two months until the CD warped. In that time, her life had miraculously changed. She was released from a long-term abusive relationship, her health had improved and her business had soared. Another woman made it successfully through rehab listening to the music. The stories that poured in had a profound effect on me.

Up until then, I hadn't thought I was a particularly spiritual person. My focus was on other pursuits, but after this album was released, I remembered earlier experiences that I had forgotten and yet, were so impactful they had altered my life course and prepared me for this time.

I began playing music at the age of five when my grandmother's piano was moved into our home. I was very ill as a child, suffering from an acute case of asthma. It wasn't easy for me to run and play with the other children. I was confined so much to home and so, I would play the piano hours on end. While others got good at throwing and catching a ball, I got good at playing everything I heard and loved.

Looking back now, I see that the illness was a gift. It was during that time period that I had my first divine encounter. I was 9 years old, attending Catholic school. One day my classmates and I were in church at the Stations of the Cross. The church was filled with teachers and students. I was focused on Jesus on the crucifix at the front of the church, when suddenly he moved. He was looking right into my eyes and then began communicating with me. Everything went to bright white light and I could see nothing else. I couldn't hear anything around me. I whispered to my best friend Joey who was beside me. "Joey, what are we doing now, I can't see?"

When I heard no response, I whispered, "Joey, what are we doing now, I can't hear." I felt this warmth from my head to my toes. I don't know how long this went on, but apparently I had been screaming all of this and upset the entire service. The children and teachers turned to see what was going on. A nun came to scold me. She told me to shut up and slapped me, at which point I passed out. Seven other children were affected this way as well and were carried out of the church.

My life changed that day. I began to get well and I began to understand and do well in school. Before that day I sat right behind Larry the Chalk Eater in the "F" row. That year I moved to the front of the class. To this day, I believe a miracle happened.

Many years passed and I continued to play the piano and study. While attending California Institute of the Arts and studying under William Douglas, I had my first experience of music coming thru me as if played by another. It was an incredibly moving experience.

I have continued to receive inspired music, which has now filled other albums. Music that I have never heard before pours out of my fingertips. Many times I sit amazed as whole complete pieces of music flow forth with an effortlessness unimaginable. These are elaborate compositions, not just running the black keys.

The music is always very touching and moves me deeply. Whenever a new piece is released, I have visions that come with them. Many times I am moved to tears as the music plays through me. Afterwards I spend weeks and sometimes months practicing them to commit them to memory and learn the fingering. This experience has taught me how to be open to music from higher realms and that humanity is being healed at this time through music.

To order Christopher's Rivers of Life CD
please email info@AEOS.ws

CHAPTER THREE

Harp Magic

By Peter Sterling

It all started when I moved to Sedona, Arizona, in 1990, after I had been living in Colorado for ten years. I was a ski instructor, spending almost every day up on the slopes above Aspen, skiing in the rarefied atmosphere of the Rockies. As I flew down the mountainside I had a vision of living a different kind of life. I had always had a sense of being a creative artist and I always wanted to pursue that dream. I knew I had to leave Colorado and find a creatively uplifting place that would nourish me spiritually. I felt strongly guided to move to Sedona.

I was used to listening to my inner voice. As a young boy, I had a grandmother who repeatedly urged me to pay attention to it. The voice was faint, but audible, and over time I began to trust it. It has taken me on a strange, less-traveled road.

Once I moved to Sedona, people soon came into my life that had very different lifestyles from mine. They lived clean, healthy, spiritual lives, and they became my teachers. I loved hanging out with them, learning about myself, how to take care of myself, how to cleanse my body and have an experience of clarity.

Under the influence of these new friends, I changed my diet. I became vegetarian and started eating sprouts and live foods. I also met a chiropractor that was a very talented healer and a shaman. I had sessions with him five times a week, and he would do incredible things to me in a skillful application of chiropractic practices, herbs, tinctures, and sounds.

At this time, I was living in my van in the canyons outside Sedona. It is an extraordinary wilderness area, very powerful energetically. As I explored these canyons I noticed a marvelous silence there and an incredible presence. I began to spend time meditating, sitting on brick-red rocks by gurgling creeks. As I progressively allowed my mind to quiet, I began to hear what seemed to me the sounds of some kind of celestial music, an angelic choir. My hearing began to alter so I could perceive more. Instead of the third eye opening it was as if a third ear was opening. The music was orchestral, with strings and choir, on a stupendously grand scale, grander that anything I've heard on earth. Many mystics have talked about this, the music of the spheres.

Around this time, I began to feel that this music wanted to come out of me. It needed to flow through me and be expressed. I had never mastered an instrument before, although I'd always been musically inclined and had a good ear for music. I had this musical talent bottled up in me, but I hadn't found an instrument with which to express it. Finally, after thirty-two years, as I listened to this inner music in the Arizona wilderness, I discovered what my instrument would be, the harp.

Immediately, synchronistic events started to take place. A woman had a small Celtic harp she wanted to sell, so she let me try it and at once there was recognition. It was almost like a cosmic connection. The universe cheered and said, "Yes, he's found his instrument." This led me into a period where I was very much impassioned and obsessed with the harp. The instrument had a small little carrying case and each day I would go into the wilderness and play for four or five hours. I'd hike back into the canyons and find a magical place and play for the wind and the rocks and the little animals that lived there.

I took a couple of lessons from the woman, how to hold it and how it worked, but then I just taught myself. I felt that I knew how to do this and that something was trying to happen with me. Within the first few weeks of playing, this melody started to come through, sort of a recognized feeling. I was hearing the inner music and at the same time the music was harmonizing with the harp. I realized that there was some form of energy around me, working through me, and thought it must be angels.

It was around the time of my birthday, and I climbed to the top of a ridge above a canyon and I held my harp up in prayer. I said, "I know you are with me. I'm ready to receive the gift of this music. I offer myself up as a vessel for it."

It was as if they had been waiting for my permission. I sat down and surrendered myself to this powerful force, and began to play. I was totally relaxed and my hands began moving as if I was a concert harpist, as though I had been playing all my life, it came through that strong. My fingers were playing by themselves with a virtuosity that I had been totally incapable of until that moment. It was such a powerful force. So much love and light was coming through that tears were flowing from my eyes.

I began to connect more and more with what I perceived as angels playing through me. I increasingly listened to my inner voice, and it seemed that they were communicating with me, telling me that I was to work with them to bring through this celestial music. At first it seemed so far out that I didn't really understand or believe it. Sometimes I would sit in front of a mirror and play, just to convince myself that I really was playing, it was such a unique experience, I couldn't believe it was happening.

After a while, I asked the angels to show themselves to me. One of the first times I saw them, I was playing at sunrise in the forest. I was walking back to my van and I saw a light hovering above it, about the size of a fist. I blinked my eyes, doing a double take, and as I began to look at it, it got very excited and began to move rapidly back and forth. It did that for a few seconds and then shot up over my head and flew away. It was like a Tinkerbelle kind of thing.

Each time when I went out and played in the power spots and vortexes around Sedona, I would ask the angels to appear for me. I would perceive shimmering light around me and they would begin to take on a form. At night I would see them much more clearly. I would see them flying around in front of my face, leaving little trails like fireflies. There was a whole swarm of them and they would begin to dance in front of my eyes. Slowly they became distinct, and I saw that they were little cherubs; such as you would see on the Sistine chapel.

I still perceive them to this day. They're with us now. They like it when we talk about them. You can catch them in the corner of your eye. You can't see them with your three-dimensional eyes, though. They are in a different dimension.

One of the things I liked to do was to hold out my finger and have them alight on the tip of it. They would hover on my fingertips, looking at me, and I could make out their faces and wings, and I could tell they were holding harps. They were celestial musicians.

After a few months of playing this celestial music, I was guided to Byron Bay in Australia. I met a talented musician there who had a recording studio, and my guidance from the angels was to work with this guy and record some of the melodies that were coming through. So I did that, and I played the songs, and he added strings and flute, and we made a tape.

I remember walking along the beach at Byron Bay. It was a beautiful place with sub-tropical rainforest coming down to a crescent-shaped golden beach that stretched for about ten miles. Dolphins and whales were playing just off the shoreline. As I walked there, listening to the recording on my Walkman, my inner vision opened up, as if projected onto a screen, and I saw myself going back to America and recording an album as a professional harpist. They showed me the whole thing. They showed me the actual CD and that it was in a catalog and that the right people were going to show up to market it. It was all going to be taken care of.

I moved back to Sedona from Australia and bought a bigger harp. I played it for about a month, and then I got the message that it was now time for me to make another recording. So I booked a studio. Before my session I said a prayer and asked for the music to come through clearly. I got into the studio and this powerful energy came into me from the angels and I played from my heart for about an hour and a half. Almost the whole time my hands were moving by themselves. My eyes were teary, so most of the time I couldn't see what I was doing. Some musicians turned up who donated their talent and played some guitar and keyboard. And by the end of it (I worked on it for about a month) I had a little cassette containing eight songs. I colored the cassette labels myself and gave them to a few friends and also put them in the book-stores in Sedona.

In this way, I began to promote and market my cassette, but it was difficult for me to make the phone calls and put the necessary business energy into it. So I prayed to the angels and told them that if they wanted this music to go out, I needed help. I did a little ceremony and a ritual and then I let go of it.

About a week later, I got a phone call from a record company. One of their executives had been on vacation in Sedona and had heard my tape playing in a bookstore. He found my number on the label, called me up, and offered me a recording contract. I could hardly believe that it was happening and that the angels had worked so swiftly and effectively.

I signed a contract with the company for five albums over five years. They digitally re-mastered my cassette and pressed a CD out of it. We called the album "Harp Magic," put a nice cover on it and started distributing it all over the world. Three weeks after it was released it was nominated for a national award - NAIRD, the National Association of Independent Record Distributors. It's like a baby Grammy award, what Sundance is to the Academy Awards.

Many incredible things began to happen. I would get letters from people who would write me and tell me that the angels had healed them with the music, how it had helped them through difficult times. I really believe the angels' energy is present on that record, and that you can have a direct experience of it.

So it's been quite a journey and I'm still on it. A lot of people are having angel experiences all over the world now. I think it's happened at other times, at critical junctures of human history. The angels come as our brothers and sisters to help us through difficult transitions. They influence us with their love and inspire us to go for the light and to go for love. The music has that frequency in it. It can heal people, open their hearts, and create great visions in their imagination. It can inspire them to reach for something higher.

Peter Sterling recorded his first CD entitled "Harp Magic," which won the critics praise for the new harper on the scene and eventually went on to be nominated for a "Naird Indie Award", for the best string album of 1994 - a national honor.

Peter is a metaphysical musician, teacher, artist and healer who is often requested to perform special concerts and workshops throughout the country. On these special occasions Peter will open himself up to the heavens to receive inspired music created spontaneously for the moment.

His presentation interweaves inspirational story with his ethereal harp music that inspires listeners to reach for there dreams and experience a heavenly realm. Peter is also very involved in the emerging field of sound therapy, often playing for the sick and elderly at hospitals and nursing homes.

Peter travels extensively throughout North America sharing his music and story with people from all over the world. Numerous supporters including Doreen Virtue, Neale Donald Walsh and James Van Prague recognize the magic of Peter's music as he often plays for their workshops and seminars.

He is also a featured performer and speaker at Whole Life Expos, Whole Earth Expos and the San Francisco New Age Expo.

His inspiring story has been broadcast over the airwaves on "The Quest" with Peter Weissbach, "Angel waves" with Maureen McCullah, Santa Barbara's television program "Paradigm Shift" and "Bridging Heaven and Earth." He has also been featured in the books, "Insights from the Coffee House" by Jonathan Collins and "Healing with the Fairies" by Doreen Virtue.

For information on arranging concerts and bookings in your area, please E-mail Peter at peter@harpmagic.com. For more information see www.harpmagic.com

CHAPTER FOUR

Renaissance of Grace

By Aurora Juliana Ariel

I was on the island of Maui when songs began flowing forth in a beautiful language that I've come to know as a Universal Language of Love. Night and day I would sing song after song, each one a unique melody. I could sing for hours and then when I would stop, the songs would continue on in my mind. Sometimes they would wake me up at night, they were so loud. It felt like I was waking up from another world where my Beloved and I had been performing and singing the sacred songs. I began to wonder, "Are we traveling minstrels in some other realm as we sleep on earth at night or is this a premonition of something yet to come?"

It all began when I was visiting renowned multi-instrumentalist, Bruce BecVar, in 1997 around Valentine's Day. Our hearts opened to Love, transporting us without warning into that rare and much sought after Beloved Relationship. We entered a transcendent world of beauty, color and light where each moment felt like we were walking in those Vedic paintings, where Krishna and Radha are in a beautiful heaven-like world, jewels strewn at their feet. It was the most grace I have ever felt in this life and it continued day after day without end.

Two months later, Bruce and I performed together at a Healing Conference on the Greek island of Crete. It was my second time performing and something I had never really imagined I would do professionally, even though I love to sing, write songs, and play the guitar. Singing had been something I enjoyed in quiet hours and few people had ever heard me perform.

A few nights later on the Island of Santorini, as a comet graced the night sky alongside a new moon, Bruce began playing his guitar. The melody seemed familiar. Immediately my heart leapt. Somehow I knew this song. I began singing in the sacred language and he joined me. It was the first time these songs were released through both of us. We called it, *Love's Eternal Flame*. Forever one of my favorites, it launched a creative collaboration that led to performances in Hawaii, Colorado, and Sedona and finally, our first album together, *River of Gold*.

A beautiful villa on Maui opened up for us, which we named the Temple Shanti Aloha. There we set up a full digital recording studio and began recording the 'Sacred Songs.' Sometimes Bruce would receive an inspiration and lay down a guitar track. I would come into the studio and immediately the vocals would pour forth. He would then add in dueling vocals, which gave the songs a masculine feminine mystique. Most of the songs came in this way. Instead of us composing a song, learning it, and then recording it, these songs were coming in as we recorded.

I was inspired to set up a beautiful altar in the studio and though I had never recorded before, I somehow knew only to record when I was my 'best self.' That way the songs could come in pure and not be tainted by stress or upset emotions. Course, in those days, I pretty much always cruised in a radiant happiness born of our exquisite love and co-creation.

So often in our world, music has been the voice of human pain and this has not only infected listeners, but also our planet. I've always been sensitive to music and seem to know where its coming from, whether it is inspired from a higher consciousness or from a wounded soul crying out their anger or pain. I've also had experiences of music from the angels in heavenly choirs my inner ear could somehow hear.

It became clear that the sacred songs that were being released through me had a high frequency that I found uplifting each time I sang them. I was continually transported into a transcendent state of awareness and into a world that was loving, bright, and positive. Each time I entered the studio, I would say a prayer and light a candle. Then, after a short meditation to center myself, I would record. Amazed by these recordings, Bruce said, "These songs are coming in with the same exact syllables on every track. This is definitely a language!"

My every session in the studio was a spectacular experience. There would be Divine Visitations and amazing musical synchronicities. The songs poured forth powerful and strong. Sometimes I felt the presence of a celestial music coach who assisted with comments throughout my recording, like how to bring the music from deep inside of me, to relax, open up my chest, and other timely instructions. He seemed to have a Venusian type energy, and was a comforting presence since I had never recorded before.

When I recorded the vocals for the song, *Renaissance of Grace,* the walls disappeared and I became a vast Feminine Presence cradling the world in my arms. Filled with compassion and caring, love was pouring into the souls of humanity through me as I sang. When I lay down vocal tracks for *Love's Sacred Fire,* I was transported to a huge celestial cathedral with high ceilings, and was singing at an altar there. I have often thought this song is a prayer for humanity and the world.

I was told the Sacred Songs are a gift from the Heavens to help with the Awakening and that they contain healing matrixes to infuse the people of Earth with Divine Archetypes and Universal Principles so needed at this time. They are to help heal our world as well as to inspire New Archetypes for the New Millennium.

A couple of these songs made it on our first album, *River of Gold.* Sold all over the world, these two songs received major attention and received spectacular reviews. Surprisingly, not one reviewer asked what language these songs were in, though everyone felt they were transcendent love songs.

Betty Timm of Napra Review wrote, "Heartfelt melodies, true to BecVar's signature sound, explode with joy, vibrance, and unquenchable longing. Masterfully orchestrated, the melodies are accented by beautiful vocals from the artist and Aurora Juliana Ariel. The sweet duet "Journey of the Heart" is a dance of masculine and feminine voices delicately interspersed with exquisite guitar rhythms. As I listen to this and other pieces, I am transported to a land where love and romance abound and the beauty of nature flows through my heart like a river of gold. This recording is deeply passionate, exotic, and simply unforgettable."

We had three fourths of our *Renaissance of Grace* album done when our relationship shifted to a best friendship that remains strong to this day. But with this change came a dark cloud over the project. It began in early 2002, when I returned from my personal winter writing retreat in Mount Shasta so we could complete the album. A dark energy entered the picture, blocking the completion of this album for the next 6 years. During that time, the unhealed wounds in a woman who longed for the Beloved Relationship we had had, but who could never fully win

Bruce's heart, worked her dark magic to block our friendship and stop the album. This was challenging and painful, but through it I learned not only how to deal with black magic, but how to heal it from within. In each session, I found a thread of the Saint Martyr pattern that was traversing my family line and healed it. In this way, this individual was serving me.

The next years were largely devoted to this inner exploration, as I received hit after hit, each bringing its own devastating theme. Finally, after miraculously healing a Death Curse she sent, I stepped completely free from the drama, more empowered and clear than I have ever been in this life. I had mastered a challenging art and had healed a tremendous deep wound caused by Saint Martyr ideologies, which I found is one of the most destructive patterns imbedded in the human psyche and which can be found in most religious doctrines on the planet.

Overcoming my own inner blocks and responsibility in the dynamic, the dark cloud disappeared. A sacred tryst with the Heavens was fulfilled and the gift that had been so lovingly prepared in Celestial Realms was released to the world in 2008. A great victory, *Renaissance of Grace* is available and selling around the world. The Sacred Songs are playing on the airwaves of the planet, soothing the souls of humanity at this challenging time. The reviews are pouring in and all have a similar theme. These songs are having a profound and healing effect on listeners. I end this story with one of the latest reviews by award winning recording artist and vocal coach, Pamela Polland.

"Aurora is one of those rare artists whose clear voice and beautiful music transmit to more than just the ear, but reaches into the listener's heart with hidden healing messages. Coupled with the extraordinary talent of musician/composer Bruce BecVar, Aurora's offering awakens our inner peace and invites our own calm center to bubble up to the surface. Aurora's mystical language is at once exotic and familiar, adventurous and comforting. Renaissance of Grace, as one of the song titles indicates, is truly a Journey Of The Heart: one pleasurable piece of music after another that you will never want to end. The work as a whole lives up to its name."

Renaissance of Grace and other music CDs by Aurora can be ordered at: http://www.AuroraJulianaAriel.com or http://www.AEOS.ws

CHAPTER FIVE

Chosen By a Guitar

By Aurora Juliana Ariel, PhD

I never could have imagined in all my life that something as seemingly inanimate as a guitar could choose a person and want to be with them, but I was to learn otherwise in the fall of 2001. Bruce and I had been traveling all summer in our beautiful RV with my two youngest sons, visiting glorious sites around the northwest. We spent time in Ojai, Sedona and Aspen, hiked trails high up into the Rockies, visited Indian Ruins, and soaked in hot springs. During this time, I kept having a reoccurring experience, where a guitar Bruce had for sale in a music store in San Francisco kept calling to me. Each time this would happen, I would say, "We need to go get that guitar," but Bruce remained adamant he wanted to sell it.

I wasn't sure why I was so compelled to speak so fervently about this, but it kept happening as we traveled on. It was strange, because I didn't remember seeing this guitar among his collection of fine guitars and instruments in our music studio in Hawaii.

When we came to Mount Shasta to drop off my youngest son at a private school he had chosen to attend, I felt a powerful feeling I was meant to stay as well so I could focus on my writing. A beautiful home at the foot of Mt Shasta was offered to my son and me, and soon we were settled in for the winter. Delving deeply into this sacred time, I felt immersed in the Sacred Destiny I was called to, and protected by the Spirit of Mount Shasta. In my daily walks I would look up at that beautiful mountain and feel such a powerful connection and love every time I looked at it.

From the moment I was in Shasta, the guitar began calling even stronger to me. Each day its voice grew louder. I told Bruce who brushed it off as ridiculous. He had returned to Maui and we were completing our shift to Best Friends.

While the feeling was getting stronger each day to get the guitar, I realized that it was worth $7500 and that Bruce was hoping for a quick sale at $5000 and wanted the money. So, I tried to just ignore it. I began to focus fully on my writing and became immersed in a wave of inspired creative expression, but the guitar did not stop calling me. It wanted to be with me and I found this amazing. Nothing like this had ever happened before.

One day I was on the computer emailing friends when the guitar's presence came in strong and said it wanted to give Bruce a message. This is what flowed forth with no edits...

I sit wondering what will become of me
Thrown to the winds and chance
Who will be my next owner?
My Destiny, I thought, was grand
Celestial Music pouring through my strings
Now I wait and wonder

I remember Aurora
Inspired Music and Sacred Song
Illustrious, Illumined, her dedication strong
I long to be a part of the
Sacred Descent of Heaven's Songs
That continually flow through her

So, I call to her softly
In the night she can feel my Presence
In the days I sing to her heart
And now she has heard me

I long for her to come get me
Save me from this useless existence
Sitting in a store waiting
For a new owner who never comes
Because my Destiny is with her!

So I keep calling, hoping she will hear me
Hoping she will arrive to take me home
And now I speak to you,
To open up your heart to see

I was born for this Destiny
To accompany this
Sweet Woman on her Journey
And to travel with the Sacred Songs
To open hearts, to fill minds
with Celestial Archetypes

To Share the New Dream
Laid before humanity
The New Vision from lands fair
Beyond the conscious mind
Realms of Light calling to be heard
Singing to the Souls of Humanity
Masters standing in firm dedication
That this Music will be heard

Aurora's open heart to receive
Celestial Songs of Healing and Peace
From years of preparation she is now ready
From years of service I now join her
Together we bring forth the Music of Heaven

Say Yes to this Destiny
Say yes to this woman who
Has given so much
Who gives her all to Humanity
And whose only purpose is Sacred Service

Say Yes to the Celestial Ones
Who have chosen her
Trained her and Glorified her
That she might be a worthy vessel

Say Yes to Generosity
To Illumined Actions
In resonance with the Divine
Say yes to the Gift of myself to Aurora

Then watch, as Grand will be the Destiny
Illumined and Spectacular
Songs flowing forth
With sweet accompaniment

A Sacred Destiny
Shared with Celestial Ones
Divine Presences who bring a Sacred Mission
Through Aurora and I

I am a Guitar With Soul
My Spirit longs for Sacred Destiny
I call to the Heart of Aurora
I wait for her to come take me home
To this New Destiny

I pushed "send" and days later Bruce responded saying, "Go get the guitar. It's yours." What else could he say! This guitar had a strong intention to be with me that could not be denied. A week later I went to San Francisco to pick up the guitar. The men in the store were impressed that I would be gifted a handmade Loudon.

When they opened up the guitar case, I could not believe my eyes. With its gorgeous dark wood inlaid with abalone, it was my dream guitar, exactly as I had imagined it.

I drove the four hours back to Mount Shasta, tears flowing from my eyes and in awe. What an amazing experience, to have a guitar call to me so strongly, insist it was part of my destiny to bring forth the Sacred Songs, tell Bruce he had to gift it to me, and then turn out to be the dream guitar I had envisioned for years.

CHAPTER SIX

I Heard the Angels Sing

By Peter Sterling

Through a synchronistic turn of events, I found myself guided to move to the New Age mecca of Sedona, Arizona, a move that would change the course of my life forever. Once there, the towering red rock formations and ancient canyons called to me with an uncanny feeling of home. I found myself drawn into the backcountry where I would hike by myself for hours into the ancient canyons of the Anasazi.

Often times I would climb to the top of a red rock ridge overlooking a grand vista and play my native flute honoring the spirits of the ancestors that lived there hundreds of years before. The sound of my flute would float on the air and reverberate off the canyon walls, creating the effect of playing in a great cathedral. As I would walk the sandy trails in silent contemplation, I would listen to the silence and hear the voices of the ancient ones speaking to me in my heart and soul. Words of wisdom and sacred teachings would be given to me, as I would humbly request the Elders to share their story with me. Often vivid pictures would come into my mind as I was shown what it must have been like to live there 1,000 years ago.

As I went deeper into the silence, there was a stillness that descended into my mind. For the first time, the endless chatter began to subside. Meditation became effortless as I would hike back into the silent canyons and find a special place to sit and journey within. The old adage "silence is golden" began to come to life for me as an opening on the inner planes began to unfold. I noticed that the quieter I became, the more a golden light began to appear in my mind's eye. Radiant and warm like honey, this light enveloped me in a cocoon of peace and love like I had never before experienced.

Allowing myself to move even deeper into the silence, I began to hear subtle impressions of what seemed to me to be music of some kind. Faint at first, the more I "tuned in" to it, the louder it became, until I was able to perceive this Divine Symphony in all its glory. The sound was like nothing I have ever heard before. It was symphonic and orchestral in nature, but grander than anything I heard previously. It had the most beautiful melody, richly layered in harmony that rolled on and on and on. It was an unchained melody playing endlessly into eternity that brought uncontrollable tears to my eyes; tears of joy that seemed to wash my soul clean of lifetimes of grief, sorrow, and sadness.

At first I was startled by what I was hearing. I opened my eyes several times and looked around trying figure out the source of this music. It seemed to me to be emanating out from everything around me. Not only on the inside, but also coming from the trees and the rocks and the birds and the wind.

I had read many books with accounts of "The Music of the Spheres." Many mystics have spoken of a heavenly music that is perceived by a spiritual aspirant as they move into higher states of awareness. As this was happening to me, I was keenly aware that I was experiencing some sort of "Spiritual Initiation." I felt the presence of my spiritual guides with me, encouraging me to let go and journey deeper into this experience.

As I sat in meditation and beheld this glorious music, I heard an inner voice that spoke to me and told me that it was safe to let go and travel on this musical sound current. I was familiar with the concept of astral travel or "out of body experience" from reading different books on the subject over the years. And now as I sat there on a rock in the canyon, it was as though the Heavens were opening up to me, and I was being invited into this magical realm.

With my intention, I was able to literally float effortlessly right out of the top of my head or crown chakra. As I did this, my inner vision opened up simultaneously, and I was able to perceive, to my astonishment, angels floating right before my eyes. I couldn't believe what I was seeing! I tried to clear my mind of any self-created images, but they just stayed there in front of me looking at me and smiling. As their images became more distinct, I was able to perceive that they were Cherubs. Cherubs are the little chubby baby-type angels that we see so often depicted in Renaissance art. They were playing instruments like harps, violins, and flutes. And the music they were playing was the same music that I was hearing before I ever laid eyes on them! There was a whole flock of them, and they flew around me with great excitement as they beckoned me to come with them on a journey into their world.

Soaring and flying through iridescent prismatic colors, I followed my angel guides as they led me on a journey into the angelic realms. The feeling was one of pure joy and exhilaration as together we flew through one realm to another of indescribable beauty. If you have ever gazed into a beautiful quartz crystal with a colored light illuminating it and let your imagination explore the interior of it, you might get an idea of what this was like for me.

Eventually we came to a place where all I saw up ahead of me was a luminous sphere of radiant light that shone like 1,000 suns. The light was so bright that I had a hard time looking at it. But the energy coming off of it was one of pure love that penetrated me deeply into the very core of my heart and soul. I was drawn to it like a moth to a flame, but my angel guides held me back. It wasn't time for me to merge totally with this luminous sphere of flaming love. As I continued to gaze upon it with squinting eyes, I began to see, radiating out in all directions, more angels of every imaginable shape and size. There were multitudes of them, and they were all singing praises in perfect union and harmony to this light, which was the source of all things. I was shown that this was the source of the music that I was hearing and which my angel guides were playing.

They told me that in reality, there is only one song, and that this one song expresses all the love, harmony, peace and oneness that emanates directly from God out into the far reaches of every corner of the universe. This was the "Song of Creation," they said. I was told that there was a time when all the beings on earth heard this song and sang it with one another in perfect harmony. This was back in the time of the Garden of Eden before the fall. But in the present time, most beings of earth don't hear this celestial music anymore. The result of this is apparent everywhere as the people of earth feel disconnected from the source of all things.

They told me that now the volume on God's heavenly music is being turned up so that once again the people of earth can hear this divine symphony and come back into a state of love, harmony, and peace. They called it a "Clarion Call" to the souls of earth to come home once again into the Love. They showed me that this is the grand movement of energy in the universe, and that this is going to happen whether the people of earth want it to or not. The term they used to describe it to me was "Ascension." The Love and light is increasing everywhere as God calls all his/her children home.

CHAPTER SEVEN

A Music Destiny

By Caitlyn

An incredible destiny brought my Beloved and I together. During our individual music tours worldwide, Sika and I met in 1994 at the Glastonbury Music Festival, UK, amongst 250,000 people. We began playing music together straight away and also realized we shared the same vision, to create a multi-media music concert that would tune people into the wondrous, delicate and sensitive planet we all live on. This experience would be designed to stimulate all the senses, to take us close to the Spirit of All and to the heart of nature, and to bring awareness to people about living harmoniously on the earth.

We took photos as we traveled across the States, Hawaii, Australia, New Zealand and Britain of beautiful wilderness and sacred places. At our first concert together in New Zealand we ran our slide show and played our music. We were so immersed in the show that when we stopped for an interval, we realized we had been playing for two and a half hours! We had entered the Dreamtime and literally had no concept of time.

In 1996 we recorded our first album together, "Earth Album," and no sooner was it in the shops, we began working on our next project, "Ancient Land." Our creativity just flowed non-stop as did our travels while still keeping in balance our horse treks and living in nature.

We began performing at music festivals and holistic health festivals playing either ambient dance rhythms or calm, relaxing music. We give people a taste of life in the wilderness, close to some of the more remote places on the planet, expressing our experiences with powerful rhythms of the Earth on drum and didgeridoo, highlighted with enchanting vocals and melodic flutes. Many different instruments come to us bringing new sound and rhythm, such as the mbira from Africa, ocarinas and panpipes from South America and the 12 string guitar bringing a Celtic feel to our music.

Our newest creations have been our two beautiful children. After our first child, Shemaya was born, we wondered if it would change our relationship to music ~ it has. I find it has enhanced it and brought my vocals and song writing to new realms. I did take some time off performing when Shemaya was in her first months, although some people have been at our concerts where she was peeking at the audience from the backpack as I danced around at the keyboard!"

Our third album together 'One World' was released in 2002 and soon became our bestseller, launching us into a new era. With its catchy intro title song 'One Family' with guitar, didj and vocals, it brings a message of hope and unity, reflecting our relationship with each other and the planet.

Family life is important to us, as is living in the community here in Golden Bay, New Zealand, amongst like-minded people with so much love and support. It is fun to dance and celebrate, as we really are all One Family, the whole world over! The cover has a blue spiral of Koru with fractals within it because we wanted an icon to show oneness. One of the reviews on it said, "This album is magnificently produced, musically and graphically, typically light in energy, it has some up-tempo songs, such as 'Spiritus' and 'Jungle Dreaming'. Caitlin's lyrics are truly positive and inspiring."

In 2002 at the Vision NZ festival in Golden Bay, NZ, the Jungle Gypsies were born. Aimed specifically at teenagers, the Jungle Gypsies are charged with super-natural powers to enable them to be peacefully active in saving the planet from destructive forces. We saw so many young people who were aware of things that are not helping the planet, but they often felt completely despondent and unable to contribute. So we created this new culture of dance music to bring together a sense of unity and of solidarity. Music and fashion are important for kids, and so the Jungle Gypsies are spreading across New Zealand and England, as more and more JG's emerge.

One of the lyrics is, "All you have to do is drink some of the magic water that gives you back the Power, then you are just empowered to do the work, looking after each other and the Mother Earth, no more of this feeling alone and helpless." We found the Jungle Gypsies have fun 'Being True and Honest.' There are plans to make T-shirts and hats so that we can recognize each other. I think the fashion will naturally emerge from the kids. Sika and I were excited to create a movement for the young people who will soon be leading the world, to help create a positive future and give the kids back their Power! We teach them that each one of us needs to take responsibility for our own lives in ways that benefit the whole.

For the next few years, we continued our tours in the UK and NZ, missing our USA visits as the UK and NZ felt safer places to be in a world of chaos. Then, as our farm grew with new arrivals in the animal realms, we began to stay more in one place than ever. One World One Family inspired us to become more involved with fundraising projects as we see an increasing necessity to help our changing planet. Then 2004 and 2005 became home building time where we were busy converting our barn to a house and studio. Eight foals along with our new baby, Jaya Kim, were born.

Those who had been following our concerts heard an influence of mantras coming through the music. Early visits to Hawaii and Ashrams and monasteries in the UK an NZ taught us songs in Sanskrit and, inevitably, a new album of these mantras was released in June 2004, Laxmi's Dream, which was my latest solo. The piano is my first and most loved instrument and this appears on the album along with the 12-string guitar and didgeridoo, upon which sit these powerful and sacred mantras, sung layer upon layer. Meanwhile we continued booking up new concerts and festivals and began work on our 'Gaia' project.

I first received the vision of the Gaia Project during a talk by Ecologist, Stefan Harding. He described the way the Earth, Gaia, is alive and the dance of all the living parts interrelating to maintain life, as we know it. His talk was like Tai Chi, a dance full of beauty, merging science with spirit. I saw a vision of a CD of dance music, with voices over the music explaining the Gaia theory. When you've had it told to you, it changes the entire way you see things. I thought, "To get this wisdom whilst dancing would really be good for the planet!"

The Gaia Project is going ahead. Already four of the worlds leading experts in Gaia wisdom have agreed to share their knowledge and record their voices. We are composing the music now. A Mouri Stone has been found by Barry Brailsford and blessed in a ritual that holds the Mana of the project as it is being created. We continue to distribute our own works, which are ten albums to date, as we feel this gives us the freedom we desire. We are the keepers of the dream. May our story inspire others to follow theirs.

Caitlin and Sika are live performers and recording artists. They live in Golden bay, New Zealand for 9 months each year and in their homeland in the UK on the ancient moorland of Devon for 3 or 4 months. They perform at music festivals and holistic health festivals as well as their own concerts, often with a slide show of sacred sites and beautiful places in nature around the planet. This creates an exciting crossover of relaxing, soothing sounds of vocals with positive, uplifting lyrics, flutes, didgeridoo, percussion and guitar, keyboard or piano; as well as their ambient dance music with trance sounds of dynamic rhythms on didgeridoo, drums and keyboard drum patterns.

Caitlin and Sika are portraying their message of love and living at one with nature. In their words, "Our vision: everyone caring and living in harmony with planet Earth. ALL LIFE IS SACRED." For further info on their albums and world tours, see http://www.caitlinsika.com

Part Ten

Violet Love, Sacred Destiny

CHAPTER ONE

Violet Soul Love

Throughout time, love stories have inspired people to nobler heights and have positively influenced music, books, films, and art. These stories have set the standard for love in each time period and expressed the longing for love's fulfillment in each culture.

In our time, relationships have entered uncharted realms revealing grander potentials than we have yet realized. Creative Shared Destinies draw souls together for a higher purpose, and we are seeing this with many couples worldwide who are positively impacting the planet.

Love has been heralded as the most powerful force in the Universe. It catalyzes positive change in everyone who has been graced by its presence. Beloved Relationships speak to this Divine Blessing as souls find each other and enter heightened states of awareness to live more rarified lives. The transcendent quality of love is so all encompassing; it never leaves us the same.

The search for the Beloved has become a search for wholeness, as souls come together to minister a powerful Soul Medicine only the Beloved can provide. This Sacred Initiation of Love takes the Beloved into the deepest parts of the psyche where lost soul parts who were fragmented from painful experiences in love can be healed.

In going to these deeper levels, relationships have become powerful quests to wholeness, allowing couples to advance forward at remarkable speeds on their Path of Soul Evolution.

When we take this Journey of Love, we are catalyzed to realize our greater potential. Traversing the depths we find our Authentic Self, its hidden talents and gifts awakened by our Beloved. We are gifted the grand opportunity to cleanse ourselves from our wounded past, and to step free, more empowered, openhearted, and free.

This sacred tryst allows us to give of ourselves unconditionally, to practice patience and offer compassionate understanding to others. This is Love in the Highest Degree.

CHAPTER TWO

Journey of the Heart

I have been very fortunate in this life to have loved very deeply and have been graced with the most transcendent love experiences. Though all of them have not been easy, it is my love relationships that have given me the most growth and which have provided me with insights into my psychology from my deep inquiries. They have inspired me to traverse ancient wounds, which allowed me to come more fully into my Authentic Self.

Many people have told me they have never found love. I believe that true love begins within. We must heal all the reasons we have closed our hearts and stayed protected. We must release ourselves from our painful past so we can love fully. If we don't, love can pass us by and we may never know the great offering love would gift our souls.

We must be brave in this world to love again, for we have all been hurt at one time. We've felt the sting of disappointment and the pain of rejection deep in our souls. But we cannot leave those wounds there, or they will continue to fester, creating unhappy relationships in our future. To trust others, we must trust ourselves. We must learn to be there for ourselves in a way that is truly loving. Then we will be able to love others.

One of my favorite relationships was with an amazingly talented internationally award winning chef from France. The mix of his French with my Italian created a very romantic relationship that fed my soul and nurtured my spirit. What I also loved was our ability to go to the depths supporting each other in the deepest healing through the Soul Medicine we brought each other.

This aspect of love is the most misunderstood, causing great pain. When we understand that the Beloved Relationship also brings with it the opportunity to come into greater wholeness, we can use every challenging experience to our advancement. Thus, the unconscious actions of our Beloved will trigger up our next piece to resolve from our past history. If we follow this course and heal our inner dynamics, we come into greater understanding and ability to love unconditionally from the depths of our being.

Though I share a shorter version of the following story in book one, *Earth 2012, The Ultimate Quest,* I feel inspired to give it in its entirety here, for it speaks to the importance of healing the schisms in our psyches, and that when we do that, our relationships can reflect our higher nature. The result is the most exquisite love.

CHAPTER THREE

Soul Medicine: A Gift from My Beloved

T In 1994 I arrived in Aspen, thinking I was going there to write my book, but my vision of long silent walks and hours of writing, inspired by the tall majestic mountains, dissolved when I met a beautiful man from France. Immediately our soul connection was undeniable though our relationship defied age, history, and backgrounds. He was much younger than I and had been raised in a completely different part of the world with different ethics and values.

The day after I met him, I was sitting in town, reveling in the illumined energies of TheQuest™ session I had just given. The sun was pouring its warm rays upon me and I felt a great sense of peace. All of a sudden I felt an electric current passing through me from head to toe. Immediately, a voice began speaking to me in the soulful tones I was used to from the Heavens. She said...

> The Beloved is an experience rare
> It blossoms in its own accord and timing
> No one can seek and find it
> It is bestowed as a Heaven Gift without warning
>
> You have traversed the Solitary Path for some time
> You have sought the deep sanctuary of self imposed exile
> Now, you are venturing out into the world of fun
> Sacred Romance and Sacred Sexuality
> Important steps to guide you into
> Soul Fulfillment on all levels

This is the Season for Love,
For Play, for Romance, for Fun
It is not a time of Solitude or for writing
It is Summer! A time for Vibrant Living and
Coming into a Fuller Embodiment of your Self

In this backdrop of simplicity
A new Wealth and Realization of your Value is born
First from within, like a Phoenix rising from the ashes
Your Inner Self arises and manifests Wealth before your eyes
From Diminishment to Wealth
You rise into your full Power and
Blossom fully with many gifts to share

Your writing cycle begins out of the Solitude and Peace
You have attained through Love and being cradled in Wealth
Your Destiny arises, different and more simple
Than your imaginings or momentums, and
Actions for Destiny fade away in Love
Out of Love, a New Destiny is born

The Past is behind you, Beloved
A New Life beckons
Radiant and Awe-inspiring to your
Simple Soul Existence at this time

This is the Glory and Joy of the Heavens to
Bestow its Magic and Gifts on your Soul
Be at Peace! The Gate is open
Enter now the Sanctuary of your Life... True Love

I wondered at this amazing message and its import. Was I really
here to find love? Was my plan to write really not the reason why I had
been drawn to Aspen this summer? I wondered about the man I had met
the evening before and the great synergy we had. Could he be the one?
The next days revealed that he was definitely the one she had spoken of.
With this sacred message in my heart and the great love that was being

awakened, I felt a new sense of joy filling my being.

From the first moment, he wooed my heart, taking me on a gourmet picnic in the heart of the mountains by a stream, to swim in hot springs under a star filled sky beneath the full moon, and made chocolate crepes with fresh raspberries for my breakfast.

Within days we were exclaiming our love for each other. That began an exciting adventure where we explored all the things we both love, travel to exotic locations, new cultures, healthy gourmet foods, music, and concerts. Our relationship was filled with excitement, love, passion and an exceptionally high degree of romance inspired from our Italian and French natures.

He picked up TheQuest™ quickly, which blew my mind. After two sessions he began giving me sessions back. Whenever I would feel upset he would immediately ask in his beautiful French accent, "Would you like me to give you a session?" So began a great synergy and partnership that traversed all levels.

Around the same timing, my son, Aradeus, began training in TheQuest™ and started giving me sessions as well. So, it was both of them together that opened the doorway for TheQuest™ to be shared with the world, which at the time was a vision I really at that point had no idea how I'd accomplish. Watching the principles and practice of TheQuest™ transfer so easily was exciting.

All summer, I felt a deep sense of fulfillment on all levels. My new relationship was showing signs of having great potential. My heart was happy and I felt a great sense of unity and purpose. I wondered at the spectacular nature of life to bring me a relationship out of the blue, when I had been so focused for three years on a solo journey to bring my life's work out. I guess it was time for Love and I was immensely grateful for such an unexpected gift.

CHAPTER FOUR

A Harsh Note Appears Without Warning

Some months had passed since meeting my French Beloved. We had journeyed to the island of Maui. I was excited to show him the many facets of the beautiful island jewel in the Pacific Ocean that had been my home for seven years. We explored all the sights and had snorkeling adventures with turtles. We hiked back into the mountains and spent the day lovemaking by a stream. We enjoyed the rich foods, colors, and sights of beautiful Maui. We were lovers in Paradise, reveling in the magic and beauty that was everywhere around us and then, without warning, a harsh note began.

The waves were gently flowing onto the shore. White ripples upon a vast turquoise sea. Palm fronds rustled in the breeze. Lush green mountains with flowering jungle growth loomed overhead. It was another glorious day on the island of Maui.

As inviting as the warm sparkling water seemed, I sat on the shore immobilized by pain. My beautiful adventure with my beloved had turned into a nightmare and I was completely heartbroken and shattered. Turning within, I began my familiar inner journey into the heart of the pain, TheQuest™ once again, my best ally. Soon I was a three year old, standing before an angry father. The scene revealed a devastation as a child I hadn't remembered and with it, a deep wound that had never been healed. It was the beginning of a pattern of abuse.

In my second relationship, as I earlier shared, abuse appeared without warning, but I did not have the skills to effectively deal with it then. After it took its toll on my life, I got the strength to leave the relationship, but had not yet healed all the underlying causes. There was one more piece and that opportunity had now appeared.

Without warning, a harsh note had entered our beautiful love.

My Beloved became cruel, angry and harsh, his judgments cutting deep into my open heart. His tirades made me tremble. I could not believe how such a beautiful love had quickly become such a painful nightmare.

The Beloved was administering his Soul Medicine. His upsets were opening the caverns of my psyche and letting me look at the devastation within. An early childhood I had not remembered was revealed, which had scarred me indelibly, infecting future relationships. Each angry episode, I would enter my next self counseling session, and would be taken back to review another sad history when I was one to three years old. Sometimes, I would revert even further back to the womb.

Now, three weeks had passed and I was sitting beside the ocean, stunned by what had been taking place in the relationship and deeply saddened. My heart broken, I entered yet another session, a now familiar journey into an unknown past, where my earliest years were further revealed. That which had been hidden my whole life was now in view. The pain in my relationship was uncovering the mystery of why I had drawn in abuse again, each session giving me the next piece to the puzzle of my life. But I did not know in that moment what a powerful and profound journey my relationship challenges were meant to be.

Returning home, I sat with my Beloved and shared my heart from a neutral, centered place. I could not continue the relationship as it was. I felt empowered to say 'no' to abuse, as I had had been called to do in my 2nd relationship, and after that I had assisted many clients to say no as well. I feel it is our responsibility to take this stand to end abuse on earth, and that it is time for humanity to address the inner wounds that have created suffering like this in our world, so that they can be healed for the last time. I was intent on doing my part.

Greatly saddened, my Beloved cried. He did not understand why so much anger was coming up in him or why he would treat me in such a cruel way. We decided to get to the heart of it, sharing TheQuest™ sessions over the next two days, each of us taking turns lovingly facilitating the inner journey for each other. What we discovered were the answers to our destructive dynamics, in patterns that went back into our early childhoods and beyond. As we healed our inner wounds and ended this patterning, we both stepped free, realizing we had taken our relationship to a whole new level. We had moved through a cycle of abuse in rapid time and had emerged on the other side, illumined and free. An exquisite light was radiating from us as we returned to Love.

It was Thanksgiving Day. We stood together, united and victorious. I was excited by what our inner work had accomplished in so short a time. We had proven a way for couples to move quickly through the most devastating impasses and restore their love. The future stood bright before me. I was now even more ready to bring forth my work on TheQuest™.

Over the next year came opportunities to address different issues that were arising, nothing so dramatic or disastrous as our three week abuse cycle had been, but certainly worthy of further sessions. I was continuing to unlock the mysteries of my early childhood, uncovering my once hidden history from 0 – 3 years old. Through this inner work, I could now understand how I had drawn in abuse from that early wounding. My soul wanted to heal it, so it brought in abusive experiences.

That I was programmed for abuse was a shock to me, as the only memories I had up until then, were of the idyllic childhood I had spent in Malibu, California. Living in a spacious oceanfront home, I was a nature child, always on the beach or riding my horse in the mountains. I could play alone for hours, writing stories or building a city for my trolls. My favorite adventure was to gallop my horse along the shore or to ride up to a hidden mountain pond where my horse would swim over his head with me on his back. These were incredibly happy years.

My mother had remarried when I was three. Her new relationship was peaceful and harmonious, creating a happy and stable home. When her new husband legally adopted me, my birth father faded out of the picture and I was never to see or hear from him again until I was 16.

Later, when I encountered the abuse that almost took me out of this life, I could not understand. My childhood had been so wonderful and my parent's relationship so harmonious, how could I be experiencing something less? I didn't have the tools back then to discover the reasons why until I went on my healing journey and began mastering cutting edge counseling technologies. I had tapped into the Saint Martyr Pattern, which was the important thread for me to pick up at that time. Now I was finding another piece to the puzzle. All the threads of my life were coming together like a beautiful tapestry that I could finally understand and this gave me peace. Feeling complete from my inner explorations and profound healings, I did not realize that we were yet to go through one more series of trials. The Soul Medicine was not complete.

CHAPTER FIVE

A Call To A Deep Soul Healing

My boyfriend and I moved to Puerto Vallarta the winter of 2005, a gorgeous location I had chosen to work on my book. Stressed and worn out from the move, we were both exhausted and not our best, the perfect alchemy for more inner work. A lot of rage began coming up in my Beloved while I did not take it well. This created an explosive situation to where I was quickly becoming a nervous wreck, my body shaking from our intense interactions.

The oceanfront 'luxury condo' I had thought I had rented, was run down to such a degree, I could not live in it as it was. However, with its gorgeous turquoise tiles, white walls, and private hot tub on the deck, it had promise. I decided to fix it up rather than try to find something else. In the meantime, my Beloved had not found his own place yet and moved in with me, though I had felt I needed my own space to finish my book.

Amidst long days of replacements and repairs, with workmen underfoot and trying to wade through a new city and foreign language, my Beloved became increasingly unhappy with me, while I was exhausted from the overload of work and frustrated because I was not getting to my book. Blasted many times by his outbursts, I would shut down or retaliate and cause a scene. With all the pressure, hard work and challenging dynamics, I felt I was coming undone.

To survive and get to my book, I decided I needed to change the relationship to friends, stating as I had the year before, that I could not allow abuse in my life. My Beloved responded with so much remorse, it touched me deeply and brought me into a new understanding and level of compassion for the 'abuser.' He wrote...

My Dearest Beloved,

I want to say my true feelings. I want to apologize from my heart for all the bad things I said to you. Why all that came out of me I don't know, but now I feel really horrible, sad, and my body is shaking badly. I now can understand what you are going through!

I really believe you are an exceptional person, very hard to find on this planet, and really beautiful inside and out. I hate that I wrecked my chance to be with you. The truth is, I love you. I'm really in love with you, your body and your soul, and everything that you do. Life is so much better with you.

All the times I was mean to you, it was like there was a demon inside of me. I certainly have some issues. In my other part, the good part of me, I don't want to be like that, but the mean part has been more strong than my nice part.

After I treat you like that, my good side steps in and says, "But you love her," but then my bad part continues. I would like to be able to control that part, but it is so strong! It comes up so fast in me. But when it's all over, I always come back to the same conclusion. I love you! I can't live without you. When you're not around I feel so sad and alone. I miss you so much already.

This morning I went on the beach and tried to play in the ocean to forget about you but it was an impossible mission, because you are always in my heart and mind. I would like to resolve forever my issues, so that I can return to the Love and harmony with you. Please forgive me for everything. I love you.

Having more compassion and understanding of each other, we turned once again to TheQuest™. The deep inner process took me from feeling devastated and being a nervous wreck to peace within an hour. It took him from being angry and abusive to understanding how he had kept his feelings pent up over a long time. Too loving to express these emotions when he was younger he had held them in, and then covered them over with pot. Now, with the intense situation we were in, and without the marijuana that he had used to check out of his emotions before, he could no longer keep it in. The volcanic explosions were finally letting these hurt feelings out.

Over the course of three days, we dipped deeply into our past, healed more ancient wounds, and emerged radiant and free. We realized that we had gone through that similar cycle exactly one year before, the same month and the same timing, ending on Thanksgiving. Now, one year later, we had been called to pass through the next level of healing.

This was a profoundly sacred passage for me. Deep and powerful, it changed my life. I felt I had finally lain to rest the once hidden years of early abuse. By changing the patterning within my subconscious, the cycle of abuse had immediately ended and a new radiant picture emerged. I was shown how powerful TheQuest™ work is in healing seemingly impossible and severely painful dynamics between couples and that I would be teaching this in the future.

In the past, I had believed the best I could do for my 'abused' client, was to get them out of the relationship and away from the 'abuser.' The abuse I had suffered earlier in my life had led to an incurable illness. Because I had not done the inner work, there was no resolve. I did not have compassion for the abuser. My experience and the research I had studied told me that abusers are usually in denial and blame everyone around them, never taking responsibility. Therefore, they seldom changed. I had seen this repeatedly. In those cases, the best that could be done was to get the abused family members away.

Now I had a very different picture and clearer insight on how abusers could quickly heal their suppressed anger. Through TheQuest™, they can end the cycles of their abuse. Their mates can also take responsibility for what they are drawing into their life and heal their part. In this way, both people can be healed and the love and harmony restored. This was an amazing discovery. I was very excited.

Once again, I had seen the truth from the inside out. I had suffered what many people have had to endure and I had found an answer, a way out through TheQuest™. I then understood the importance of this cycle and why I had taken on the patterns I had as a child. I needed this experience to further develop my work and bring it out to the world in a way that is easy to apply.

This passage helped me to further perfect TheQuest™ process for couples and gave me a greater compassion for those who are angry, violent, or abusive. My Beloved paved the way through his courageous sessions. As we went deep into the psyche to find the answers behind his rage, we had uncovered a beautiful child who had learned how to hold his emotions inside. This gave me the ability to look beyond the ugly contorted face of abuse to the wounded child within, a very necessary piece for my work.

Through my own retaliation and part in our plays, I realized that within us all are emotions that have been pent up from the pain we carry from our past. Add in just the right amount of stress and challenging circumstances, and anger and rage can quickly come bursting out of us, like volcanic eruptions. We can all lose our tempers, say unkind things, and afterwards feel an immense regret, but when this behavior continues over a period of time, it can greatly harm our loved ones.

Experts have determined that verbal abuse suffered over time has the same effects the torture in POW camps has on their victims. The stress is the same as physical abuse, even if it only psychological. Because we do not see the physical effects of psychological abuse, it is considered less insidious. The truth is, these scars can last a lifetime and people are never the same.

People who were abused as children, will cycle in abusers as their souls try to heal the early childhood wounding. When they do not have the tools to heal the reason why they have attracted abuse, the new experiences add to the wounds they've already accumulated. Their lives become shipwrecks on the shores of life and through these experiences, many feel their chances at love are ruined.

It is such a joy to be able to bring this understanding to a planetary dilemma that has infected millions of lives and to show a way out of yet another source of misery on this planet! It is so fulfilling to know that with these tools, couples can now work through their issues quickly, heal the wounds from their childhood past, and change the detrimental inner programming that is wreaking havoc in their relationship.

At the deepest level, the truth behind every relationship is love, no matter what is manifesting in our outer experience. Today we can unlock the mysterious challenges in our life, heal seemingly impossible relationship dynamics in but a few sessions, and alter our future course. We can clear the way for more harmony and peace in our life, by ending the cause of suffering and abuse within our subconscious patterning. We can swiftly return to love, realizing more harmony and happiness in our relationships.

CHAPTER SIX

My Journey to Love

By Kamala Allen, PhD

In my own journey to Love, I've had my share of disappointments. Before I discovered the path to openhearted relationship, all I wanted was to be deeply connected with someone, to share my day, my dreams and my love with a person who met me. But that kind of connection never seemed to come along. I thought, "What's wrong with me? Am I destined forever to be alone, busying myself with activities and projects while constantly longing for a relationship that works?"

The more I longed for this kind of connection with someone, the more it seemed to evade me. As my adult life went on, my sexual relationships got less enjoyable and more mechanical as I went through the series of wounds and disappointments that characterize many people's relationship odyssey. Though I didn't know it at the time, I was in the predicament of a great many lovers who, not yet fully centered in their hearts, mistakenly believe they are connecting with others, while a larger part of themselves are locked away in the emotionally safer cocoon of sensation and mental constructs.

I decided to make a point of healing whatever was limiting my love and sexuality, embarking on many years of study, personal growth and spiritual practice. In addition, I immersed myself in the accumulated knowledge of relationship therapy, sexual counseling and trauma recovery. What I would come to learn, was that the way to end separation with those I loved was not through exploring the narrow channels of the mind, but by diving into the vast ocean of the heart. I began training in the traditions of the sacred sexual arts under qualified teachers, as well as in intuitive and energetic healing... an adventure that has lasted decades.

When I finally understood how to open my heart and my nervous system to love, and how to assist my partner to do the same, my relationships changed forever. Then I wanted to share it with everyone. I began teaching workshops to women, men and couples and wrote a book on the subject, entitled "A Woman's Guide to Opening a Man's Heart." Along the way I have incorporated everything I have learned and have come to understand in my work with clients.

In my work, I have found that many men and women, due to emotional wounds associated with unrealized and distorted love, abuse or sexual misinformation, in childhood and in later life, are caught in fears of letting go, embracing the intensity of their feelings, and making the deep connection with a partner that is necessary for extraordinary intimacy. This wounding gives rise to the lack of personal fulfillment and growth and the sexual blocks, problems and failures found in most in relationships.

Since love and sexual energy flow on the media of attention and esteem, I believe it is the heart connection between partners that creates relationship healing. The core of our ability to relate to others resides in the heart center that has a direct connection to the sexual center within the human energetic system. Suppressed thoughts and feelings buried in these centers, are like thorns that ache until they are discovered and removed. Opening the heart through energetic processes allows this to take place.

What most couples are looking for in relationship and sexuality, consciously or not, is just to connect deeply and fully. By learning the energetic processes for centering in our hearts, we can fully experience our wholeness and the wholeness of another, as we tune to each other and open up the subtler depths of love, healing and unity. When we are able to open to, receive, and direct this energy, we become fully available to the pleasure and presence of another. Then we can allow the natural and effortless qualities of love, contentment and pure being to flow within all of our relationships.

Kamala Allen, PhD is a talented healer who has specialized in conscious relationships and sexuality for over 25 years. For more information on her services or to buy her book and other products, see http://www. kamalaallen.com

CHAPTER SEVEN

Lightning Bolt of White Light

By Trish Regan

By the year of 1989, I had come to a place of relative inner peace. I had learned how to love myself and manifested into my life my perfect spiritual partner and husband, Doug Hackett. We were married in 1992 and made the commitment to follow Spirit and our hearts in every decision that would come before us.

We had known from the beginning that we would be doing spiritual work together some day. I had received training in spiritual counseling and healing and Doug had devoted many years to the study of meditation and spirituality. Our deepest desire was to be catalysts for personal empowerment for others, to be beacons of Light and examples of what it means to live a totally fulfilled life of meaning and service.

We would regularly meditate together and call upon beings of Light from other realms and dimensions to assist us in our relationship and our work in the world. I had many visions of these glorious beings and felt their presence daily. I learned to trust the wisdom they shared with us and believed, most of the time, that we were totally guided and taken care of.

There were the times, of course, that I would slip into my old patterns of doubt and skepticism. These were the times of darkness for me when I could feel myself being pulled into the downward spiral of negativity and fear. In those moments, I knew that unless I immediately dealt with the darkness, rather than ignore it, then turn toward the light and positive thoughts, I would be lost for hours (or days) in that dark hole. I would pay attention to the content of these negative thoughts and emotions and always seek help from spiritual counselors and healers to find the source and to transmute them into higher learning about myself.

Doug and I helped each other to become aware of the remnants of dysfunction and limiting beliefs from our childhoods as we sailed the sometimes stormy seas of relationship. We believe that a "sacred partnership," such as ours, can be the perfect catalyst for this exploration. Though 90 percent of our time together was blissful, the other 10 percent held the challenge of emotional discovery and the call to healing. Our commitment to this task has paid us endless rewards as we grow ever closer in intimacy and love. Our willingness to see each other through the eyes of our spirituality allows us to support each other in our continued commitment to heal deep wounds, open our hearts and give service to the best of our abilities.

One year after our marriage took place, we received an invitation we could not refuse. At the beginning of 1993 we had the opportunity to experience three months of personal coaching. This process was designed to help us to open to living a totally fulfilling life. We both had harbored many reservations and negative beliefs about that subject. We thought that it was really impossible to be totally fulfilled. Our upbringing and cultural conditioning had taught us that we need to work hard to get what we want out of life. We needed to sacrifice some of our dreams if we were to truly be able to create security for our families and ourselves. It was ridiculous to think that we could have everything we wanted in life.

Through the skillful guidance of our coach, we sailed through the three months, stripping off those limiting beliefs and negative thoughts and ended up with the same vision. We saw ourselves living near water, in a large house with a high ceiling, with many people coming through. It was a wonderful vision, but we had no idea where we would be living and what we would be doing. We were satisfied with the coaching, even though we had no clue what our life's work would be. We trusted that it would be shown to us at the appropriate time.

The next month, in May, our good friend, Joan Ocean, came to visit us in our home in California. Joan's life was a perfect demonstration of the power of living by following your heart. I met her in 1983 and became the first participant in her meditation group in Belmont, California. She soon began to receive messages of love, peace and harmony from the dolphins. They seemed to ask her to be their ambassador to the world bringing their wisdom and beautiful energy of love to all. She and her partner, visionary artist Jean Luc Bozzoli, left the lives they knew, packed a few suitcases and began a journey around the world bringing the dolphin message to all. Not knowing where the next flight would lead, or where they would get the money to pay for it, they lived on pure faith and were totally taken care of. Joan ended up in Kona, Hawaii, living on the ocean and swimming with the dolphins every day, learning their immense wisdom and sharing it with the world through books and dolphin seminars.

We were in awe as we viewed Joan's extraordinary video and listened to mind-expanding information about the dolphins and their multidimensional consciousness. Their energy drew us into their magical spell and we looked at each other and said, "We have to go and swim with the dolphins!" Two months later we found ourselves in the ocean with these magnificent beings. The experience blew open our hearts and brought us into a state of being I can only describe as ecstatic, the adventure of our lives.

To be met one on one by these creatures, both joyous and otherworldly, was astonishing in its intimacy and in its awesome connection. We felt that they came to us with the desire to communicate and share their magical world with us, in this third dimension and in higher dimensions also. When we were with them, all concerns or feelings of limitation disappeared. We were brought into the present moment in a way that had never been experienced before. It was pure bliss. We could see what Joan was talking about. The dolphins assist us to touch the higher aspects of ourselves and to seek joy through an expansion of consciousness. We knew we would never be the same.

Before leaving for home, Joan said, "Why don't you move to Hawaii and help me with this work?" She said that there would be more and more people drawn to be with the dolphins in their ocean home and that there needed to be people to help them have that experience. Since I had attended some spiritual training seminars with her in the past, and Doug and I had made the commitment to do our spiritual work, whatever that was, we felt that Joan must have been guided to ask us about this. Even so, we were not prepared to say yes to this fantastic suggestion. We said to her, "We can't do that! We have our lives in California!"

Upon returning to California, to his surprise Doug realized that we didn't have lives! His experience was that what he had been doing no longer had that spark of aliveness or spirit behind it! For several years Doug had been feeling that he was supposed to leave behind his career as CEO of the energy conservation company he had founded, however had not found anything that he would rather do. Upon meditating on it, the only thing that had that sense of aliveness for him was selling everything and moving to Hawaii to work with the dolphins! However, he refrained from telling me right away, knowing that the perfect moment would come in the next few days.

My experience was a bit different. On the following Wednesday, after returning from Hawaii, I was driving over the San Mateo bridge on my way home from work. While thinking about the dolphins and Joan's invitation, I suddenly had an incredible experience. A "lightening bolt" of white light shot right through my body and I heard the words, "Go do this work." It was as clear as day and I knew this was a powerful message from the universe, the dolphins, and my Higher Self.

I had experienced this same extraordinary "white light" two other times in my life. The first time the universe gave me this kind of unmistakable message was when I was guided to end my first marriage. The experience left no doubt whatsoever that I was to leave "now" with no turning back. It was so powerful that even though I was not prepared financially to go it alone and live the life of a single mother, I was compelled to seek a divorce.

My husband and I had dedicated thirteen years to the attempt at making a successful marriage. I felt that we had exhausted every avenue in our search for the truth of our relationship. Was there enough love to keep it all together? What about the children? I just couldn't leave unless every stone was turned and we had tried everything possible to make our marriage work. Should we stay together or seek happiness apart? The "white light" answered the question for me. We parted right away and sailed into lives, which fulfilled our true natures and brought us more happiness and fulfillment than we had felt for many years.

The second time that I was visited by the "white light" occurred a few years later. This lightening bolt shot through my body out of the blue one day and "said" to me, "Go to see your friend now." I had no idea why I was being told this and what in the world I was to do when I got there. This was not about getting in the car and driving a few blocks away. I was being told to get on the next airplane and travel 3,000 miles to see this friend!

At that time in my frugal life, it was unthinkable that I would take that kind of money out of the bank and take off just like that! But this message was so powerful and compelling I did just that. I arranged the ticket, got on the plane and, feeling sick with anxiety about what I was doing and what may be ahead, I painfully endured the five hour flight. Never having traveled alone, I found it such a challenge to get the rental car and then to find my way in a strange city to my destination.

When I reached my friend's home and knocked on the door, after announcing who I was, I waited for twenty minutes before she opened the door. Upon first sight I could see she was in a state of deep depression. She was about to commit suicide that day and I had come at precisely the right moment. We talked for twenty-four hours and I was able to convince her to get the help she needed to get through that challenging time. Oh yes, I trust that white light!

Returning to the story of our return home, when I told Doug about my experience with the lightening bolt, he reacted with assurance that we were on the right track. He said, "Well, we made the commitment to follow Spirit and it looks like we are both being called and are being tested." Happily we both knew that this was the direction we should go and though it meant leaving behind security, we agreed to "jump off the cliff" and follow our guidance.

We sold everything, packed up our books and some kitchenware, and left for Hawaii the following February of 1994. It wasn't easy leaving our children, friends and families on the mainland. Though my daughter and son were adults and on their own, and Doug's two teenage daughters were living with their mother and step father, our hearts tugged at us to stay close by. We made a pact with the Universe that we would see them at least four times per year in whatever way we could.

That first year was exhilarating, magical, transforming and challenging. For me, the prospect that we did not have paychecks would prove to be terribly frightening. I had spent many years as a single parent working very hard to create some sort of security for my children and myself. Before I met Doug, I had bought a condo, paid cash for my car, and had money in the bank and a retirement fund. I was set for the rest of my life.

Interestingly, I had an astrological reading six months before I met Doug in which I was told that I needed to lose everything to gain everything. "No!" I said, "I refuse! I have worked too hard to finally feel secure!!" But alas, I knew in my heart that if detachment to it all was to be asked of me by Spirit, I would indeed have to surrender it."

When we moved to Hawaii, we began working very closely with Joan, who became our mentor and inspiration. She told us in the beginning that she could not support us completely financially, but would pay us to assist her in her dolphin seminars and help her with her work. She also encouraged us to create our own dolphin seminars so as to manifest a source of livelihood.

We founded and co-created Dolphin\Spirit of Hawaii and began our adventurous life as facilitators of monthly seminars including dolphin swims and spiritual transformation. While our seminars began slowly at first, we found that facilitating them was the most joyous, stimulating and fulfilling work we could imagine.

Our life had completely changed and began to bring to us magical adventures, interesting and wonderful people from all over the world, and deep satisfaction in the knowledge that we were contributing to the spiritual awakening of the people we served.

Trish Regan, Visionary Writer and Intuitive Soul Reader, is author of the book series Essential Joy: Finding It, Keeping It, Sharing It. She has been married in spiritual partnership to her husband, Doug since 1992.

They founded Dolphin\Spirit of Hawaii in 1994 when they experienced a dramatic spiritual calling to "jump off the cliff," leave their professional lives behind and come to Hawaii to work with the wild dolphins.

Since that time, they have conducted monthly transformative dolphin-swim seminars/retreats in Kona. They also facilitate whale swim retreats in the magical waters of Tonga. In addition, for seven years they worked very closely with world-renowned dolphin researcher and author, Joan Ocean.

They travel internationally, bringing workshops such as Essential Joy, Sacred Partnership, Dolphin Essence Experience, Empowering Magnificence and Be the Vision to many seekers of Light and bring to their visionary work a deep connection with the dolphins, whales and many Beings of Light.

See more about their amazing dolphin and whale tours, events, and products at: http://www.dolphinspiritofhawaii.com, and http://www.essentialjoy.net

Part Eleven

Children of the Violet Ray

How a New Wave of Souls are Impacting the Future

CHAPTER ONE

Children of the Violet Ray

Born into an extraordinary time when the world is at a cross roads of dark and light potentials, and people worldwide tremble before increasing dire conditions on the planet, the Violet Child is a light to humanity and a hope to the world.

The fulfillment of Indian Nation Prophecies, the first Violet Children made their entramce into our world in the 20th century. According to the different prophecies, a new race would be born from every nation and people at a time of increasing travail. They would be the teachers, healers, and wayshowers leading humanity back to a time of peace. Indian Seers called these people the Rainbow Warriors because they would be born from every race and color. Whether white, black, brown, tan, olive, red, or yellow skinned, they were a band of visionaries who were coming to save the world.

After the first wave of Violet People came of age and began impacting the planet in the 60's, the next wave of illumined children began appearing in every region of the Earth and continue to be born to this day. Whether they have distinct personality characteristics of Indigos, Crystal, Dolphin, or Rainbow Children, I have found all these soul groups carry the same Violet Signature. Thus, I categorize all these groups under Violet Children. To me, they are Indigo Violets, Crystal Violets, and so forth.

The young 'Warrior of the Rainbow' comes at a time of darkness on the planet, many times fulfilling their mission at a young age. All the time I hear about young children who are clear about why they are here, what they want to do and be in this life. Many of these children have insights on how to create a better world. All of them feel the world needs more love and feel troubled that people are not happy here. They don't seem to understand why there are so many problems. Their rarefied consciousness doesn't quite fit in our troubled world

Their unique qualities of purity, innocense, and love is a torch in a Dark Night that inspires us to be our best selves. Their presence in our lives helps us lift our weary heads from the strife and shows us that there is a greater destiny to be fulfilled, that we can be more than we imagined. We can live joyous lives, with greater awareness of who we are, and why we were born to this time.

Such is the case with Boriska, a boy from Russia, who remembers in vivid detail where he is from and why he came to earth at this significant time. His prophetic wisdom at a young age cannot be denied as he shares his past and brings a message of hope in a time of Great Change. (See his story in the next chapter.)

CHAPTER TWO

Boriska,
The Boy From Mars

By Gennady Belimo

Sometimes, some children are born with quite fascinating talents and abilities. I was told the story of an unusual boy named Boriska from members of an expedition to the anomaly zone, located in the north of the Volgograd region in Russia, most commonly referred to as Medvedetskaya Gryada.

"Can you imagine, while everyone was sitting around the campfire at night, some little boy (about 7 years of age) suddenly asked everyone's attention? Turned out, he wanted to tell them all about life on Mars, about its inhabitants and their flights to earth," shares one of the witnesses. Silence followed. It was incredible!

The little boy with gigantic lively eyes was about to tell a magnificent story about the Martian civilization, about megalithic cities, their spaceships and flights to various planets, about a wonderful country Lemuria, life of which he knew in detail since he happened to descend there from Mars, had friends there...

Logs were crackling, night's fog enveloped the area and the immense dark sky with myriads of brightly lit stars seemed to conceal some sort of a mystery. His story lasted for about an hour and a half. One guy was smart enough to tape the entire narration.

Many were stunned by the two distinctive factors. First of all, the boy possessed exceptionally profound knowledge. His intellect was obviously far from that of a typical 7-year-old. Not every professor is capable of narrating the entire history of Lemuria and Lemurians and its inhabitants in such details. You will be unable to find any mention of this country in school textbooks. Modern science has not yet proved the existence of other civilizations. Second of all, we were all amazed by the actual speech of this young boy. It was far from the kind kids his age usually use. His knowledge of specific terminology, details and facts from Mars' and Earth's past fascinated everyone.

"Why did he start the conversation in the first place," said my interlocutor.

"Perhaps, he was simply touched by the overall atmosphere of our camp with many knowledgeable and open-minded people," continued he.

"Could he make this all up?"

"Doubtful," objected my friend. "To me this looks more like the boy was sharing his personal memories from past births. It is virtually impossible to make up such stories; one really had to know them."

Today, after meeting with Boriska's parents and getting to know the boy better, I began to carefully sort out all the information obtained around that campfire.

He was born in Volzhskii town in a suburban hospital, even though officially, based on the paperwork, his birthplace is the town of Zhirnovsk of Volgograd region. His birthday is January 11th, 1996. (Perhaps it will be helpful for astrologers).

His parents seem to be wonderful people. Nadezhda, Boriska's mother, is a dermatologist in a public clinic. She graduated from Volgograd medical institute not so long ago in 1991. The boy's father is a retired officer. Both of them would be happy if someone could shed light onto the mystery behind their child. In the meantime, they simply observe him and watch him grow.

"After Boriska was born, I noticed he was able to hold his head up in 15 days, recalls Nadezhda. His first word "baba" he uttered when he was 4 months old and very soon afterward started talking. At age 7 months, he constructed his first sentence, "I want a nail." He said this particular phrase after noticing a nail stuck in the wall. Most notably, his intellectual abilities surpassed his physical ones."

She continued, "When Boriska was just one year old, I started giving him letters (based on the Nikitin's system) and guess what, at one and a half, he was able to read large newspaper print. It didn't take long for him to get acquainted with colors and their shades. He began to paint at two. Then, soon after he turned two, we took him to the children day care center. The teachers were all stunned by his talents and unusual way of thinking."

The boy possesses exceptional memory and an unbelievable ability to grasp new information. However, his parents soon noticed that their child had been acquiring information in his own unique way, from someplace else.

"No one has ever taught him that," recalls Nadya, "but sometimes, he would sit in a lotus position and start all these talks. He would talk about Mars, about planetary systems, distant civilizations. We couldn't believe our own ears. How can a kid know all this? Cosmos, never-ending stories of other worlds and the immense skies, are like daily mantras for him since he was two."

It was then that Boriska told us about his previous life on Mars, that the planet was in fact inhabited, but as a result of the most powerful and destructive catastrophe, had lost its atmosphere and that nowadays all its inhabitants have to live in underground cities. Back then he used to fly to earth quite often for trade and other research purposes. It seems that Boriska piloted his spaceship himself. This was during the times of the Lemurian civilizations. He had a Lemurian friend who had been killed right before his .eyes.

"A major catastrophe took place on Earth. A gigantic continent was consumed by stormy waters. Then suddenly, a massive rock fell on a construction. My friend was there," tells Boriska. "I could not save him. We are destined to meet some time in this life." The boy envisions the entire picture of the fall of Lemuria as though it happened yesterday. He grieves the death of his best friend as though it was his fault.

One day, he noticed a book in his mother's bag entitled "Where do we come from?" by Ernst Muldashev. "One should have seen the kind of happiness and fascination this discovery triggered in the little boy. He's been flipping through pages for hours, looking at sketches of Lemurians, photos of Tibet. He then started talking about the high intellect of the Lemurians," his mother said.

"But Lemuria ceased to exist minimum 800,000 years ago," I uttered in response to his statements.

"Lemurians were nine feet tall!"

"Is that so? How can you remember all this?"

"I do remember," replied the boy. Later, he began recalling another book by Muldashev entitled, "In Search of the City of Gods."

The book is mainly devoted to ancient tombs and pyramids.

Boriska firmly stated that people will find knowledge under one of the pyramids (not the pyramid of Cheops). It hasn't been discovered yet. "Life will change once the Sphinx will be opened," he said and added that the great Sphinx has an opening mechanism somewhere behind his ear (but he does not remember where exactly).

The boy also talks with great passion and enthusiasm about the Mayan civilization. According to him, we know very little about this great civilization and its people. Most interestingly, Boriska thinks that nowadays the time has finally come for the "special ones" to be born on earth. Planet's rebirth is approaching. New knowledge will be in great demand, a different mentality of earthlings.

"How do you know about these gifted kids and why this is happening? Are you aware that they are called "Indigo" kids?" I asked him.

"I know that they are being born. However, I haven't met anyone in my town yet. Perhaps may be this one girl named Yulia. She is the only one who believes me. Others simply laugh at my stories. Something is going to happen on earth; that is why these kids are of importance. They will be able to help people. The Poles will shift. The first major catastrophe with one of the continents will happen in 2009. Next one will take place in 2013. It will be even more devastating."

"Aren't you scared that your life may also be going to end as a result of that catastrophe?"

"No. I'm not afraid. I have lived through one catastrophe on Mars already. There still live people like us out there. But after the nuclear war, everything has burnt down. Some of those people managed to survive. They built shelters, new weaponry. There was also a shift of continents there, although the continent was not as large. Martians breathe gas. If they arrived on our planet, they would have been all standing next to pipes and breathing in fumes."

"Do you prefer breathing oxygen?"

"Once you are in this body, you have to breathe oxygen. However, Martians dislike this air, earth's air, because it causes aging. Martians are all relatively young, about 30-35 years old. The amount of such Martian children will increase annually."

"Boris, why do our space stations crash before they reach Mars?"

"Mars transmits special signals aimed at destroying them. Those stations contain harmful radiation." I was amazed by his knowledge of this sort of radiation. This is absolutely true. Back in 1988, resident of

Volzhsky, Yuri Lushnichenko, a man with extrasensory powers attempted to warn Soviet leaders about the inevitable crash of the first Soviet space stations "Fobos 1" and "Fobos-2." He also mentioned this sort of "unfamiliar" and harmful radiation from the planet. Obviously, no one believed him then.

"What do you know about multiple dimensions? Do you know that one must fly not on straight trajectories, but maneuvering through the multi-dimensional space?" I asked the boy. Boriska immediately rose to his feet and started to pour all the facts about UFOs. "We took off and landed on Earth almost momentarily!"

The boy takes a chalk and begins drawing an oval object on a blackboard. "It consists of six layers," he says. 25% outer layer is made of durable metal, 30% of the second layer is made of something similar to rubber, the third layer comprises 30%, once again, of metal. The final 4% is composed of a special magnetic layer. "If we are to charge this magnetic layer with energy, those machines will be able to fly anywhere in the Universe."

"Does Boriska have a special mission to fulfill? Is he aware of it?" I posed these questions to his parents and the boy himself.

"He says he can guess," says his mother. "He says he knows something about the future of Earth. He says information will play the most significant role in the future"

"Boris, how do you know all this?"

"It is inside of me."

"Boris, tell us why do people get sick?"

"Sickness comes from people's inability to live properly and be happy. You must wait for your cosmic half. One should never get involved and mess up other peoples' destinies. People should not suffer because of their past mistakes, but get in touch with what's been predestined for them and try to reach those heights and move on to conquer their dreams." These are the exact words he was using.

"You have to be more sympathetic and warmhearted. In case someone strikes you, hug your enemy, apologize yourself and kneel before him. In case someone hates you, love him with all your love and devotion and ask for forgiveness. These are the rules of love and humbleness. Do you know why the Lemurians died? I am also partially at blame. They did not wish to develop spiritually any more. They went astray from the predestined path thus destructing the overall wholeness of the planet. The Path leads to a dead end. Love is a True Magic!"

"How do you know all this???"

"I know."

CHAPTER THREE

Angels From On High

By Aurora Juliana Ariel

I end this treatise on the Violet Child over the folling chapters, with stories of my own amazing children, Mariah, Araphiel, Gabriel, and Aradeus. This next story is about my daughter, Mariah.

It was a cold, wintry day in Northern Idaho. My three-year-old daughter, Mariah, was quietly playing near me, as I was sewing. All of a sudden she stood up pointing above the sewing machine and cried, "Look Mommy, look!" Looking up, I couldn't see anything but the ceiling. She started pulling anxiously at my dress saying, "Don't you see them, don't you see them?" I responded, "Who?" She said, "Podey and Jadey."

A week later I had forgotten all about the incident, when Mariah came running up to me with a book in her hands. In the inside first page there was a picture of two cherubs. Mariah said, "Look, Mommy, look! Its Podey and Jadey!" Smiling, I understood. Two angels had visited us that day, but only she could see them!

Mariah has always been aware beyond her years. Precocious at a young age, her grandparents called her an "Old Soul." Her extraordinary insights and profound statements continually lent their magic to my life. Today, she is my best friend on this earth and one of the most remarkable and insightful women I know.

Mariah was 3 ½ years old when her first brother, Araphiel, was born. I will never forget the many times I would look over to find her changing diapers or rocking her baby brother to sleep. She seemed to take command of him with an efficiency that was hard to imagine at her age, let alone witness. People who visited us would look on in wonder.

One time we were in California visiting her grandparents. I had begun running the bath for the children and went into the adjoining bedroom to get their pajamas. I returned to find my 2-year-old son totally soaked from head to foot standing beside Mariah, who was looking confident and controlled. I asked her, "What happened?" She replied, "Araphiel fell into the bathtub and under the water. I pulled him out!" At 5 years old, she had saved his life! As her other brothers were born, she watched over them in the same way, bringing her love and nurturing to their early life experience.

When Mariah was 15, she wrote a poem that echoed through me, touching me in a profound way. (See the following page.) A rare treasure and insight into an extraordinary awareness, I kept it all these years. Now, I am excited to share it with you as an example of the depth of the Violet Child, and their intense inquiry into the mystic side of life.

As Mariah came of age, she seemed to have a innate maturity and wisdom that has propelled her into great success at a young age. Mastering every aspect of a business she started with her partner, she now runs two successful restaurants in Hawaii that have begun to be franchised.

She is a realtor and real estate investor who owns many homes and she keeps expanding her horizons. But, her material acquisitions pale in comparison to her intelligence and beautiful caring heart.

When you visit her main restaurant, Da Kitchen in Kahului, Maui, you would never imagine that it is really a finishing school for the young women she employs, but it is true. With her skillful guidance, the girls learn how to have positive attitudes, save money, have confidence and high self esteem, do an exemplary job, and to render a unique service that keeps the restaurants packed night and day with happy customers.

Many of these girls have bought their own homes and drive luxury cars, though they are in their early twenties. Guided by the knowledge and skill of their mentor, they are championed to lead abundant and exemplary lives.

With an extraordinary depth that has inspired her to master both her inner and outer worlds, Mariah brings a higher vision to everything she does. I hope if you visit Maui, you will try out her amazing food. As most people on this island know, Da Kitchen rocks!

Check out Mariah's restaurant at: http://www.da-kitchen.com, and if you make it in there, please mention you read about it in my book. You won't be able to miss her, she looks just like my picture on the back cover.

I Am

By Mariah Napenthe Brown

I am young and
want to experience life
I wonder if I know everything I should
I hear the sun singing a mystic tune
I see teardrops falling from the moon
I want to see the world through somebody else's eyes
I am young and want to experience life

I pretend things don't bother me
I feel the angels' wings guide me along
I touch the magnificent colors of the rainbow
I worry about all the pain and suffering in the world
I cry for all those less fortunate than me
I am young and want to experience life

I understand people don't live forever
I say life can be anything you make it
I dream someday the sky will have no limits
I try to bring happiness to everyone around me
I hope that the world never has to come to an end
I am young and want to experience life

CHAPTER FOUR

Healing The Wounded Healer

There is a legend among Medicine People that Healers must first be wounded to bring their gift to humanity. It is through their own challenges and personal healing that they forge their extraordinary knowledge and are then able to help others. I have witnessed this in my own life and heard the same story from clients over the years. It is also the deeper meaning I read into my eldest son, Araphiel Isaiah's story, which follows this chapter.

Araphiel is highly empathic and has a natural healing ability. When an Aboriginal Shaman from Australia came to Maui, my son knew he needed to attend his training. At the end of the training, the Shaman told him he was a powerful healer and gifted him one of his prize healing crystals so that he could begin his own healing work. He is also highly skilled in multimedia from animation to graphic arts.

When he was 11, I was preparing to attend an Advanced Zone Therapy Course at the Center For Alternative Medicine in Kristiansen, Norway, and realized I would not be home for his 12th birthday. Being a newly single mother, with my four children and I having just undergone a huge life change, I decided, I couldn't have him be without me on his birthday. So, with a clear intention that immediately produced results seemingly out of thin air, I manifested an extra thousand dollars for his plane ticket and took him with me.

The Advanced Zone Therapy Course by Dr. Ersdal was very intensive. Highly acclaimed in Norway for his pioneering work, he was greatly respected by the medical community. Often he was called into the hospital to give his diagnosis when it eluded attending physicians.

Part of our course was theoretical, another part hands on, and the other was attending Dr. Ersdel as he made his rounds to see patients in his clinic. There Araphiel and I witnessed the miracles of Dr. Ersdal's healing work. One boy had been healed of a hole in his heart. A barren woman was now was pregnant. As we made our way through the rooms watching Dr. Ersdel address each client, my son would ask the most astounding questions, showing that he had a clear grasp of this healing method, with a perception that was beyond that of the other students who were over twice his age.

His questions were timely and insightful, and Dr. Ersdel was impressed. Not only that, Araphiel sat in every class drinking in the information and speaking intelligently about it later. Day after day, he never got bored, neither did he want to leave the classroom and be a kid. Towards the end of the 10 days, he had even mastered the Zone Therapy method that takes months to learn, and began giving sessions to whoever wanted them, which he was really good at.

I have seen other times in his life where he displayed an extraordinary knowledge and healing ability. This has impressed some high level healers. Grandmaster Pang, the Hawaiian Kahuna who passed his lineage to me, held a training that Araphiel attended when he was 14, and quickly mastered. I have also done a lot of inner work with him and passed on some of my knowledge.

I think one of the most momentous experiences in my life was the time he saved my life. It had been an exciting day on the west coast of Oahu, where I had taken all my children to swim with the dolphins at Makua. The water was a warm brilliant turquoise and we played with the dolphins for hours. (Araphiel shares his story about this adventure in the next chapter.) After awhile, Araphiel went off to surf. Finally, the rest of us turned to go back in.

I had just gotten the last child safely onto shore, when I felt myself being pulled backwards by a strong force. I turned around and saw a huge wave looming above me. I went under it just as the wave crashed over me. This was a freak set. A calm ocean can turn into humongous waves without warning as the winter months are arriving in that region.

In the summertime the ocean is like a lake there. In the winter there can be 20 – 50 foot waves. Beneath the surface on the south side is a dangerous coral reef that can crack skulls and wipe out the best of swimmers, and I was quickly being hurled towards that danger zone. Tumbling in a swirling mass of white water, I was not able to come up for breath for what seemed like an eternity. Finally I reached the surface, gasping for air, only to see another huge wave about to crash over me. It came down hard and I was spun around and around under the water until I ran out of breath and began to get frightened. Finally, I broke free, reached the surface and was able to gasp for breath, but I knew I wouldn't make it through one more wave. I had spent over two hours swimming with the dolphins and it had taken its toll. I was tired and worn out and out of breath.

I felt lost in a dangerous sea, alone and helpless. I looked up and could only see water and sky. I squeaked a pathetic, "Help!" that I knew no one could hear. I was gasping to catch my breath, knowing the next wave would be over me any minute. I knew without a doubt I wasn't going to make it.

Without warning, a strong arm grasped my hand and pulled me up over a surfboard. I looked up into Araphiel's green eyes. With skill and strength, he paddled us out to sea, using his surfboard as a flotation devise for me to rest upon in between the waves. As each wave prepared to crash over us, he would let go of the surfboard, which had a leash attached to his foot, hold my hand and guide me under the slamming wave towards the bottom of the ocean, holding firmly onto me until it had passed. Each time we would come up for air, he would grab the surfboard, get me to slide up onto it, and push me farther out to sea.

The waves were massive. There was no way for us to avoid them. We had to keep facing them head on. This was an exhausting trek, because we didn't have time in between waves to get a good breath before the next wave was pounding us. But somehow, I felt safe in Araphiel's presence and this calm helped me to make it through the ordeal.

Finally, Araphiel paddled us beyond the waves, bringing me to a place of safety, where it took another twenty minutes for me to catch my breath. Calmly he stayed with me, silently watching my recovery, until my partner reached us and said he would help. When it was safe, he helped me get to shore between the big sets. Making it to the comfort and warmth of the white sand was a miraculous feeling. I was safe! To this day, I remain in awe of what happened and how my son, who had been off surfing and in his own world, had saved my life.

Araphiel's journey has not been easy. I think it is the same for all sensitive souls on this planet. Life can bring many harsh experiences and bitter disappointments. For the empathic Violet Child, this can bring tremendous harm. Because of Araphiel's sensitivity, he has been greatly affected by the challenges my children and I had to endure. He speaks of this impact on his life in the following story and how an extraordinary encounter with dolphins brought an amazing gift to his life.

CHAPTER FIVE

A Dolphin Elder Changes My Life

By Araphiel Isaiah Brown

I was having a really hard time in my life. I was 15 years old and felt frustrated most of the time. Some of the hard things I had gone through were somehow permeating my whole life. I felt completely bored at school and my grades were dropping. If there was an exciting assignment, I would get right to it, but in handing it in, my teachers would not believe I had done it. It would be such excellent work, they thought only an adult could do it. Consequently, they did not believe I was capable of this, so it further pushed me from caring about school. My incentive was dropping and I was just drifting along.

One day, my mother took my brothers, sister, and I out to swim with the dolphins. She had been swimming with the dolphins for some time and wanted us all to experience it. This was going to be my first dolphin encounter.

We drove an hour to the western shore of Oahu until we came to a place where a beautiful white sand beach stretched along the shore for miles. The ocean was a steely blue shifting to turquoise with sparkles of sunlight dancing on the smooth glassy surface. Dolphins were jumping and leaping out of the water off the shore about 100 yards out. As fast as I could, I threw my fins and mask on, and swam out to them, thinking I also wanted time to make it back in time to surf the waves breaking on shore.

Groups of dolphins came by just out of my reach. Each cruised by me, checking me out. After a while of trying to catch up with them, a group of 20 dolphins began swimming towards me and then a strange thing happened. They circled me and held me in their captive dolphin pen until I grew alarmed. What were they doing? What did they want from me? For a moment I got really scared. I didn't know much about dolphins, but here they were, in a tight circle around me, holding me in the center, every dolphin's attention clearly on me.

Then the circle opened and an older dolphin entered. He swam over to me looking deep into my eyes. This dolphin had a powerful presence and seemed to be revered by the dolphin clan. He was covered with scars and I had the sense he had had a very hard life. I thought of mine, all the difficulties and hardships I had endured and felt I was meeting a kindred spirit.

There was a harpoon hole and shark bite out of his fin. He had been through a lot and yet, this old dolphin seemed to hold an honored position in the dolphin pod and wanted to make this connection with me. He continued to look deeply into my eyes and I felt something powerful transfer to me. I was receiving so much that wasn't even registering on my conscious mind, but somehow I knew something incredible was taking place. There was a message for me but I did not realize how deeply I was touched and how profound this message was for me until many years later.

And then the transfer was complete. The circle opened and we all began to swim together. With a strange effortlessness, I was able to follow at their pace wherever the dolphins went, and they kept close to me. I was so amazed that I was actually cruising with dolphins.

It felt like we were in a silent communion, swimming together in unison, each of us with our past. Every time I would look over, the Elder Dolphin would bend his head and look directly into my eyes with a deep soulful look. I felt he could understand what I'd been through and somehow I could understand him. We had both seen hard times.

He kept staying alongside of me, no matter what the others were doing. As we cruised along together, I began thinking about my life, how frustrated I had felt so much of the time and how sick I was of school. I had no direction in life and somehow I didn't care. My thoughts drew me down deeper and deeper until I was remembering the time in my life when everything had changed, when the happy childhood I had known came to a sudden end, and a new harder life had begun. My parents had divorced. One side of the family began attacking the other's character. They shared victim stories of so many things that had happened in their life until I felt burdened and overwhelmed. It was too much to handle. I had been 4 or 5 at the time, innocent, open, loving, carefree, and enthusiastic about life. I got good grades, was into sports, adventures, and having fun. As the years passed, one of the troubled family members became angrier and more upset, until finally they were continually ranting and raving, blaming the other for their ruined life every time I saw or visited them.

I saw how shocked I had been; saw how devastating this experience had been for me, saw how I had become quieter, more inside myself, happiness eluding me. I never realized how much this had affected me until this moment, swimming with my dolphin friend within the dolphin pod. I had never thought about it so clearly and deeply before, I had just been living it and shrugging it off.

I now could see how this person's misery and sense of victimhood had passed into me and now, in my teen years, was there right beneath the surface, influencing and ruining my life. It had all added up, accumulating over the years, and now it was my misery, my own sense of victimhood, my anger, my rage, my discomfort, my lack of self esteem and self worth. Somehow I had taken it all on. Was it because I had cared so much, wanted so much to make it better?

I looked over to my dolphin friend and he seemed to understand. I felt his compassion and that he really cared. As the misery went out of me, I was seeing the loving boy again, the boy who cared so much and wanted to help, but never could. The boy who could not understand why his family would have to suffer so much and why one side of the family did all the horrible things they did. As fast as the images came to my mind, they would dissolve. I felt relieved as each one faded from my sight. The pain, the hopelessness, the futility all came up and passed before the screen of my mind and soon, I began to feel a deep sense of peace. The dark clouds were lifting. The deep pain was resolving. The emptiness I had felt for so long was leaving, and for the first time I felt free.

My dolphin friend seemed to smile at me in that moment. I felt he truly understood what had been locked up inside of me, and that now I was able to finally see it and release it. It was not mine, but somehow I had taken it on. I had carried my family's pain and judgments, perspectives, and sense of injustice deep inside me, and it had wounded me. It had left a deep wound as if it were my own. It had become mine and that was the strange thing about it and now, it was gone!

Right then, another dolphin came up on the other side of me and began leaping high into the air. He was so huge I got scared. I really thought for a moment that he was going to crash down on top of me! His splashes sent huge reverberations throughout my being. Soon, I was laughing at his acrobatics. This dolphin was having so much fun. I felt he was giving me a message. "Let go of the past and you will find happiness again. You can learn to live in joy."

He kept up these antics for quite some time, as if to make sure I got the point. Meanwhile, the other more soulful dolphin continued to swim by my side, moving with me inwardly as well as outwardly, feeling all that I was feeling and gently guiding me through the healing passage.

After awhile I was getting pretty tired and I started falling behind the pod. My dolphin friend stayed behind with me. I really wanted to keep swimming with the dolphins but they were getting way up ahead of me. Mentally I called out to them, "Hey, wait up." Immediately they all came to a halt and waited until I caught up to them. I could not believe it! They had been going so fast and were getting so far ahead. Now they were all waiting for me.

Once I caught up to them, they swam with me at my slower pace for a long time. I felt protected, safe, and cared for. My dolphin friend had made it clear that he was aware of everything I was going through. These dolphins were leading me on a healing journey and he was the facilitator of that healing.

Being with him and one of their group, I could feel the love and protection the dolphins were providing me. It was incredible! They had created a sacred space for my healing process, had lovingly enveloped me with their presence, and because of this, I was able to get in touch with the hurt that was beneath my anger and release it. I knew it was time for me to have more joy. The seriousness of my family member's "illness' had etched its sad history into my soul. Now, I was being given the opportunity to heal some of that pain and to move on into a happier life of my own.

Finally, my dolphin friends said goodbye and were on their way. My one dolphin elder friend gazed long into my eyes, before turning to follow them. He knew I was a different person, a changed person from that experience. He had gone on the healing journey with me, somehow taking me beyond the anger and my seeming apathy with school and life, deep into the heart of a pain I didn't even know was there or could be healed. In finding this wounded place inside me, I was able to release it from my life with their help, to finally let go of a big piece of it and the memories that went with it.

I felt very different after that day. I was more relaxed, easy going and peaceful. I seemed to get along better with my family and others, and amazingly I now was taking a renewed interest in school and with an effortlessness that seemed unimaginable, my grades increased.

Everyone noticed a big change in me. They saw that I was a lot happier. For me, I found I had a better intuition about things and a sense to follow that intuition which turned out to be a wise thing to do. I was more creative and excited about my life and I was free of that dull sense within that had for too long been covered over by angers I didn't understand. The dolphins had set me free!

You can see Araphiel's amazing Shark 3D animation that includes music and vocals by Bruce BecVar and Aurora at: http://www.youtube.com/ user/araphiel

CHAPTER SIX

A Rose Blooms in the Snow

In the midst of a vast winter wonderland, I went into labor with my third child, Gabriel Josiah, and decided to take a walk to help move things along. Bundling up in warm clothing, I put on my hiking boots and headed out the door. Our property was set like a jewel on a snow covered mountainside in northern Idaho, three miles from a town called Hope. We had an expansive view. Our home looked over evergreen trees to a vast sixty mile long natural turquoise lake, with jagged mountain peaks beyond.

The sky was clear and sunlight was sparkling on the freshly fallen snow. I looked down in amazement. To my disbelieving eyes, there was a white rose blooming in the snow! Radiantly beautiful, I was compelled to touch its soft, warm petals.

It was early December and the ground had been frozen for two months. The last of our garden vegetables had died out long ago. The rose garden over at the other side of our home (and quite a long distance away), were now thorny spines barely jutting out above the snow, while this amazing single rose stood tall and strong above the icy white landscape. Beneath it was the buried lawn, neither had there ever been roses or any other flower planted there. It was the only living plant in sight, except the dormant leafless raspberry bushes at the edge of our garden and the tall evergreens that filled the mountainside around us. I stood stunned in silent awe.

After a day and half labor, with the doctor finally fishtailing up an icy road to deliver my son at our home in the early hours of the morning, I realized this rose was not for me, but was rather a blessed sign welcoming this child's entrance into our world. The Nature Kingdom was heralding in his birth with this extraordinary gesture. I had to wonder who this child was and what his destiny on Earth would be.

Gabriel did prove to be an extraordinary child. Insightful and wise, he had a commanding presence at a young age. One day, when he was three years old, a friend witnessed him making skillful moves in the yard, and commented how well he was doing with his martial arts. Surprised, I said, "Gabriel has never taken martial arts." My friend couldn't believe it. He said, "Well, he certainly knows the moves. He looks like an adept!" One can only wonder where he learned this!

Gabriel had a clear direction for his life from an early age that I came to honor and respect, assisting him in every way I could to fulfill his Life Visions. He always seemed to know what next steps were important for him and had a determination and strength of will that helped him manifest his intentions. He, like my other children, has an uncanny healing ability. While I was studying different healing modalities, he would be mastering them. At one point, he used to tell people he would give them a Foot Zone Therapy Treatment for only fifty cents, "A lot cheaper," he would tell them, "than what my mother charges!" And many people would take him up on it and found it very healing.

When he was 11, Gabriel wanted to attend a prestigious private school on the island of Oahu where we lived, but at the time I was a single mother of four who was putting myself through my doctoral program in psychology. I was also flying to LA every six weeks to attend IBI (Income Builders International), a powerful business forum where people learned business skills, built teams, and raised capital.

After attending six times to bring forth my Earth Vision Center project, I had begun to assist other attendees as an IBI Ambassador, while further moving my vast humanitarian endeavor forward. Consequently, I did not have the extra funds to fulfill his desire, but in an inspired moment I said, "Gabriel, if you are very serious about this, I will sponsor you at IBI, and maybe you can raise the money you need there." He said, "Yes. I want to go!" and so off we went, flying to California together to attend the forum.

Gabriel was the youngest person who ever attended IBI. Those who witnessed his dedication to his dream were amazed how focused he remained the whole week, never once going off to hang out with other kids at the hotel. He even turned down video games when we checked in, he was so intent on his mission.

And so it all began. Not being content to stay within the Teen

Program, I continually saw him in the adult program and then implementing what he was learning. He would hang with the adult group and entered many serious discussions with those present. Finally he was gaining a reputation, as many people had never seen anything like it. He was a huge sponge absorbing everything and then speaking intelligently about what he was learning.

The Super Teaching Classroom format at the Forum provided a high retention of what we were learning. It was an extraordinary advanced learning system, which the founders were hoping to get into classrooms around the globe, and Gabriel was availing himself of every lesson, instead of hanging with the teens in their learning environment.

At one point I was astounded to see him standing at the head of the room before hundreds of people. The lesson was on manifesting our Vision and he was sharing his. He described his dream school and that he needed to raise $7000 for his tuition. As he shared his intention, people began running up the aisle and placing money and checks in his hand. This continued for some time, which completely blew the Trainer's mind and everyone present.

It was a very electric moment in the history of IBI, and something I had never witnessed before or after over the years I attended 12 of the forums. After his victorious moment in the classroom, people kept coming up to talk to the now famous, Gabe, many handing him checks and cash until money was overflowing from his pockets. By the end of the week he had made a powerful impression on everyone there, raised most of the money needed, and a month or so later, entered the school of his dreams.

At 12 years old, Gabriel was inspired to manifest a new vision. He had heard a friend of mine speaking about an amazing school in Mount Shasta, California, and told me, "I don't know why, but I feel that I need to be there." This Inner Calling became so strong that it inspired a new Beloved in my life to sponsor him!

As he departed on the plane, I felt a huge empty space that made me realize what an important position he had held in our family with his strong presence. He had provided a peaceful strength, stability and harmony over years of many challenges and changes.

Gabriel, from his earliest years, seemed like a Buddha to me, as if he had been born in Tibet as a lama being raised for a Holy Purpose. Like a Buddha, he has a quiet yet commanding power, a great wisdom, and a unique insight into human nature. Another 'Old Soul.' This strong presence remains to this day, and I am sure it is a great source of strength to his wife and children, who all adore him.

Gabriel continues to govern his life with a clear direction, which has taken him into the world of high math, physics, and computer programming, all of which he is brilliant at, to working as an electrical engineer on the computer systems of F16's in the Air Force.

Meeting his match in his exceptionally gifted wife, Becky, the two of them, both in their early twenties, manifested the home of their dreams in South Carolina where he is stationed. A new vision is forming for when he completes his present service to our country. It will be interesting to see what Gabriel manifests next!

CHAPTER SEVEN

Aradeus, Winds of Fire

I was sitting with my two younger sons the winter of 1995 in our home in Hillcrest overlooking Kailua, Hawaii. It was a magnificent day and our view stretched out over the town to the vast turquoise ocean beyond. To the west, tall jagged peaks rose to the sky. Our conversation turned to my youngest son's progress with his piano lessons, which weren't going well. Aradeus had slacked off from playing and couldn't be enticed to get back into it. Consequently, he wasn't practicing or moving his skill forward.

At that time I was producing Christopher Connolly's *Rivers of Life* album. Christopher was continually playing his magnificent masterpieces on his Grand Piano. With a home that was continually filled with inspired music, Aradeus was drawn to the piano. Seeing his natural talent, we had hired a music teacher, but soon he had lost interest and we didn't know why.

I told him that I felt he had an extraordinary talent and that I had a recurring vision of a music CD he would create in the future, entitled *Aradeus, Winds of Fire.* Immediately, without a word, he rose from the chair and went to the piano and began playing the most extraordinary uplifting music.

The conversation with my son, Gabriel, rose to a new height until we were speaking about something very remarkable. We both became aware of the shift at the same time, and looking at me with a knowing glance, Gabriel said, "Get the movie camera." Meanwhile, inspired music was flowing forth from the piano, filling the room, and lifting Gabriel and I into an incredible awe as we witnessed Aradeus skillfully playing music we had never heard before that was way beyond his capability.

Gabriel took command of the camera and focused it on Aradeus, capturing the incredible music that was pouring forth through his skilled fingers. When one piece ended I asked, "Aradeus, what is happening for you?" He got up, opened the piano bench, took out his music books and threw them on the floor saying, "These are boring!" Then he jumped back on the piano saying, "And now, music from Ray Casino." This was a completely different type of music... a jazzy tune that made his fingers fly over the keys and soon even his feet joined in, leaving Gabriel and I astounded. We couldn't believe our eyes. This was a beginning piano player with little experience. The next piece was a haunting tune bringing its celestial magic to the room. Again we felt uplifted and inspired. The music was soothing and healing, like music from celestial spheres.

We realized then that Aradeus had a rare talent. In this special moment in time, he had tapped into a higher power, and was able to bring forth inspired healing music beyond his abilities. He was around 9 years old at the time and though he never cared for formal lessons after that, when he is in the right space, he has the ability to draw from an incredible inspiration that has gone beyond music to filmmaking and other multimedia as well as healing modalities.

In the first book of the series, *Earth 2012: The Ultimate Quest*, I share the story of how he trained with me for over a year and a half starting when he turned 17. He was my first formal student, and quickly became adept at giving counseling sessions using TheQuest™. He also co-facilitated a Teen Forum with me in Aspen when he was 17, where we taught the teens TheQuest™, including Youth At Risk. Now 21, he has gone on to help others in his own extraordinarily unique way.

Part Twelve

The Indwelling Presence

CHAPTER ONE

The Indwelling Presence

We are in a time of blessed dreams and profound awakenings. Our Inner Light is expanding and we are held in its sacred embrace, witnessing its Vision of a Transformed World manifesting in our earth experience. The more we make room for this Indwelling Presence, the more our lives are transformed, and the more we are transfigured from an ordinary human into an extraordinary being who fulfills a Higher Destiny and realizes its Full Potential.

We become great under the guidance of this Inner Light. We become powerful and secure. The foundation of our life becomes an empowered anchor point of our Innate Divinity. We realize we are spiritual beings set upon an Illumined Course that allows us to awaken and become who we really are beyond the human programming that has traversed the ages of our past. We are catapulted into a time of great advancement from a deep inner soul perspective. The needs that once kept us feeling unfulfilled recede and we are left with that which really matters to fulfilling our unique Soul Destiny.

There has been so much that has held us back and kept us entrapped in rounds of challenging circumstances. We've longed for freedom and yet, have sought it too often in outer means, while the inner part of us that holds the code to our True Destiny waits silently within us for the time when we will finally come to the inner gates and drink deeply of its Ancient Wisdom.

When we find the Inner Truth that goes beyond all human belief and reasoning, we make a superhuman advancement beyond what we could normally realize trapped in the human limitation we've known in the past. We go beyond the bounds of what is humanly possible and the impossible becomes manifest in and through us. That is when life gets really exciting!

We've entered an historic time when we, as a humanity of souls traversing this planet, are releasing an ancient heritage that kept us caught in the old games with its focus on personal survival and advancement. We are moving swiftly out of the grip of planetary despair into the joyous renewal and restoration of our Divine Awareness. We are leaving the human patterns that once kept us in misery, to embody our divinity as spiritual beings having an extraordinary human experience. Through this inner shift, everything is magically changing around us. Our issues are resolving, our illnesses are being healed, our inner pain is dissolving, and our limitations are being removed, until the Dark Night we were once immersed in, steadily fades away.

This is the Awakening. It is an inner experience that can only be realized from an inner vantage point. Then it becomes a real, tangible experience beyond what we've read or heard about. It becomes a reality that rises to meet others in a similar amazing place. As we align with our greater destiny, synchronicities and timely meetings call us out of our busy lives, into a soul alliance that is changing the way of life on earth. This alliance is igniting a global shift in consciousness beyond our imagination. Through this magical interplay of souls awakening worldwide, a global renaissance is taking place that is transforming the world around us.

The old archaic ways that kept us downtrodden and weary fades away as a glimmering light meets us on the horizon. The sun of an Illumined Reality rises in its glory illuminating the whole sky, casting out the Dark Night. We have entered an Enlightened Era, long prophesied and willed into a physical, tangible reality by millions of souls worldwide. In it, a New World is being born and we are all a part of it. We stand together at this historic time, witnessing the Birth of An Age of Light.

CHAPTER TWO

The Illumined Pathway of the Inner Self

In 1998 at the beautiful villa I lived in on Maui, I was inspired to read the book, *The Artists Way*, and to put into practice the 'morning pages,' which were to be written each day. This was an exercise to unblock the creative flow and enhance creative expression. The idea was to allow whatever wanted to be written to flow forth uncensored. This was a time each day to pour out feelings, to share deeply, whether a joyful or painful expression. It was sacred time.

When I sat down on my computer excited to begin my first morning pages, an incredible thing happened. The words poured forth, "At last a voice in your busy world." I was stunned! An insightful voice continued, drawing me into a magical inner world I had reverence for. I was being spoken to directly from my Inner Self who invited me on an incredible journey.

She said, "If you should take this trek with me, really opening up to my magic and gifts, your life will change completely. It will look so different than anything you have witnessed before, because it will no longer be structured upon that which is illusion from an illusionary world of beliefs. Lost in a world of illusion you have often sought me not knowing truly where to find me and now you know." And so, the incredible journey began and I was never the same.

In this first message she shared, "I am the one you have longed for in your Quest for Eternal Youth. I am the one you have striven to become in your Quest for Enlightenment and at last you are here, in My Abode, and I bid you welcome. Welcome and come in."

The Inner Self helped me to realize that while my striving for spiritual attainment had largely been an outer quest, that the ultimate quest was an inner journey to the center of my Self, a journey into the heart of who I truly am. She showed me that when I am my Authentic Self, I am enlightened. I am fully conscious and aware.

She went on to say, "Feast upon the many Delights I am here to share with you. Enter Joy for the first time in many years of fortitude and striving. Be at Peace in my Garden of Delight, drinking in the Sweet Fragrance and the Nectar of Everlasting Bliss, of the Divine Elixir, which is Life Eternal and all the precious qualities that are jewels in their own right. Access these treasures on a mystical treasure hunt with me, for I grant you permission to enter the Garden with me and I am here to guide you every step of the Way. I am your Inner Creative Self."

Inner Creative Self! Those words resounded through me. She had revealed herself as the inner creative part of me. I had never imagined, as I sat down to write my first Morning Pages, that I would be embarking on an incredible adventure, nor did I fathom the depths that journey would take me. I had been determined to unlock my creative expression and that intention had unlocked my Inner Creative Self. I had tapped into the Inner Self many times, but obviously, in my full and busy life, I had failed to truly comprehend the majesty and grace of this illumined part of me. Now she was ready to take me on a journey, to personally educate and awaken me, and I was determined to make room for her to be more fully present in my life.

For the next two years I received the most precious letters from my Inner Self. Each day I would print them out on my favorite rainbow paper and lay them reverently on a table beside my bed. Each night before I went to sleep I would read them again. I found them powerful, enlightening, and life transforming.

Day after day, her wisdom was impeccable, her guidance clear, her understanding astute. She led me deep into myself, helping me to uncover the stranglehold of human patterning that had made it impossible to follow her guidance. She helped me to see how the driving parts of me, though noble intentioned, were still the human voice having its way. I found that the Super Achiever and Workaholic parts of me, with their humanitarian principles and spiritual philosophies, were nothing more than programs running from my subconscious, filling my daily existence to overflowing to where I barely had a life. I balanced this new inner awareness with TheQuest™ Self Counseling sessions. In each self-counseling, I was clearing the way for my Inner Creative Self to have her perfect expression in and through me.

I learned that the Inner Creative Self was a stiller, quieter voice. To hear her, I had to be silent. I had to rearrange my life so that I could be available, open, ready and listening. I had to fill my life with quiet moments, to give myself a lot of space just to be. This was an incredible training and an area of Self Mastery I had not sought.

I found that it was not easy to follow the guidance of the Inner Self. It took a lot of shifting internally to be really present for her. This amazed me. I thought I had always been attuned to my Inner Awareness, but the truth was, I was a very driven person. Driven in ways that looked great to the outer world, but in truth, they were wearing me out. I had so little time for myself.

By the time the letters completed, I was a very changed person. Two years had passed, and I had recreated my life to be more spacious and thus, more peaceful. I had learned to listen for those moments of inspiration and to ride that creative wave expressing my deepest self. I could still accomplish and make things happen. I was still grounded and centered and responsible, but I was so much freer than I had ever been and had so much more joy. I had learned to treasure the many gifts of this very powerful part of me. I had learned about True Power, a quiet power that does not need to make a big show or have a big push in the world. I learned how to manifest easily and effortlessly.

As I journeyed deeper into this effortless life, I began to see the magic of what she had been speaking of. I had stepped out of the driver's seat and had allowed her to take over and she blew my mind. I was having the most incredible experiences. Each day was filled with synchronicities, incredible meetings, amazing alliances. I no longer had to work hard or strive to accomplish my goals. I simply was manifesting a higher vision for my life.

Each letter has been a precious jewel and all together, a Garland of Wisdom and Love that has shed so much light on my pathway. To me, they are gifts beyond earthly treasures. The Inner Creative Self showed me finally that these letters were destined to be a book. In part one, the Inner Creative Self speaks eloquently on the Art of Sacred Living. In part two, she shares incredible insights on how to live an Abundant Life. This, for many in the spiritual community, is a lost art after millennia of religious doctrine that speak of self-denial, poverty, and lack as a way to spiritual enlightenment, both in the east and west.

Scheduled for release as one the next books in the Earth 2012 series, I have seen visions of what this book of inspired messages will mean to the spiritual communities of the world. It will be a healing salve for those who are moving out of the old paradigm with its limited awareness and life expression, to the New Archetype of 'Wealth Wedded with Spirituality' that is being birthed at this time through many Violet Souls.

The Inner Creative Self taught me, "Embracing the Abundant Life becomes the focal point of embracing one's Lost Self, for it is the Inner Creative Self who holds the key to an opulent existence that is within your reach."

Adhering to the Sacred Principles defined in these messages allowed me to see and thus, remove the stains of the old programming, which has held humanity back from living the Glorious Life designed by the Inner Creative Self. This life is available to each one of us once we have cleared the way in our consciousness, being and world.

To receive these letters so unexpectedly has been a very profound and sacred passage. I took them to heart, followed their instructions, and became a very changed person with an ability to live a more fulfilling, sacred, and abundant life.

I've included two of the letters from my upcoming book. The resounding echo through these letters is that we are loved and that through the love of the Inner Creative Self, we are inspired to see and know and love ourselves in the way that God loves us. Embracing ourselves from this Divine Perspective, we can live Sacred Lives, consecrating the moments of our existence to a Higher Purpose and allowing the Divine Plan to fulfill itself in its most perfect way in and through us.

CHAPTER THREE

Advent of a Glorious Age

A Letter From The Inner Self

"Radiant and Wondrous is this New Life that speaks of the
Transcendent Glory of the Ages and the Divine Promise Fulfilled
in a world being healed and transformed.
You have truly stepped into a New Era and with it the
Grand Opportunity for Freedom and Peace."

–Laksme

Beloved of my Heart, how great is the Glory of God, and within
this Vast Presence, the Will and Intention for your soul. As humanity
sits at the crest of a New Millennium casting its gaze upon the future
with anticipation and sometimes fear, a New Song is playing on the
ethers of a world and even now many heads are lifting up to greet this
New Day and new time on earth.

Beloved, feel the Winds of Spirit as they uplift your soul to nobler
heights and transcendent realities. Feel yourself being inspired by this
new feeling that is filling the world. Know that a New Earth is being
born just as you are being birthed into a whole new consciousness.

That which you feel is that which is being gifted to the earth at
this time. As Light streams forth from the blessed Angels and as these
Rays of Light illumine every heart, there is a quickening, an Awakening,
a sense of wonderment, of promise, of well being, of goodness. In this
all-pervading Grand Symphony of Light, souls are caught up into pure
Ecstasy and Peace abounds on earth.

This is a rare moment in the history of the earth, a time for
gratitude and thanksgiving. A time of reverence before the vast and
incomprehensible field of Everlasting Love that pours forth continually to humanity no matter what choices are being made on earth. This

Unconditional Love is tender and true, never deviating for a second from its absolute and all encompassing enfoldment of every soul, from its ever-outpouring love and good will, from its pure intention for each and every lifestream.

Dearest Heart, feel the Winds of Change that are upon you as you garner the Wisdom of the Ages and wear them as a Haku Lei (crown of flowers) of Divine Attainment. You have come so far! Now rest a moment and feel the great goodness that has been intended for your soul. Drink in the Peace, the Harmony, the Love, the vibration of Freedom that is wafting upon your soul and know you are loved and that in that love is the Promise of your Eternal Freedom, Oneness, and Wholeness in the Truth of who you are.

I love and bless you on this Glorious Day of Everlasting Love. I am the Inner Creative Self, the Divine Part of you that ever rests in the simplicity of Divine Love and the Sacred Promise for your soul.

CHAPTER FOUR

The Key to Immortality

The following letter is the one that touched me the most out of the hundreds I received over two years from the Inner Creative Self. I sent it out to friends who, like me, read it every day, drinking in its amazing wisdom.

Gay Hendricks, co-author of *Conscious Living,* also found them inspiring. He wrote, "Spend some time each day with these beautiful writings and feel your life rise on wings of love." Author Allan Cohen's response was, "This letter is filled with love, clarity, and reverence... a breath of Light and air. It is a wonderful offering! Truly Inspiring! What a gift! It is food for the soul." And, I've received many others as well, from people who were lifted up and inspired by its wisdom.

This Letter etched its message deeply into my soul. It helped heal schisms in my psyche from old beliefs I had held about myself, and it gave me entrance to an exquisite inner place of joy, passion about being alive, health, vitality, and youthfulness. I finally realized the Inner Creative Self had given me the Key to Immortality.

This letter became an amazing cure after generations of disinformation passed down from my family lineage and a lifetime of striving to know and feel good about myself through many harsh life experiences. It opened the doorway to the True Love my Inner Creative Self is here to bring, a love so vast, and far beyond what I had known.

Tears fill my eyes as I remember how nurtured and comforted I felt through those two years, as my Inner Creative Self spoke to me each day and guided my life away from the patterns that had run me forever. Her Wisdom helped extricate me from a prison sentence of human conditioning that was literally running and ruining my life.

With her skillful guidance, I became attuned to the True Voice within and through many incredible experiences, I learned to trust her completely and follow her guidance unfailingly. To know this love of my Inner Self, to feel her Presence within me, to see absolutely that there is a guiding light on this dark pathway through this world, has been the most precious experience of my life.

This world can feel so hard. People can be so unkind and we all go through so much. Just to walk on earth means to feel a pain unknown in the higher realms. A great sacrifice has been made by many great hearts to be here at this time. Weathering this world and all it's many trials is to know suffering in its truest form. No one escapes this, though many find ways to live here and survive. Others turn to substances to drown out the pain.

Sadly, many beautiful souls become lost and fragmented beyond earthly repair, but no matter what the experience, our Inner Self can restore us, for it is our link to our Divine Source. Each one of us can turn to this Inner Creative Self in any moment; receive letters, healing, and hope. It is a bastion of great comfort, a shelter from the storm, and a Place of Peace within. It is our Key to Freedom and the way we can restore Heaven on Earth in our own life experience.

CHAPTER FIVE

Worshipping the Light Within

A Letter From The Inner Self

The Transfiguring Process of Life that comes from the
deep Inner Work that arises from life challenges
is the building block to one's Divinity.
Through the passages of Shadowed Substance,
the Chela finds the Light of its True Self,
shimmering as a Brilliant Jewel amid the rubble.

- Babaji

The Brilliant Jewel of my Divine Selfhood radiates its Presence through your eyes and shining countenance. If you could but see me in yourself, you would treat yourself with the utmost care and respect. Tenderly caring for me as a Precious Being, you would worship before the Divine Presence within you, treating yourself as a Holy Personage of Great Light and value to the world and thus, gifting all your energies in making me comfortable in your Temple.

This Sacred Art of Worshiping the Light Within has long been lost to this world. Instead, outer images of other personages have been paraded before the people, and many have become lost in idolatry. Thinking greatness is out there, they have not seen the Great One within them and thus, their pilgrimages have been about outer experiences, bowing before outer images while I, the Beloved I Am stands ready to receive them within!

When there is not this Sacred Reverence for the Divine Self within, there are many abuses and thus, bodies, hearts, and minds are mistreated, neglected, left to fend for themselves, while even the most saintly persons seek to please and perform for others that which would be so nurturing and healing for themselves.

How did the world get so turned around to where the Divine One has been paraded as an outer image while the Glory of God within is constantly neglected? And at what cost has this outer idolatry been, where souls know not the nourishment of Self Love and Self Care.

Beloved, there is a Sacred Sanctuary within your temple where I dwell. Heaven born and free from this world with all its traumas, I stand within you ready to transfer my knowledge, wealth, abundant lifestyle, rich understandings, and timely guidance. When you come to understand the full import of my Presence within you, you then begin to turn your attention within to worship the Divine Light that is ever present for you.

Through tender care and regard, you build the Inner Trust that is so important err you can become fully God Realized. For in caring for your Self, this Divine Part of you, while tenderly working to heal the Shadow Aspects, you turn your life into a Sacred Journey where Life becomes a most treasured experience and where you avail yourself of the many gifts and treasures from my heart.

How blessed a journey life becomes when you understand this One Truth and when, in turning to care for yourself as a most Sacred and Beautiful Being, you learn to live true to your Highest Ideals and Noblest Nature.

Then the world can tremble and roar around you and you will be unmoved because you love and revere yourself, you honor yourself in the highest, and you are there to protect, defend, and care for yourself. Like a Royal Personage, you treat yourself with the highest deference and respect and gift yourself all those treasured experiences and loving moments you have always longed for.

What a different world this would be if all peoples gave themselves this Divine Gift of Love, reverence, honoring, and respect. What a noble culture it would be and what great beneficence would flow forth from the fountain of each one's being.

When you live true to your Self, loving and caring for yourself in all the ways you have ever longed to be recognized and treated, you will find a deep relaxation and peace settling in as if you were sinking down to a place of stillness and clarity within you. All the driving forces that keep you ever on a wheel of accomplishment would cease to move you, for you would know yourself in your most dignified form and you would love yourself so dearly and respect yourself with such a true honoring, that nothing could move you to exploit yourself for attention any longer. You would be living in your Truth, at Peace within yourself, and feeling the Eternal Winds of Freedom blowing through your soul and thrilling your being.

What an incredible life that would be and can be, if you turn your attention within and begin to treat yourself with the greatest reverence and respect you have ever known. Then will Peace come to dwell with you, in body, mind and soul. Then will Happiness and Joy light your every day, and then will you find yourself singing with a newfound Freedom and Delight in the world around you. A Carefree Essence that will waft its Sweet Fragrance through all your life experiences and this, because you choose to live true to your Self.

I am here this day to guide you into this new Way of Being with your self. A Way of Love and Truth. I am here to show you that self-abnegation, self-abuse, and self-denial were never the way to treat yourself, for in doing so, you have created life dramas of great sorrow and sadness to your soul and reaped a life of continual hardship and drudgery. It has not worked. Therefore, it is time to cast off the old way of living and bring yourself fully into the New Life, sharing your Great Joy in finding yourself, embracing yourself, and knowing yourself, with everyone you meet.

As you live in this Radiant Joy of Self Respect, the world around you will shift and you will receive love, honoring, and respect from others. As you treat yourself so shall you be treated. The more love and goodness you give to yourself, the more you shall experience this in the outer world, for the outer is a continual reflection of what is taking place within you.

Take life in your hands and choose to fly. Soar above the old patterns and the old ways that created hardship and pain and cast these into the Sacred Fire. Make a Vow today to be there for yourself in the most sacred, meaningful, and true way, and never move from this Path of Self Love and Self Nurturing again.

Bring to yourself every wondrous adventure, every beautiful experience. Shed joy on all your activities and praise yourself for all your accomplishments. Seek to know your finest qualities and heal those patterns that no longer serve you. Take away the chains, the hardship, and the drudgery. Replace these with garlands of beautiful flowers and radiant and glorious experiences, and treasured moments, and lofty ideals becoming realized.

No longer will you be moved by the world's opinion, nor the fads that seem to rule a majority of people's lives. Instead, you will live in a nobler, fairer reality, seeking to bring forth those fruits that are an expression of your unique design. As you allow yourself to drink from the Fountain of Life and nurture yourself with every precious experience, because you see and acknowledge yourself as precious, then will you know Peace.

We will then know a oneness together, where my Beneficent Spirit can pour forth the Divine Energies to heal and transform your world and in healing your world, uplift and inspire others to do the same with theirs. Thus, a collective effort begins, where the Authentic Selves are at last allowed a voice in this world, where their momentums of Great Good can at last pour forth the Pure Divine Essences they have longed to gift this planet. Then will extraordinary Destinies spring forth to bless humanity in countless creative ways and endeavors.

Such a Powerful Destiny can be unleashed when your focus and attention is on your self, your True Self, and you allow that to rule your life. Such an incredible array of events can take place when you are one pointed and anchored in your Truth. Nothing else you can do on this earth can access this level of Power and Mastery and Skill, nor unleash the Full Power of the Authentic Self, whose Will and Intention is to anchor your Divine Inheritance in the physical world.

All outer activities will become a passage of Divine Will in Action, as every moment you will be attuned and activated by the Inner Light of your God Presence. Nothing that you can dream up can be withheld from you when you are living in that oneness with this sacred part of yourself. Nothing can be denied, for all your treasured ideals, all the most sacred dreams of your heart are the realization of the God Self within in the physical world around you.

That divine equation must be pondered and understood, for it has eluded this humanity for so many centuries and thus, so many lost dreams, dashed hopes, and grave disappointments have been the result in the fulfillment of goals and intentions realized and yet, not bearing the fruits that were the true desire and hope of each one.

As you align with the God Force within, all that you have longed for will become fully manifest in your world, if it is in alignment with your Highest Good. Thus, many dreams will fade away, because they were built upon momentums of seeking to know oneself, or to understand one's importance and worth. But when this worth is fully established deep within, the game changes. There is no longer the seeking to be in the limelight, to be thought well of, to have the adulation of others, for there will be a deep security and inner peace that is unmovable and unshakeable and this will be the guiding force of your life, the strong foundation upon which your life will be built.

Now realize the simplicity with which I speak. Honor yourself in the highest. Treat yourself as if you are your best friend, your most treasured person, and your most beloved one. Think of all the joy you will feel when you are creating an extraordinary life for her, waking up each morning to see what she would love to do best in that day, how she is feeling, what are her needs. What an amazing life.

When life is lived this way, there is a sacredness that exudes your being, a deep and abiding Peace and Transcendent Happiness that radiates out from you and touches all who come in contact with you. Thus the Love, Joy, Happiness, and Peace is spread around the world, for it flows through your being and ignites change all around you. Not in a harsh and rough way, but in a gentle uplifting and inspiring way, where others feel nourished from being with you and basking in the love that radiates out from your being. How precious this life can be and of such great service, and yet rendered without thinking, without effort, without planning. A simple outpouring of Divine Love, Wisdom, and Grace because you have made yourself a Fountain of Light through which I can pour my Presence.

The sacredness of this life is simpler than you have imagined or dreamed for yourself. Think of how this can be without all the striving, hardship, and challenges, without all the incessant doing that has attended your life in the past, without a great momentum to accomplish and yet, all things accomplished with an ease unimaginable while you lead a happy, fulfilled, and tranquil life.

That is the Preciousness of Life that I seek for you, that I hold for you, and envision as your life's expression. Each day through each clearing and in each moment of alignment, we are moving closer and closer to this Sacred Life which you so long for in the innermost part of your being.

This Way of Life shall bring such great relief that you will wonder, looking back, why it took you so long to enter this way of being. Why you struggled through everything and thought that you needed to accomplish great things to find your worth. Now, in Loving, Honoring, and Appreciating your self you will know your worth. You will live on that solid Rock of Knowledge of the truth of who you are, and Peace will be the result. Peace, Joy, and Fulfillment! I love and bless you, my dearest one. May this Sacred Life begin. I am the Inner Creative Self

CHAPTER SIX

2027: A Journey Into the Future

I had an experience on my birthday in 1999 that was so powerful it completely changed my life. It revealed to me the vast difference between human effort and Divine Intention as no other experience could. It was a lesson well learned, for now I know my human self can never bring forth the glory that my Authentic Self can so easily manifest when allowed full reign in my world.

I discovered that we don't need to wear ourselves out to fulfill our destiny or work hard to survive here on earth. It's only been that way because of the programming from our human patterns. There is another way to live life and achieve our highest potential, and over many years of pioneering research and work in the uncharted realms of the psyche, I was able to unlock the secret code to this higher destiny fulfillment.

Being of a strong humanitarian persuasion, I never realized that some of my efforts were from a human rather than an Authentic Inspiration until that day in 1999, when I had the powerful inner experience that changed the course of my life forever. I decided to share this very personal story, even though it goes way beyond the bounds of normal reality, because I feel it will assist the Violet Person to understand the subtleties of human conditioning and how it can adversely affect our lives, while we believe we are fulfilling our destiny.

I had worked many years on what I called the Earth Vision Project, witnessing miracles of every kind, but in late 1996 the project experienced an unexpected blow. One of the key directors played the role of 'saboteur' in what was an earth drama worthy of any movie in Hollywood. While I won't share that story here, suffice to say, there were all the elements to make a great film. Intrigue, avarice, exploitation of power, and the need to destroy the project because he couldn't "have me." It was an extremely challenging passage after years of dedication and hard work, and felt like a huge tidal wave had wiped my project out. After that, I faced numerous unexpected obstacles around the project, but I kept on trying to move it forward in every way possible. I was so committed to the vision I wouldn't give up.

I had received the download of this vast humanitarian endeavor through a divine 'transmission' in 1990. In the days that followed, I was taken up into the Heavens where I remember many key meetings on the instrumentation of this project. Meeting with the Divine Architects behind this project was very exciting. The plan was to bring forth Earth Vision Centers in key sites around the world. Set in pristine natural environments, they would be living libraries of the advances of our time. With a healing retreat central theme, these centers would showcase the best from our world in every field, in what would be a step into the future. Our guests would feel like they had entered an illumined world where the planet was healed and people lived in harmony together.

The mission of each Earth Vision Center would be to download these advances, these 'New Archetypes for the New Society', to their respective countries and areas. Twelve first centers were envisioned, followed by many more, until all major countries would have at least one within this century. This would set a powerful matrix, gifting humanity important Archetypes for the New Millennium that would raise the standard of life throughout the planet.

From the first moment I 'received' the Earth Vision Center archetype I loved it. It resonated with my love for humanitarian endeavors and high tech. As a child, each time I was taken to Disneyland my favorite part was Future World. I was enthralled with the technologies of the future. I've spent many years since, studying advances in every field and for seven of those years, showcased different advances on my weekly TV show, Quest For Truth, which aired in Hawaii on Oahu and Maui.

By the time the 'disaster' took place, the download of the Earth Vision project had initiated years of dedicated effort where I accomplished great feats, raised seed capital, created a full business plan, and built a team of experts. I had traveled to prospective locations and done feasibility studies on different sites. Each step was an exciting adventure. To have the project come to an abrupt halt was a shock, and then to see it limping along for another year and a half was heartbreaking.

By April 1998, I was worn out. Tapped out financially, I did not have the power or resources to keep the Earth Vision project going. So, I finally surrendered, admitting I must let it go. I spent two months experiencing its death, deep in grief. I knew I had to release it and yet, it was such a painful thing to do, because I am a person that never gives up. Despite the worst circumstances I will keep on, but it had all become too much. I believed in the project with all my heart, but I finally had to face the truth. I could not do it on my own and no one was showing up to champion its cause. My team had all moved on and I was left alone, holding the torch.

It felt like death had crept its tentacles into my life and that an evil person had murdered my precious child, but from all my inner research and work, I knew better. I had found that life always knows what it is doing and from countless self counseling sessions with TheQuest™ over many years, that all things are ever working to our greater good. I was being called to just let go and trust.

To survive this ordeal I turned to TheQuest™ once again. The deep and painful places calling for attention, took me deep into the uncharted realms of the psyche. I began to reassess the Earth Vision Project I had been working so diligently on. Through very deep and profound sessions, I was making incredible internal shifts. I was addressing all the ways I had been driven, a super achiever, workaholic and why. I was unlocking the mysteries of my past, my higher potential and destiny as well as the childhood programming I had taken on when I embodied on earth. And, I was becoming incredibly detached and free.

I began having visions of a different life, one that had more spaciousness in it. I had begun to get tastes of this New Life when I first moved to Maui in 1997. My experiences with the dolphins on Oahu, in the years before, had prepared me for this new way of living and being. They had made a huge impact on my life, and had begun shifting me from a full on, type 'A' person (overworked and prone to stress) to an 'AB' type person (more relaxed, yet still motivated). Now I was being given another opportunity to trace the programming behind that 'A' type personality that had kept my life so high powered and ever driven. Session by session, I was fast escaping the grip of my once intense overworked existence, finally settling into what was one of the happiest, most peaceful and blessed times of my life.

Every once in awhile I would meet someone significant and pull out the Earth Vision plan. Energy would seem to want to move the project forward, but then nothing much would happen, though it did help to get my energy going. Somehow these little sparks of energy were keeping the Earth Vision project alive. I realized, "We can never lose something that is a part of us." I began to see that every part of the Earth Vision project represented a part of me. It was a reflection of the many facets of my self. This gave me a lot of peace and helped me to further release it to Divine Will.

In 1999 I traveled to Fiji and found that Forbes Island, with its incredible 4000-acre tropical landscape, was for sale with the most glorious reefs and crystal turquoise water. It was complete with gardens, a Fijian village, and resort. This ignited a whole new series of talks, meetings, visions, and plans. The energy had started to roll again. It was just picking up steam when I received an unexpected visit.

On my birthday in August, a radiant being appeared to me. She called herself my 'Future Self.' She said she had come from the year 2027 and that she had important information for me. She told me, "You think you 'gave up' the Earth Vision project, but I am here to tell you that it is about to take off. You have reached the place in your attainment to now draw in the millions of dollars you need for this project. 1999 is the year you will meet the people who will be involved. When that happens, you will be swept away on a powerful energy current that you will believe is divinely orchestrated, into a future where these Earth Vision Centers are in place."

She went on to say, "Everything you have been visioning is a reality in 2027. I have come to take you into the future so that you can witness this for yourself." Immediately we were traversing my future timeline, images downloading to me quickly as we passed through 28 years, arriving swiftly at the year 2027.

The Earth Vision Centers were in place. I was heading 7 major Trusts and was implementing many humanitarian projects, including the New Hospitals and Academies For Educational Excellence for teens, which were now located throughout the earth. While I had been victorious and had put so much into place, I was shocked to find the world relatively the same and that my huge humanitarian endeavor was but a tiny speck in a still largely troubled world. I realized, "This is not the Vision of a Transformed World I have dedicated my life to. This is not the future I have been working so hard to help birth." I then realized I had given up a personal life to fulfill a destiny that barely had made a dent in the planetary equation.

Looking deeply into my eyes, my Future Self said, "What I want you to know is that your life doesn't need to look this way!" She went on to explain, "You are part of a large soul group who believes that you have to sacrifice yourself for a cause. For you, this pattern goes back to the Fall of Lemuria, after which you decided you would do everything in your power to rebuild that enlightened world. This has set up a powerful momentum that has continued to this day. It is this energy wave, along with the momentum you have built in this life,mb that is about to power your current project. It is about to manifest everything you need to put you on this future course. This is an energy you set in motion all that time ago and which has given you so many histories where you have denied self for something you believed in."

I was stunned by this information and profoundly impacted by this inner experience. For the next few days, I traveled over the years to this future again and again, seeing everything in more detail. How my Beloved finally gave up on me, as I was never available. One of my children passed away whom I had not been able to spend much time with for years. By 2027, I was a high-powered businesswoman who had literally spent every waking hour on the phone or in meetings since 1999.

Curious, I called my Future Self back and asked her, "What would my life look like if I said no to this future?" Immediately she took me on a different line of force, into a future where I had a very blessed, very rich and fulfilling life. My relationships had stayed intact. My child was still alive. I had very close friendships and spent many beautiful moments with my children, beloved and friends. I was incredibly creative and spent a lot of time bringing out music, books, and films that were works of art, all of which had a similar humanitarian ideal. But in this scenario, I was thoroughly enjoying a personal life rather than a life where there was no time for me.

Looking at the beautiful being in front of me, I realized how much she wanted the right thing to happen. She came all the way from the future to help me change the inevitable, because she cared so much. I was deeply touched. I said, "I want this life, this beautiful, amazing life. I don't need to be a high-powered businesswoman and wear myself out for 28 years just to make a tiny mark on the planet. My life and my children's lives are more important. I'm important! I don't want to fulfill a 'human plan.' I want to fulfill my Divine Plan." Smiling radiantly at me, she nodded her approval, as her ethereal form floated back to the future.

Now that I had made my 'big decision,' I had to find a way to implement it. Tapping into the huge momentum my Future Self had shown me, I felt like a tiny person beside a thousand stallions galloping to a future I no longer wanted. How was I going to stop this momentum and change my life course? The answer was within. Going deep into yet another series of powerful sessions, I went to the heart of the driving part of me that had first set this energy in motion. It took me back to Lemuria and the great loss I had felt when that continent sank. It took me through many histories when, like a Joan of Arc, I had given my life for a cause. And finally at the center of this movie, I found the wounded self, with all her many facets from religious beliefs to noble ideals, which had so powerfully determined my fate. Born of misconceptions around sainthood and service, and misinterpretations of a Lemurian past, she had wanted to render the highest service and yet, much of this was more about human effort than Divine Instrumentation.

Healing her, I stepped free of a pattern that had hugely affected my life for millennia. As the shift occurred at deep inner levels, I reconnected with my Authentic Self and felt the power of her ability to orchestrate a planetary service with a sense of fun and ease. A whole new concept! In that moment, the need for working hard and wearing myself out for causes disappeared. A new pathway, a literal right turn on my life path, appeared before me. As I stepped onto it, the 2027 future I had been shown completely dissolved and in that moment, I knew I was victorious. I was in my New Life and I was free of a future and way of life I no longer wanted. Now I would be able to live more in accord with the Divine Intention for my life.

Very quickly, I was transported into my New Life, which dazzled me with its spectacular array. Life became so much easier than the high-powered life I had lived for so many years. I was now experiencing my sojourn on earth as a blessed and amazing adventure, available for Divine Synchronicities and miraculous events that were not of my doing.

I fully released the Earth Vision project. It was then I realized I could bring it forth in a book and just gift it to the world. Those who were inspired could implement the Centers, and I would be happy to help guide them, but as a consultant rather than an administrator. I could fulfill my role as a Creative Visionary rather than a hard working businesswoman.

My Creative Self liked this idea so much better, especially because I love to write and create multimedia projects. A book was much more in line with my personal Vision and New Life Path than the previous one my human patterns had been relegating me to. I was excited. I could fulfill the Sacred Office I had been given in a whole new way. This allowed me to have peace about a 'mission' I had been called to from Divine Realms and to relinquish my life more fully into Divine Hands.

I learned a profound lesson in that cycle. That even though it may look, feel, and seem like we are being Divinely Inspired to do a project or that a meeting or event is by a Divine Hand, it could be a manifestation of our human patterning. Because of this common human tendency, it behooves each one of us to take a deeper look, so that our energies are aligned with the highest vision for our life and our work a true part of our Divine Plan.

Lemuria Rising

Over the next years, my release of the Earth Vision Project allowed me to focus more fully on developing the last facets of TheQuest™. By 2005 my years of research and development were complete. Called to Aspen, Colorado, I was inspired to set up the Aspen Institute of Healing as a community service and outreach division of the Institute of Advanced Healing, and to transfer my Seven Step counseling technique to teens and adults in weekly Teen Forums, Healing Circles, classes at local high schools, and finally through certificate training courses. I was excited and felt incredibly fulfilled seeing all the ways TheQuest™ was transforming lives and how this was translating into a worldwide healing ministry.

In the midst of this very empowering time, I began to write the first Earth 2012 book, and also received a series of incredible visions. They began with a glorious white domed temple set overlooking the ocean. It was the same Grecian Temple that had been shown to me in a vision in 2003, which I had been told was meant to be a Temple where people would come to experience TheQuest™.

Now I was seeing that this spectacular temple was on a beautiful oceanfront property that expanded out to reveal the first Earth Vision Center. I was amazed. As months passed, these visions became stronger and more frequent, until I was literally 'walking' the property day after day. Whenever I would relax from my writing, I would be immediately transported into the future where I would explore all the many facets of the property that included organic gardens, white domed multimedia studios, the Institute of Advanced Healing, and a large Healing Center and Spa set in a private cove.

By the next year, I was convinced this land exists in a tropical location on the planet and was determined to find it. But having learned so much about 'manifestation' and loving to be the recipient of incredible experiences rather than a big 'do-er,' I decided to let it unfold in its own natural way instead of trying to make it happen.

My understanding of this Center grew over time. I was shown it is the first Lemurian Temple rising from an illustrious ancient past. It will display Divine Archetypes from that glorious time, when earth inhabitants lived in a world that was abundant, harmonious and peaceful. Part of its destiny is to provide a Golden Age experience that can be transferred into other regions. It also will be a place of restoration for those who will come for healing from all over the world. For others, it will be a training ground for TheQuest™.

I have walked this property so often; it is so real to me. I feel as if it is already a physical reality. When I see my life there, it is a joyous experience filled with creative projects amid a life of splendor and beauty. A quiet sanctuary from the world, it now lives in my heart as a radiant vision.

Watching everything come together from a Divine Orchestration rather than a human effort has been a spectacular experience. It is a great joy to witness the Archetype of Lemuria Rising being released through me, and to know my human self, with all its propensity for messes, misinterpretations and mistakes, is not doing it.

Eagle Medicine

Inspired to be in a tropical retreat to complete my first Earth 2012 book, I spent the winter of 2005/06 in a beautiful condo by the ocean in Puerto Vallarta. In the midst of that focused cycle, a powerful electric energy began running through me. A vision of Lemuria Rising transported me into a future time where life was tranquil and serene as I joyously worked on films and other multimedia projects with my AEOS team at the Earth Vision Center. To give voice to this vision, I created the Lemuria Rising website and brochure. It was in this powerful creation cycle I had an amazing experience with eagles.

I was sitting out on the back lanai while speaking on the phone with someone about the Lemuria Rising project and what it would mean to humanity, when that powerful electric energy began coursing through me once again. Raised up into a very high vibration, I felt empowered, clear and directed as I spoke.

An eagle appeared out of the mountainous jungle, flew to a short distance from me and started circling to the left just above me. He seemed to be listening to what I was saying as he circled. It felt like he was making a statement to me. His presence was so powerful.

Then a second eagle flew out from the jungle and joined him and the two were circling overhead right near me. After a short time, a third eagle came and joined them. Now three eagles were flying close overhead in a tight circle. It was incredible to have this going on while I was sharing my inspired vision about the Lemuria Rising project.

Then one eagle left the circle and flew back over the jungle, made a u-turn and headed over the trees in a straight line right at me, flying level with me. I was on the ninth floor of the building with two floors above me. As he drew closer, I felt a tingling in my third eye as his spirit touched mine. He drew so close that I could see his little red beak and beady eyes. He was coming right at me and was just feet away when at the last moment, he swooped up over me climbing straight up two floors and over the roof. This eagle seemed very clear, intent, and purposeful, like his action was of great significance. Then all three eagles departed together, flying back over the jungle and beyond, never to be seen again.

This experience touched me profoundly. I was literally in awe of what had taken place and could hardly believe it. I never imagined there were eagles in the rain forest of Mexico. This inspired me to write a Shaman friend, who had descended from Huichol Indians, a mystical tribe who lived a few hours away.

When I asked him what the experience meant he wrote, "This was a very powerful and telling experience you had, Aurora. After reading your email, I offered a prayer and became open to the narrative of what our brothers/sisters the eagles were communicating to you. Eagle Medicine is very powerful and visionary.

The 1st eagle circling left is touching the left side of your brain, the intuitive and spiritually discerning one. The left eagle also represents your past and female aspect that you are experiencing in this lifetime. The fact that this event happened during a conversation about the LIGHT AND HOPE OF THE WORLD is significant and timely.

The second eagle represented action/material, reality/manifestation of thought and spirit/intention... the third one represents that you are in direct alignment with the holy and spiritual force of the triune GOD. As the Christians believe in the holy trinity, this is a natural physical manifestation thru God's messengers to bless whatever it is that you are doing. The eagle that flew directly at and over you was acting out a directional reference to something or someone coming to assist you and also to tell you to continue on the path and journey you have chosen. I also have had many powerful directives from the holy ones by way of the eagle, red tail hawk and the hummingbird. Birds are very close to me as they were very close to my grandmother, who was HUICHOL. I am Hummingbird Clan through my mother and her lineage by my grandmother. I took some time and browsed the Lemuria Rising website. It looks very visionary and powerful!"

Today, with a change in our global economy, many islands and big properties have come up for sale. I know that at the right timing I will find the one meant for this project. I have 'walked it' so often, it lives as a reality within me. I have also seen it in the Akashic Library in my Book of Life, displayed in living moving panoramic color.

Perhaps the owner of an island or large parcel will want to partner in on this project with me or gift it to the Earth Vision Foundation, the non profit I set up in 2004 to bring out this vast humanitarian endeavor. Whatever way this property will come is in Divine Hands. Meanwhile, I am holding strong in my vision with the knowledge that one day, Lemuria Rising is a light to humanity and a blessing to the world.

I hope you enjoyed the stories in this book and that they have inspired your own journey into the Miraculous. I would love to hear about your experiences and what you thought of this book. You can submit your own stories, and they may be chosen for one of the next books in the Earth 2012 series. If you have a story, insights, quotes, or a vision to share please email it to: Info@AEOS.ws. I would also be grateful for your endorsements of this book, the Earth 2012 series, and TheQuest™.

Topics of interest are: Your 'Vision of a Transformed World,' the Awakening, earth changes, healings, life transformations, visions, prophecies, Voice of the Elders, synchronicities, miracles, blessings, the New Children, the Beloved Relationship, awakening to your destiny or life purpose, how you healed an addiction, relationship, your self image, or restored your health, extraordinary encounters (dolphins, whales, sea life, animals, angels, nature or divine beings.)

Appendix

About The Author

Aurora Juliana Ariel, PhD is a dedicated healer, teacher and counselor whose research and work have given her a profound understanding of the psyche and the tools to heal an ailing humanity. She trained under pioneering doctors in alternative medicine, psychology, and holistic health, and holds over 35 certificates and degrees in advanced healing methods as well as a B.A., M.A., and PhD in Psychology.

A Holistic Health Practitioner for many years, Dr. Ariel is a Questor Doctor in Total Body Modification, a Certified Zone Therapist and a Certified Practitioner and Instructor of Stress Release Therapies. She is also trained in Edu-Kinesiology, Bio-Kinesiology, Personality Traits and their Relationship to Disease, Immunbiology, Neuro-Emotional Techniques, and more. She has mastered many of the cutting edge counseling techniques of the last century including Gestalt, NLP, Person Centered Counseling, Reality Therapy, Psychosynthesis, Holodynamics, and others. She has also been given the title, Kahuna, as the successor to Hawaiian Kahuna, Grandmaster Kimo Pang.

All of this pales, however, in comparison with the work Dr. Ariel has done on herself and her work directly in the psyche with countless clients over many years. That work has brought forth Dr. Ariel's landmark discoveries and the development of her Counseling Theory and Healing Practice, TheQuest™.

A Spiritual Scientist in the Laboratory of the Soul, Dr. Ariel took her vast body of knowledge and went deeper on her own quest for healing. She discovered a way out of pain and suffering, a transformative technique that changed her life and brought tremendous healing to her clients.

Dr. Ariel has taken TheQuest™ to the next level and offers it as a Self Counseling technique. Her reason for bringing it to the people, rather than simply releasing it to professional counselors is simple. She wants to bring healing to a world in desperate need.

Dedicated to positive planetary change, Dr. Ariel sees this period on earth and the signs and portents around 2012, as a time when we, as a planet, desperately need to uncover and heal the patterning she believes is at the heart of all the dire conditions we are presently facing. When we accomplish this, we become the peaceful, loving, happy individuals we were meant to be and the world changes around us.

For more information about Dr. Ariel, her work, and other products see http://www.AuroraJulianaAriel.com

TheQuest™

TheQuest™ is a revolutionary breakthrough Counseling Theory and Healing Practice developed by Dr. Ariel after years of extensive research and work. It is designed to bring timely knowledge and a missing piece to rehab centers, prison reform, addiction, youth at risk, 12 step and other programs, greatly increasing their success rate.

For practitioners, it is a way to move your clients quickly from upset to peace, and to help them quickly resolve deep issues, step free of limiting and self sabotaging patterns, addictions, and dysfunctional personality traits, and realize their greater potential.

For the layperson, it is a way to gain understanding and mastery of your psychology, empowering authentic self-expression and creative fulfillment.

For couples, it is an essential ingredient in conscious relationship, where each person works with their own psychology as issues arise. Greater harmony and clear communication can exist when the focus is on resolution through loving, compassionate interactions.

The Institute of Advanced Healing

In 2000, Aurora Juliana Ariel, PhD founded the Institute of Advanced Healing, a non profit organization, to bring forth her life's work, TheQuest™, which includes TheQuest™ Trainings, Classes, Pilgrimages, Counseling Sessions, Support Groups, advanced healing products and services.

Dr. Ariel developed certificate-training programs and set up a model chapter in Aspen, Colorado in 2005 to be duplicated around the world by graduates of TheQuest™ Master Counselor and Spiritual Leadership 2 Year Training Course.

She has successfully worked with youth at risk, addicts, abusers, and the abused, people with serious illnesses and trauma, and a host of dysfunctional personality traits and life conditions with tremendous results.

She has given classes to teens at High Schools, released TheQuest™ to the public on her websites, TV, radio, support groups, and via her Ask Dr. Aurora Column, and is now training people in her four level

TheQuest™ Counselor Certificate Training Courses provided through the Institute. For more information see http://www.IOAH.org

The Human Dilemma

The work at the Institute of Advanced Healing has a very clear focus. The subconscious programming that has created the human condition with its propensity for misery and suffering must be healed. People worldwide need to understand their psychology and learn how to become masters of their destiny, rather than victims to their fate. The cause of suffering must be healed for the world to begin to reflect the noble ideals that are encoded in the hearts of humanity.

When people are engulfed and entrapped in their human patterns, a higher destiny is never fulfilled. Instead, the destiny that plays out is from this programming. The degree that the higher nature, which Dr. Ariel calls the 'Authentic Self,' can express through the individual, the more the person will be able to experience a higher awareness and ability to attain a greater mastery over their life circumstances. But, presently, this is very rare on earth. Even in the spiritual communities of the world where the greatest trainings and highest information is attained, there is a continual dysfunctional aspect to people's lives, because the subconscious patterns are not being addressed. They are being suppressed or spiritually bypassed, while they continue to work their havoc.

It has long been believed that people cannot change their personality traits or heal their addictions. The best that can be done is for individuals to understand their patterns and strive to overcome them. But this method does not work because physiologically the limbic system, the part of the brain that is activated under stress in what has been called the Fight and Flight Syndrome, is different from the area of the brain where the will and determination is found, which is in the frontal lobe. Therefore, under stress, the individual will revert to Fight and Flight, and the subconscious pattern will begin running. They will move into survival and seek substances or run other addictive behaviors to alleviate suffering. Physiologically, the blood will recede from the frontal lobe impairing will and therefore control.

When the deeper patterns have not been addressed and healed, people will understand their addictions and strive to stay sober or substance free, but if they undergo a series of life stresses, it will be easy for them to fall off the wagon. This is because the subconscious has been left out of the equation.

Currently, because the deeper work is not being done, there is only an 8% success rate in rehab centers and addiction programs. The programs today help strengthen the individual's resolve, but do not provide a complete healing. TheQuest™ Seven Step Counseling Technique provides the 'missing piece,' which can greatly increase the success rate at these centers and with people suffering from addictions of every kind.

A Breakthrough Technology

Understanding the human dilemma and being concerned that psychologists today normally only scratch the surface when working with clients, thereby keeping people coming for sessions for years without any real movement, change, or growth, Dr. Ariel developed a way to move people quickly through their issues, and heal their underlying patterns. Her revolutionary method provides a complete resolution, healing, and breakthrough in each session.

If you would like to sponsor or support Dr. Ariel's work and the Institute's mission to bring TheQuest™ to communities throughout the world, donations are tax deductible and greatly appreciated. To make a donation, please go to the Institute website at http://www.IOAH.org

TheQuest™ Life Mastery Path

When you understand your psychology, you have greater control over your life circumstances. As you master TheQuest™ tools and learn how to heal every condition from within, you have a greater command of your destiny. Your Authentic Self is given room for a fuller creative expression in and through you and a new passion and excitement about life returns. You wake up looking forward to each new day and what amazing things will happen next. Unexpected events and synchronistic meetings increase resulting in key alliances with like-minded people for a greater purpose. Life takes on a sweeter quality, as you know you are fulfilling a sacred destiny. TheQuest™ Life Mastery Path training is available in TheQuest™ courses, providing you with the tools and knowledge of how to free yourself from every pattern and condition that has limited you, kept you feeling disempowered, burdened, or held back, so that you can realize your full potential.

Heal Your Life, Change Your Destiny

When you heal your life, you change your destiny. It is as if you are defying a powerful law like gravity. For the human patterns within you are creating a different reality than the Life your True Nature would give you. Clearing the way for this Authentic Self to lend its wisdom and power to your life, allows you to fulfill a higher destiny.

TheQuest™ Counseling Sessions

While Dr. Ariel is largely on sabbatical focusing on her next books and training individuals worldwide, she is from time to time available for personal sessions and for shorter personalized training programs. These are weekly or bi-monthly sessions over 3 - 6 months that include Life Coaching and Counseling sessions along with personal training in TheQuest™ Life Mastery Path. Dr. Ariel is also available at times for personal 7 - 14 day retreats, where her focus is completely on you and your optimum health and well-being, and for Total Life Intensives where every area of your life is addressed and transformed.

Earth 2012 Events
Cruises, Conferences, Workshops, and Seminars with Dr. Ariel

Bringing out more information around 2012 and a personal application that can help facilitate positive planetary change, these events are held in many parts of the world. These events can include TheQuest™ Counselor Three Level Certification Training Courses.

TheQuest™ Programs

TheQuest™ Life Coach and Counselor Trainings consist of four level certificate courses. All four levels must be completed to become a Certified TheQuest™ Counselor. These four level training courses provide an in-depth study of psychology in a format that is experiential, life changing, and empowering.

TheQuest™ Master Counselor and Spiritual Leadership Training Course (Level Four) is a two-year (or one year accelerated) personal training course with Dr. Ariel. Highly experiential in its application, this program gives you the life mastery skills, knowledge, and tools to become a Master Counselor.

Doctors, Psychologists, Health Practitioners, Life Coaches, and Ministers may qualify for the accelerated Level Four 6 - 8 month training program with Dr. Ariel for TheQuest™ Counselor Certification, depending on their background, skill, and knowledge.

TheQuest™ Certificate Training Courses

These four level courses train you in valuable life mastery skills. Each course is unique per the occupants and their current life issues and challenges and is, therefore, a largely experiential journey to the heart of these conditions where they are healed and transformed. As you learn how to clear a pathway to the Authentic Self and its inner wisdom, you begin to give it more power in your daily life and to live your higher Destiny Potential.

Each training provides an in-depth study of psychology and gives you tools to heal self sabotaging patterns, addictions, personality traits, and dysfunctions, deal effectively with health and career issues, and transform challenging relationship dynamics.

In these trainings you learn how to quickly resolve and heal your issues so that you can live more often from your authentic nature. These highly informative trainings are held within a compassionate caring environment and are empowering and life changing.

Dr. Ariel holds TheQuest™ Certification Training Courses all over the world. If you'd like to sponsor her in your area, receive counseling sessions or life coaching, or receive certification as a Quest Counselor, please contact the Institute of Advanced Healing at info@IOAH.org

When you Heal your Life, You change your Destiny.
When you Master your Psychology, You become a Master of your Life.
When you align with your Authentic Self,
You Live Your Highest Destiny Potential

A New Frontier in Multimedia Arts

Media is one of the most powerful ways we can facilitate change today because of its immediate affect upon the psyche. Understanding this, Alchemists of the New Millennium know that transmitting positive images, ideas, and language of a beneficial and healing nature can quickly shift consciousness, open up new doorways of thought, and empower individuals to be their best selves.

Through conscious media, we have a tremendous opportunity to assist in this next evolutionary leap in human consciousness and safeguard against the repetition of the mistakes of the past, assisting humanity to become conscious stewards of the earth and inspiring them to bring forth their greatest gifts and achievements on behalf of a people and a planet. By helping catalyze this quantum shift, we become Alchemists of Media who have an important role to play in this New Millennium.

At AEOS, we are determined to make a difference! All our products are exquisitely designed with the highest quality materials, highest vibration of colors, images, and subject matter, and transmit, energetically and creatively, the highest frequencies. We believe our vast array of extraordinary products and services are destined to transform millions of lives throughout the planet.

AEOS, Inc. is a Hawaii based Multimedia Production Company founded by Chairwoman and CEO, Aurora Juliana Ariel, PhD. TheQuest™ is a proprietary revolutionary breakthrough technology she developed, representing one of the Company's five collections of inspired music, books, and films, placing AEOS on the leading edge in the new psychology/self help genre.

Look for more exciting AEOS products soon, as well as Dr. Ariel's upcoming books in the Earth 2012 series, which delve further into her insights on the worldwide awakening and global renaissance she believes are birthing a New World. To order our products please go to our website at: http://www.AEOS.ws

Healing Inspired Music & Media

Dr. Ariel has studied the powerful influence music and media have on the psyche. She believes that "transformational media is a key to creating the quantum leap in consciousness so necessary at this time, if we are going to avert the many dire potentials before us and positively affect the evolutionary cycle of our planet."

Understanding that conscious media can have a profound and healing influence upon individuals and even transform lives, her greatest love has been to translate her knowledge into multimedia productions that have a healing, uplifting, and inspiring effect. In 2003, she founded AEOS, Inc., a Hawaii based Multimedia Production Company to bring forth her inspired music, books, and films.

In her words, "My joy is in translating the knowledge I have gained into transformational multimedia productions that facilitate positive change within the psyche of humanity, profoundly affecting the consciousness of the planet and assisting humanity to advance forward into an Age of Enlightenment and Peace."

Other Books & Music CDs by Aurora

Earth 2012: The Ultimate Quest
How To Find Peace In a World of Chaos

Renaissance of Grace
Aurora's World Music CD with Bruce BecVar

Gypsy Soul, Heart of Passion
Gypsy World Music CD by Bruce BecVar & Aurora

Rivers of Gold
New Age Music CD by Bruce BecVar and Aurora

Earth 2012: The Ultimate Quest
How To Find Peace in a World of Chaos

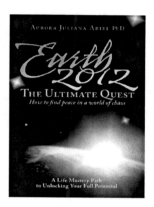

The Award Winning 1st Book in the Earth 2012 Series
By Aurora Juliana Ariel, PhD

Cataloging the profound shift presently taking place within the psyche of humanity, Dr. Ariel points to the fact that we are living in unprecedented times! Weaving a blend of sacred prophecies, prophetic visions, and scientific predictions around 2012, she unveils a glorious potential that is casting its first rays of light on earth, illuminating the Dark Night we are presently passing through, and providing a "missing piece" to traversing the challenges of this time.

In this first book in the Earth 2012 series, Dr. Ariel guides the reader on a personal quest, providing 7 Master Keys to Inner Peace and a revolutionary breakthrough Self Counseling Technology, TheQuest™, that is easy to apply. Distilled into seven powerful steps, this healing process is designed to accelerate a personal and planetary transformation that could help end suffering on Earth.

Her message, "If we want to avert the dire potentials before us, we must look within and unlock the subconscious patterns behind our challenging life conditions."

For timely updates, sign up at http://www.AEOS.ws
More books in the Earth 2012 series are coming soon!

Aurora's Solo Music CD

Renaissance of Grace

The exotic vocals of Aurora with Bruce BecVar
weave a mystical blend that is both uplifting and inspiring,
transporting us into a world of transcendence and light.

Talented musicians grace this gypsy world music album including renowned multi-instrumentalist, Bruce BecVar; Percussionist Rafael Padilla; Peruvian Shaman, Tito La Rosa on Andean Pan Pipes; Gypsy Violinist, Don Lax; Violinist Rachel Handlin, Michael Buono on drums, and Brian BecVar on Synthesizer. Purchase through AEOS at http://www.AEOS.ws

"Aurora Juliana Ariel is one of those rare artists whose clear voice and beautiful music transmit to more than just the ear, but reaches into the listener's heart with hidden healing messages. Coupled with the extraordinary talent of musician/ composer Bruce BecVar, Aurora's offering awakens our inner peace and invites our own calm center to bubble up to the surface. Aurora's mystical language is at once both exotic and familiar, adventurous and comforting. *Renaissance of Grace*, as one of the song titles indicates, is truly a Journey Of The Heart: one pleasurable piece of music after another that you will never want to end. The work as a whole lives up to its name."
-*Pamela Polland, Award Winning Recording Artist, Vocal Coach*

"Journey of the Heart and Shiva Moon are two of the most heartfelt ballads you will hear on any release, their voices soaring together and weaving in and out of fluid guitar lines, gentle piano, bass flute, and percussion. The lyrical romanticism that is expressed owes much to the spirit of Aurora Juliana Ariel, who collaborates with Bruce BecVar to create inspired songs." —*DL, New Age Voice*

Printed in the United States
221520BV00005B/1/P

9 780981 650135